BTEC FIRST
Applied Science
STUDENT BOOK

John Beeby
Lyn Nicholls
Chris Sherry
Kevin Smith
Nicky Thomas
Gemma Young

Collins

William Collins' dream of knowledge for all began with the publication of his first book in 1819. A self-educated mill worker, he not only enriched millions of lives, but also founded a flourishing publishing house. Today, staying true to this spirit, Collins books are packed with inspiration, innovation and practical expertise. They place you at the centre of a world of possibility and give you exactly what you need to explore it.

Collins. Freedom to teach

Published by Collins
An imprint of HarperCollinsPublishers
77–85 Fulham Palace Road
Hammersmith
London
W6 8JB

Browse the complete Collins catalogue at: **www.collinseducation.com**

10 9 8 7 6 5 4

ISBN-13 978 0 00 748842 1

British Library Cataloguing in Publication Data
A Catalogue record for this publication is available from the British Library

Commissioned by Letitia Luff
Edited by Jane Roth
Proofread by Tony Clappison
Typeset by Ken Vail Graphic Design, Cambridge
Index by Jackie Butterley
Cover design by Anna Plucinska
Production by Rebecca Evans

Printed and bound by L.E.G.O. S.p.A. Italy

Acknowledgements

The publishers wish to thank the following for permission to reproduce photographs. Every effort has been made to trace copyright holders and to obtain their permission for the use of copyright materials. The publishers will gladly receive any information enabling them to rectify any error or omission at the first opportunity (t = top, c = centre, b = bottom, r = right, l = left):

p10 Ekem/WkiMedia Commons, p11 leonello calvetti/Shutterstock , p13 mdavid/Shutterstock, p14 Masson/Shutterstock, p15r evantravels/Shutterstock, p15l Danomyte/Shutterstock , p16 Anton Gvozdikov/Shutterstock, p18 Dudarev Mikhail/Shutterstock, p20 Blend Images/Shutterstock, p22 Art_man/Shutterstock, p24 CSU Archv/Everett/Rex Features , p25l Charles D. Winters/Science Photo Library, p25r Charles D. Winters/Science Photo Library, p26 pzAxe/Shutterstock, p28t Kuttelvaserova/Shutterstock, p28c Collins Education, p30 Power And Syred/Science Photo Library, p32 Oliver Hoffmann/Shutterstock, p33 Andrew Whittle/iStockphoto, p34 Andrey Nyunin/Shutterstock, p35 Ecelop/Shutterstock, p36c mediablitzimages (uk) Limited/Alamy, p36l David J. Green/Alamy, p36r Robert Neumann/Shutterstock, p37 Collins Education, p38t Alan Freed/Shutterstock, p38b szpeti/Shutterstock, p39t nostal6ie/Shutterstock, p39cr Novastock/Science Photo Library, p39br Vitalii Nesterchuk/Shutterstock, p39cl photo video the same object/Shutterstock, p39bl Jack W. Aeby/WikiMedia Commons, p40t Brian Knight/John Baggott/Southwest Strongman, p40b Shawn Hempel/Shutterstock, p41t Matt Antonino/Shutterstock, p41cl MCarter/Shutterstock, p41cr Andrew Buckin/Shutterstock, p41b NASA, p42 Joggie Botma/Shutterstock, p43c takayuki/Shutterstock, p43b Diego Cervo/Shutterstock, p44t Stephen Bures/Shutterstock, p44c i4lcocl2/Shutterstock, p45tl a9photo/Shutterstock, p45tr PhilipLange/Shutterstock, p45c Zeljko Radojko/Shutterstock, p46t Chris Butler/Science Photo Library, p46c Shutterstock, p47 Willyam Bradberry/Shutterstock, p48tr Tony Mcconnell/Science Photo Library, p48tl Howard Sayer/Shutterstock, p48c Christopher Halloran/Shutterstock, p48b krivenko/Shutterstock, p49bl ejwhite/Shutterstock, p49br abimages/Shutterstock, p49t NASA, p50t Losevsky Pavel/Shutterstock, p50cr Jason Stitt/Shutterstock, p50cl Eamon Curry/flickr, p50b R. Michael Ballard/Shutterstock, p51t itsmejust/Shutterstock, p51c Ints Vikmanis/Shutterstock, p51b ISM/SCIENCE PHOTO LIBRARY, p53 Serdar Tibet/Shutterstock, p54 iStockphoto, p55 Shutterstock, p54-55 iStockphoto, p56 iStockphoto, p57t Andrew Lambert Photography/Science Photo LIbrary, p57b Collins Education, p58 Charles D. Winters, p60 Photograph reproduced with kind permission of De Beers UK Ltd., p62 kentoh/Shutterstock, p63 Shi Yali/Shutterstock, p64 Gyrohype/Shutterstock, p65c Dmitriy Shironosov/Shutterstock, p65b Vasilyev/Shutterstock, p66cl Andrew Lambert Photography, p66t Daboost/Shutterstock, p66cr craftvision/iStockphoto, p66b Squareplum/iStockphoto, p67t Shutterstock, p67c diephosi/iStockphoto, p68b bunhill/iStockphoto, p68t TRL LTD./Science Photo Library, p69t BORTEL Pavel/Shutterstock, p69b Glen Jones/Shutterstock, p70 Charles D. Winters/Science Photo Library, p71 Charles D. Winters/Science Photo Library, p72 Elena Elisseeva/Shutterstock, p73 Vasiliy Koval/Shutterstock, p74t Shutterstock, p74c Shutterstock, p77t JoLin/Shutterstock, p77c aida ricciardiello/Shutterstock, p78 Green Chemistry Centre of Excellence, based at the University of York. The Centre aims to promote the implementation of green and sustainable chemistry into new products and processes (www.greenchemistry.net), p78 D.A.R./Shutterstock, p79 Dirk Wiersma/Science Photo Library, p80t ronen/iStockphoto, p80b eyeidea/iStockphoto, p81 Shutterstock, p82 hammondovi/iStockphoto, p83 NASA/Science Photo Library, p86 Frizi/iStockphoto, p87 hepatus/iStockphoto, p88 tiburonstudios/iStockphoto, p89br Carlos Caetano/Shutterstock, p89t Shutterstock, p89bl ROBERT Brook/Science Photo Library, p90 danielschoenen/iStockphoto, p91 Shutterstock, p94 Shutterstock, p94-95 Shutterstock, p95 Shutterstock, p96 Website of The Israel Museum, Jerusalem/Photograph by Ardon Bar Hama/WikiMedia Commons, p98 Antonia Reeve/Science Photo Library, p100 Kevin Carden/Shutterstock, p101 Propaganda/Alamy, p102 Mikhail Nekrasov/Shutterstock, p103c OxfordSquare/iStockphoto, p103t Danicek/Shutterstock, p104 Adambro/WikiMedia Commons, p106t InnerShadows/iStockphoto, p106b Shutterstock, p107 TItan120/iStockphoto, p108b patpitchaya/Shutterstock, p108c Tpopova/iStockphoto, p109 Fertnig/iStockphoto, p110 clearviewstock/iStockphoto, p111 Manfred_Konrad/iStockphoto, p112 Merikanto/WikiMedia Commons, p112 NASA, p113 NASA Goddard Space Flight Center/COBE Science Working Group, p116-117 iStockphoto, p116 Shutterstock, p117 iStockphoto, p118 Norman Pogson/Shutterstock, p119t Uryadnikov Sergey/Shutterstock, p119b Evgeny Murtola/Shutterstock, p120 Wonderlane/flickr, p121c Heiko Kiera/Shutterstock, p121t Steve McWilliam/Shutterstock, p122 Jeff Davies/Shutterstock, p123c Portokalis/Shutterstock, p123tl D. Kucharski & K. Kucharska/Shutterstock, p123tr Shutterstock, p123br nialat/Shutterstock, p123bl Shutterstock, p124t SEFSC Pascagoula Laboratory; Collection of Brandi Noble, NOAA/NMFS/SEFSC, p124b EcoPrint, p124ctr Vinicius Tupinamba , p124cbr Shutterstock, p124cbl Shutterstock, p124cc Shutterstock, p124ctl XAOC/Shutterstock, p125cr Henk Bentlage, p125bl Tania Zbrodko, p125br Lusoimages, p125cl Nancy Nehring/iStockphoto, p125cc Henrik Jonsson/iStockphoto, p126 arindambanerjee/Shutterstock, p127t NASA, p127bl Petr Vopenka/Shutterstock, p127br Rich Carey/Shutterstock, p128 Keith A Frith/Shutterstock, p129bc Borislav Borisov/Shutterstock, p129br Jens Stolt/Shutterstock, p130 Keith A Frith/Shutterstock, p131t Pontus Edenberg/Shutterstock, p131ctl Jonathan Billinger/WikiMedia Commons, p131cl Felix Andrews/WikiMedia Commons, p131b Petrafler/Shutterstock, p131cr alle/Shutterstock, p132t Photo Courtesy of The Heart of England Forest Project, p132b Jonathan Billinger/WikiMedia Commons, p133 Gorshkov25/Shutterstock, p134t hjschneider/Shutterstock, p134b Bob Castle/WikiMedia Commons, p135c MarkMirror/Shutterstock, p135b PJC&Co/WikiMedia Commons, p136t Shutterstock, p136b Institut Pasteur/Unite Des Virus Oncongenes/Science Photo Library, p137c Saturn Stills/Science Photo Library, p137t Brian Chase/Shutterstock, p138 Sue Robinson/Shutterstock, p140 khz/Shutterstock, p141 Bsipvem/Science Photo Library, p142c Medical-on-Line/Alamy, p142t Shutterstock, p144 Lisa F. Young/Shutterstock, p146 iStockphoto, p148c Shutterstock, p148t Maridav/Shutterstock, p149 digitalskillet/iStockphoto, p152-153 iStockphoto, p152 nikkytok/Shutterstock, p153t iStockphoto, p153b iStockphoto, p154c Courtesy of Canland UK (Hot Pack) Ltd. Producers and distributors of Hot Pack Self Heating Nutritious Meals. TM and Non Magnesium Flameless Ration Heaters, p154b Jan Otto/iStockphoto, p156 Phil Date/Shutterstock, p158t Towards Fawley/WikiMedia Commons, p158b David Hay Jones/Science Photo Library, p160b JeffreyRasmussen/Shutterstock , p160t Shutterstock, p161 Martyn F. Chillmaid/Science Photo Library, p162 mevans/iStockphoto, p163c Gualberto Becerra/Shutterstock, p163b Tomas Pavelka/Shutterstock, p164t Volker Steger/Science Photo Library, p164b Benjah-bmm27/WikiMedia Commons, p165 Shutterstock, p166t Lori Martin/Shutterstock, p166b Norman Pogson/Shutterstock, p167b PhillipMinnis/Shutterstock, p167t Gordon Ball LRPS/Shutterstock, p168 Richard Majinder/Shutterstock, p169tl Martin D. Vonka/Shutterstock, p169tr Andrew Lambert Photography/Science Photo Library, p169tc Adisa/Shutterstock, p169c Hywit Dimyadi/Shutterstock, p170t Elena Aliaga/Shutterstock, p170c Ecelop/Shutterstock, p171t Shutterstock, p171c Stephen Aaron Rees/Shutterstock, p171b Graça Victoria/Shutterstock, p172c Jerry Mason/Science Photo Library, p172bl Andrew Lambert Photography/Science Photo Library, p172br Martyn F. Chillmaid/Science Photo Library, p172t sportgraphic/Shutterstock, p174c PAUL Rapson/Science Photo Library, p174t Vidux/Shutterstock, p175t Silvere Teutsch/Eurelios/Science Photo Library, p175b Robert Brook/Science Photo Library, p176 NASA, p177c sgame/Shutterstock, p177t Michael Ströck (mstroeck)/WikiMedia Commons, p178t IsaacLKoval/iStockphoto, p178b Valua Vitaly/Shutterstock, p179c Glenda M. Powers/Shutterstock, p179b Wade H. Massie/Shutterstock, p180 Shutterstock, p181 Philippe Plailly/Eurelios/Science Photo Library, p182t Nejron Photo/Shutterstock, p182b Shutterstock, p183 Shutterstock, p186-187 iStockphoto, p186 iStockphoto, p187 iStockphoto, p188t tirc83/iStockphoto, p188c VisualField/iStockphoto, p190t fstop123/iStockphoto, p190c Shutterstock, p191r thad/iStockphoto, p191l LUke1138/iStockphoto, p192l colleenbradley/iStockphoto, p192r Soubrette/iStockphoto, p193b NASA, p193t Silvia Antunes/Shutterstock, p194t Firehorse/iStockphoto, p194c PeterMooij, p194b Display bookshelf reproduced with kind permission of Daniel Eatock, p195b jhgrigg/iStockphoto, p195c Andrew Blight/Flickr, p196 Shutterstock, p198t Rob Cottrell/Shutterstock, p198b Shutterstock, p199 Mark-W-R/iStockphoto, p200 NASA, p201l Shutterstock, p201r Shutterstock, p201b Shutterstock, p202t elisemeyers/iStockphoto, p202c BlackJack3D/iStockphoto, p204 chrisboy2004/iStockphoto, p205 gmnicholas/iStockphoto, p206 TACrafts, p207 ostill/Shutterstock, p208 borisyankov, p209 Mr Fergus Paterson, Knee Surgeon at the Bupa Cromwell Hospital, SW5 0TU, p209 Pasieka/Science Photo Library, p211c Shutterstock, p211t Seattle dentist Ethan Janson, p212 Shutterstock, p214t tattywelshie, p214b Shutterstock, p215 photobank.ch/Shutterstock, p218t istockphoto, p218b iStockphoto, p218-219 iStockphoto, p219 iStockphoto, p220b DUSAN ZIDAR/Shutterstock, p220t Ieva Geneviciene/Shutterstock, p221t iStockphoto, p221b Shutterstock, p222 Ã?Â??mit Erdem/Shutterstock, p223 Shutterstock, p224 Shutterstock, p225t Joe_Potato/iStockphoto, p225c AlexSava/iStockphoto, p225b Shutterstock, p226t Shutterstock, p226br Shutterstock, p226bl Alistair Scott/Shutterstock, p227t iStockphoto, p227b John Panella/iStockphoto, p228 Shutterstock, p229 Shutterstock, p230 Africa Studio/Shutterstock, p232t Shantell/iStockphoto, p232bl Shutterstock, p232br Shutterstock, p234 dagfrida/iStockphoto, p235b Sage78/iStockphoto, p235t WikiMedia Commons, p235c WikiMedia Commons, p236t NI Syndication, p236b Iwona Grodzka/Shutterstock, p237 Lisa Eastman/Shutterstock, p238 WikiMedia Commons, p239 Dr P. Marazzi/Science Photo Library, p240l Shutterstock, p240r Shutterstock, p241l Centers for Disease Control and Prevention's Public Health Image Library (PHIL), p241r Linde1/iStockphoto, p242 maska/Shutterstock, p243 Science Photo Library, p248t A. Dowsett, Health Protection Agency/Science Photo Library, p248b Health Protection Agency/Science Photo Library, p249t Adam Fraise/Shutterstock, p249c tln/Shutterstock, p249b Guntars Grebezs/iStockphoto, p250t lculig/Shutterstock, p250br Sebastian Kaulitzki/Shutterstock, p250c JMiks/Shutterstock, p250bl Ecelop/Shutterstock, p251t vilax/Shutterstock, p251c Scientifica, Visuals Unlimited/Science Photo Library, p251b Patrick Landmann/Science Photo Library, p252c Nomad_Soul/Shutterstock, p252b David Sprott/Shutterstock, p253 Andrew Lambert Photography/Science Photo Library, p254 Pascal Goetgheluck/Science Photo Library, p255 Pascal Goetgheluck/Science Photo Library, p256 .shock/Shutterstock, p259 Charles D. Winters/Science Photo Library, p260 TRIG/Shutterstock, p261 Andrew Lambert Photography/Science Photo Library, p262 l i g h t po e t/Shutterstock, p264 Rob Cottrell/Shutterstock, p266 Guillaume P./Science Photo Library, p268 Maurizio Milanesio/Shutterstock, p269 Kzenon/Shutterstock, p270 auremar/Shutterstock, p277 Pixel 4 Images/Shutterstock.

Contents

Unit 4 Biology and Our Environment — 116

First Award in Application of Science

Unit 5 Applications of Chemical Substances — 152

Unit 6 Applications of Physical Science — 186

Unit 7 Health Applications of Life Science 218

Unit 8 Scientific Skills 246

Preparing for exams 277

Carrying Out Scientific Investigations 278

Glossary 284

Index 295

Welcome to Collins BTEC First Applied Science!

This Student Book aims to help you achieve Pass, Merit and Distinction in the new BTEC First Awards. Units 1–4 build towards the Award in Principles of Science, and Units 5–8 towards the Award in Application of Science. The book is filled with exciting, relevant science content and many useful features to give you the knowledge and skills you need to succeed in your assessment. This overview shows you how to make the best use of your BTEC First Applied Science Student Book.

You will need to pass an **exam** to gain your BTEC First Award. Unit 1 and Unit 8 are assessed by exams worth 25% of your final mark. Examined units are highlighted in red. The science you need to know for your exam is bought to life with real-life examples and clear illustrations. You need to learn as much as you can.

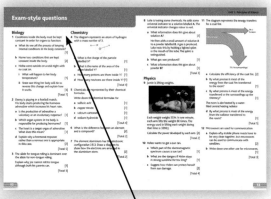

Exam-style questions found at the end of Units 1 and 8 let you practise your answers and check how much you can remember.

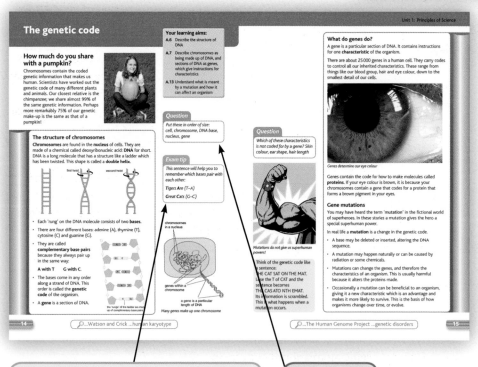

Some hints and tips for exams can be found on page 277.

Exam tips give you useful information to help you to prepare for your exam, like ways of remembering key facts.

Questions help you check your understanding.

Other BTEC units are assessed using **assignments** that your teacher will set you in class during the year. Typically, the assignments will describe a scenario with you as a worker in a science-related industry. You will be asked to carry out specific work-related tasks that will meet your grading criteria. You will be expected to work steadily and independently to meet assignment deadlines. This is probably different from most courses you have taken up to this point and present you with new opportunities to learn, and maybe some new challenges.

The **real-life introductions** to each topic will help you see how the science is used in a science-related industry.

The **Assessment Criteria** show you what part of your assignment you are learning about. At the end of the unit, you can use the **Assessment Checklist** to ensure that you have covered everything.

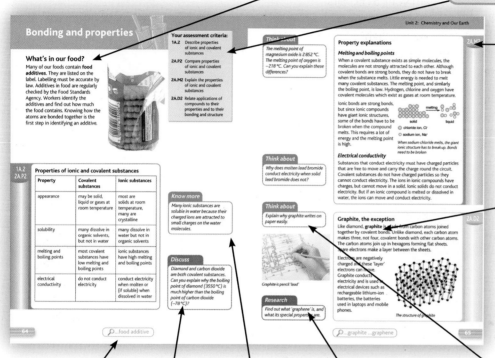

The content is divided into **Pass**, **Merit** and **Distinction** in bronze, silver and gold boxes. The Merit and Distinction boxes will give you good starting points for your further research and study.

Scientific terms can be frightening. Even some everyday English words can be difficult to understand. All the bold words have been explained in the **glossary** (p. 284) to make sure that you understand all the content.

The **Internet** will be a valuable resource when you do research for your assignment work. But it can also give you endless unnecessary information if you don't search carefully. We have supplied search terms on every page to help you to find the right information quickly.

Extra interesting **facts** help you build a good base of science knowledge.

There are starting points for **independent study** to help you progress and do well in your Merit and Distinction assignments.

See if you can **think like a scientist** to find solutions to problems.

Science can lead to interesting **debates**. Discuss ideas with your classmates. Find out their opinions and make sure that you voice your own.

You will find lots of useful information about carrying out scientific investigations in the practical work section which starts on page 278. Planning and investigation, carrying it out, collecting and displaying data and working safely are all covered.

Unit 1 **Principles of Science**

Be able to explore cells, organs and genes

- The human body contains about 200 different types of cells which carry out their own function

- Genes carry codes to control inherited characteristics such as blood group and hair colour

- You can work out the probability of children inheriting characteristics from their parents

Be able to explore the roles of the nervous and endocrine systems in homeostasis and communication

- If you swim in icy cold water your body will start up processes to make sure your body temperature does not decrease too much

- Organs and tissues in the body communicate with each other via impulses along nerve cells or by hormones flowing in the blood

Be able to explore atomic structure and the periodic table

- The periodic table contains the names and symbols of all known elements

- Lithium, sodium and potassium are so reactive that we have to store them under oil

- Argon gas is so unreactive that we use it to blanket metal-arc welding

- The hydrogen in heavy water has extra neutrons in its hydrogen atoms

Be able to explore substances and chemical reactions

- The human stomach contains hydrochloric acid to help digest food; stomach pains are sometimes caused by insufficient acid which should not be treated with an alkali

- It is said that if you put vinegar on a wasp sting it will neutralise the alkali in the sting, and bee stings are acidic so can be treated with toothpaste; in reality a wasp sting is almost neutral and a bee sting has many complex chemicals which contribute to the pain

Be able to explore the importance of energy stores, energy transfers and energy transformations

- The Sun is the ultimate source of energy on Earth

- Renewable energy sources include cow dung and peat

- Many refrigerated lorries are painted light colours; this reduces energy absorbed by thermal radiation so the energy needed to keep the lorries cool is reduced

Be able to explore the properties and applications of waves in the electromagnetic spectrum

- Some animals have eyes that are not sensitive to visible light; some snakes, birds and fish 'see' using infrared radiation, while some birds, fish and insects use ultraviolet radiation

- The first X-ray image was accidently produced in 1895 by Wilhelm Röntgend; he called the rays 'X' because they were unknown

- In 1974, scientists sent a coded message towards a star system near the edge of our galaxy to see if there was intelligent life there; the reply is not expected for 40 000 years because the distances are so large

Cells and tissues

Your learning aims:

A.1 Describe the basic structure, function and adaptations of plant and animal cells

A.2 Describe the functions of cell components

A.3 Identify cells, tissues, organs and organ systems

From one cell to trillions

The photo from a microscope shows a sperm being injected into an egg in order to fertilise it. This tiny fertilised egg is only one cell but will it grow into an adult with around 100 trillion (10^{14}) cells.

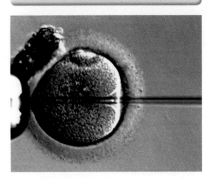

The structure of cells

Like a house is built out of bricks, most living organisms are made up of many **cells**. A cell is made of different **components**. Some components are found in all cells; other components are found just in some cells but not in others.

Most animal and plant cells contain the following components:

* a **nucleus** that contains the chromosomes, which carry genes that control the activities of the cell

* **cytoplasm**, a jelly-like material which gives the cell shape; it is where chemical reactions take place

* a **cell membrane** which surrounds the cell and controls what goes in and out

* **mitochondria** where sugars are broken down to release energy in a reaction called respiration.

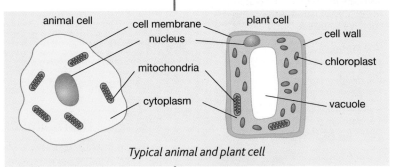

Typical animal and plant cell

Plant cells also contain:

* **chloroplasts** where photosynthesis takes place

* a **cell wall** which surrounds the cell membrane and gives the cell its rigid shape

* a **vacuole** which contains a liquid called cell sap; this provides extra support for the cell.

Different types of cells

Sperm and egg are both types of cells but they look very different from each other and from the typical animal cell shown above. They have special structures, or **adaptations**, that enable them to carry out a function.

> **Question**
>
> *Why do muscle cells contain lots of mitochondria?*

> **Exam tip**
>
> *You might be asked if a cell is from an animal or a plant. Only plant cells have two outer layers: the cell membrane and the cell wall.*

> **Exam tip**
>
> *Make sure you can explain how a special feature of each cell allows it to carry out its function.*

...cell structure ...plant and animal cells

The human body contains about 200 different types of cell. Some are shown here.

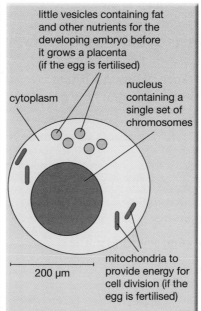

little vesicles containing fat and other nutrients for the developing embryo before it grows a placenta (if the egg is fertilised)

cytoplasm

nucleus containing a single set of chromosomes

mitochondria to provide energy for cell division (if the egg is fertilised)

200 μm

Egg cell
Function: forms an embryo when fertilised by a sperm

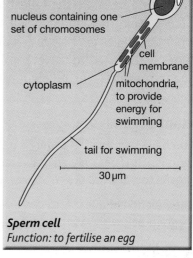

vesicle containing enzymes, to digest a way into the egg

nucleus containing one set of chromosomes

cytoplasm

cell membrane

mitochondria, to provide energy for swimming

tail for swimming

30 μm

Sperm cell
Function: to fertilise an egg

cytoplasm containing haemoglobin, which transports oxygen

cell membrane

5 μm

This is what the cell would look like if cut in half. The shape is good for taking in and letting out oxygen. Notice that the red blood cell does not have a nucleus.

Red blood cell
Function: to carry oxygen around the body

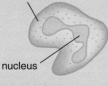

cytoplasm contains enzymes to break down the microbes

nucleus

White blood cell
Function: to kill disease-causing microbes that enter the body

Tissues, organs and organ systems

In an animal or a plant, a **tissue** is a group of similar cells that all work together to carry out a particular function.

Organs, like the stomach, skin and heart, are made of tissues. Each organ contains many different tissues.

For example, the heart contains:

- muscular tissue, which contracts and relaxes to produce the pumping action of the heart

- nervous tissue, which controls the beating of the heart

- epithelial tissue, which covers the outside and the inside of the heart.

An organ system is a group of organs that performs a particular function. The heart and blood vessels make up the **cardiovascular system**. Its function is to carry blood around the body.

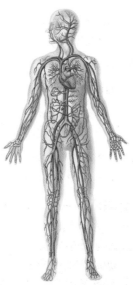

The cardiovascular system

Question

Arteries are a type of blood vessel that contain different types of cell, including epithelial and muscle cells. Are they a type of tissue or organ?

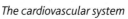
...specialised cells in the human body ...human organ systems

Plant organs

A long journey

Giant redwood trees are the tallest plants on Earth. Water has to travel from their roots and up their trunks in a constant stream to supply the leaves at the top – a distance of around 100 m! Why does water need to travel through the tree and how does it manage to make this incredible journey?

Plant organs

You have seen that an **organ** is a structure with a particular function. It is not only animals that have organs. Plants have organs too, such as stems, leaves and roots.

The function of a leaf is to carry out **photosynthesis**. The diagram below shows the inside of a leaf.

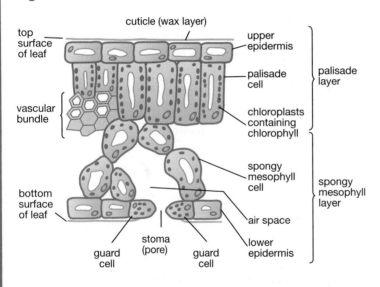

The different **tissues** in a leaf work together so photosynthesis can take place.

- Water and dissolved minerals reach the leaf from the roots through **xylem**.

- Carbon dioxide gas from the air enters the leaf through tiny holes called **stomata** (each one is called a stoma).

- Photosynthesis takes place in the chloroplasts of cells. Light is used to provide energy for the reaction between water and carbon dioxide. A sugar called glucose is made.

- Glucose is the plant's food. It is transported around the plant in **phloem**.

Stem – transports substances up and down the plant, and holds the flowers and leaves up in the air

Leaves – where a plant makes food by photosynthesis. They are usually wide and flat so they can get plenty of sunlight

Roots – anchor the plant so it doesn't fall over; also absorb water and minerals from the soil

The main organs of a plant

Question

Why do cells in the leaves contain lots of chloroplasts?

Exam tip

Be clear about how the different organs work together to provide the plant with food.

...photosynthesis ...plant organs

Adapted plant cells

The plant tissues are made up of cells that are adapted to carry out their function. Some of these cells are shown below:

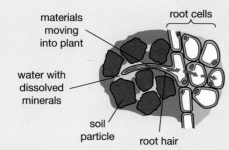

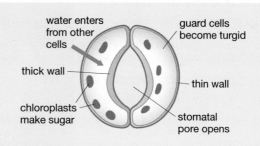

Root hair cell
Function: has a fine hair-like extension that increases the uptake of water and minerals from the soil

Guard cell
Function: controls the opening and closing of the stoma

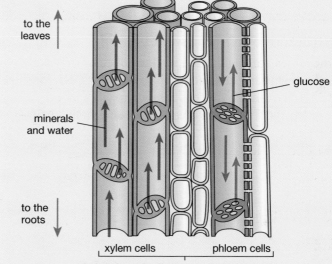

long tubes of cells that run inside the stem

Xylem and phloem cells
Function: xylem carries water from the roots to the leaves and flowers; phloem carries glucose to all parts of the plant

Question

Greenfly are tiny insects that feed on the contents of a plant's phloem tubes. Why might this kill the plant?

Water travels up xylem like a drink up a straw

Transpiration

Water moves through xylem because of **transpiration**. Water evaporates into a gas called water vapour, exiting the leaves through the stomata.

Water is absorbed by the roots and travels up the xylem to replace what has been lost. A similar process happens when water is drunk through a straw.

Water evaporates from leaves more rapidly on hot, dry days. This explains why plants need to be watered more often in the summer.

The genetic code

Your learning aims:

A.6 Describe the structure of DNA

A.7 Describe chromosomes as being made up of DNA, and sections of DNA as genes, which give instructions for characteristics

A.13 Understand what is meant by a mutation and how it can affect an organism

How much do you share with a pumpkin?

Chromosomes contain the coded genetic information that makes us human. Scientists have worked out the genetic code of many different plants and animals. Our closest relative is the chimpanzee; we share almost 99% of the same genetic information. Perhaps more remarkably 75% of our genetic make-up is the same as that of a pumpkin!

Question

Put these in order of size: cell, chromosome, DNA base, nucleus, gene

The structure of chromosomes

Chromosomes are found in the **nucleus** of cells. They are made of a chemical called deoxyribonucleic acid: **DNA** for short. DNA is a long molecule that has a structure like a ladder which has been twisted. This shape is called a **double helix**.

  first twist second twist

Exam tip

This sentence will help you to remember which bases pair with each other:

***T**igers **A**re (T–A)*

***G**reat **C**ats (G–C)*

- Each 'rung' on the DNA molecule consists of two **bases**.

- There are four different bases: adenine (A), thymine (T), cytosine (C) and guanine (G).

- They are called **complementary base pairs** because they always pair up in the same way:

  A with T   G with C.

- The bases come in any order along a strand of DNA. This order is called the **genetic code** of the organism.

- A **gene** is a section of DNA.

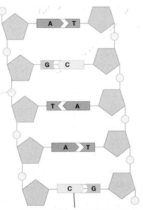

the 'rungs' of the ladder are made up of complimentary base pairs

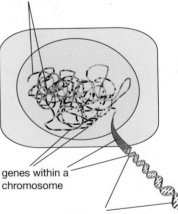

chromosomes in a nucleus

genes within a chromosome

a gene is a particular length of DNA

Many genes make up one chromosome

...Watson and Crick ...human karyotype

What do genes do?

A gene is a particular section of DNA. It contains instructions for one **characteristic** of the organism.

There are about 25 000 genes in a human cell. They carry codes to control all our inherited characteristics. These range from things like our blood group, hair and eye colour, down to the smallest detail of our cells.

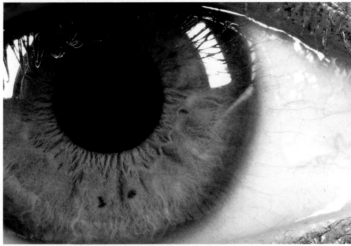

Genes determine our eye colour

Genes contain the code for how to make molecules called **proteins**. If your eye colour is brown, it is because your chromosomes contain a gene that codes for a protein that forms a brown pigment in your eyes.

Gene mutations

You may have heard the term '**mutation**' in the fictional world of superheroes. In these stories a mutation gives the hero a special superhuman power.

In real life a **mutation** is a change in the genetic code.

- A base may be deleted or inserted, altering the DNA sequence.
- A mutation may happen naturally or can be caused by radiation or some chemicals.
- Mutations can change the genes, and therefore the characteristics of an organism. This is usually harmful because it alters the proteins made.
- Occasionally a mutation can be beneficial to an organism, giving it a new characteristic which is an advantage and makes it more likely to survive. This is the basis of how organisms change over time, or evolve.

> ### Question
>
> *Which of these characteristics is not coded for by a gene? Skin colour, ear shape, hair length*

Mutations do not give us superhuman powers!

> Think of the genetic code like a sentence:
> THE CAT SAT ON THE MAT.
> Lose the T of CAT and the sentence becomes
> THE CAS ATO NTH EMAT.
> Its information is scrambled.
> This is what happens when a mutation occurs.

...The Human Genome Project ...genetic disorders

Inheritance

Your learning aims:

A.8 Describe what alleles are and how they give rise to heterozygous and homozygous genotypes

A.9–12 Work out the outcome of a genetic cross

What's the risk?

Sally's younger brother Mark has a genetic disease called cystic fibrosis. This means that it is passed down through families. She is planning to start a family with her husband and they are worried that they could have a baby with the disease. A genetic counsellor helps them to find out how likely this is.

Genes and alleles

Alleles are different forms of a gene.

You inherit a pair of alleles for each characteristic, one from each of your parents. Different combinations of alleles lead to different characteristics.

Cystic fibrosis is caused by an allele with a mutation.

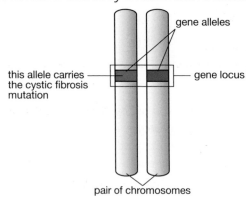

this allele carries the cystic fibrosis mutation — gene alleles — gene locus — pair of chromosomes

Genotypes and phenotypes

- Your **phenotype** is the characteristic you have. Mark has the phenotype cystic fibrosis.

- Your **genotype** is the pair of alleles that you have for each characteristic. We represent alleles as letters, e.g. A or a.

- If you have a pair of the same alleles (aa or AA) you are **homozygous** for this gene. If you have different alleles (Aa) you are **heterozygous**.

- The alleles in each pair can be **recessive** (a) or **dominant** (A). The effects of a dominant allele mask a recessive one.

- The allele for cystic fibrosis is recessive (a). This means that, to have the disease, Mark must have two copies of the cystic fibrosis allele. He has the genotype aa.

- Sally does not have the illness. She could have the genotype AA or Aa but she is not sure which.

Exam tip

Remember, other characteristics are inherited. Eye colour is an example. In simple terms, the allele for brown eyes is dominant over the allele for blue eyes. You could have brown eyes, but still be a carrier of the blue allele.

Question

Why is Sally not sure which genotype she has?

...alleles ...genetic terms

Family pedigrees

Characteristics are passed from one generation to the next. This can be shown in Sally's family **pedigree chart**.

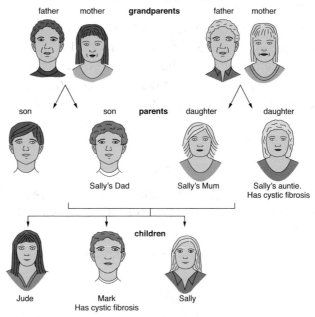

Other than cystic fibrosis, what other characteristics are passed down through Sally's family?

After seeing the chart, Sally and her husband David decide to take a test to find out their genotypes.

Genetic crosses

The results revealed that Sally has the genotype Aa. David has the genotype AA.

Sally is a **carrier** of the cystic fibrosis allele.

The genetic counsellor can now work out the chance of them having a child with the illness. She uses a genetic diagram called a **Punnett square** to do this.

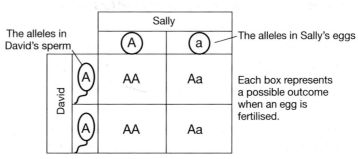

The probability that they will have a baby that is a carrier of the cystic fibrosis allele (Aa) is one in two (50%). There is zero chance of having a baby with the illness (aa).

Question

Sally's sister Jude wonders what her chance of carrying the cystic fibrosis allele is. Use a genetic cross to work this out. Hint: her parents do not have the illness, but her brother does.

Control mechanisms

Ice swimming

A traditional activity in Finland is to go swimming in water just above 0 °C. This would be dangerous if done for a long period of time, as a reduction in body temperature below 37 °C can result in hypothermia and death. However, there are claims that subjecting your body to short bursts of low temperature is actually beneficial to health.

Homeostasis

Keeping conditions stable, or constant, is called **homeostasis**.

For living things, 'conditions' means the body's internal environment.

Organs can be damaged by changes in body temperature and in the water and sugar content of the blood.

Homeostasis in the human body is controlled by two types of communication:

*   the **nervous system** communicates using adapted cells called nerve cells or **neurones**; they send messages, or impulses, around the body

*   the **endocrine system** uses chemical messengers called **hormones**.

Thermoregulation

Thermoregulation is an example of homeostasis. It is how the nervous system regulates body temperature.

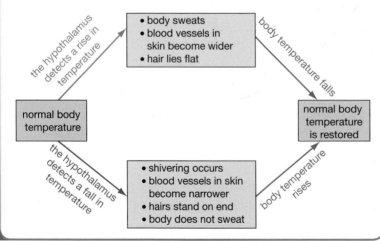

Exam tip

It is important that you learn the definition of the term 'homeostasis'.

Question

What temperature does thermoregulation aim to keep the body at?

Warming up

You decide to go ice swimming. On contact with the cold water your blood temperature will start to decrease. This is detected by an area in your brain called the **hypothalamus**. It sends impulses along neurones to the skin.

A number of mechanisms that help increase your temperature back up to normal will start.

Shivering

Tiny muscles under the skin contract and relax very quickly. Chemical reactions in the muscle cells release energy that powers their contraction. The reactions also release heat, helping to keep you warm.

Raising of body hair

Your body hair raised away from the skin traps a layer of air next to it. Air, being a poor conductor of heat, insulates the body from heat loss.

Vasoconstriction

You may notice that your skin looks paler. This is because blood vessels called arterioles running through the skin have narrowed, reducing the flow of blood through the small blood capillaries in the skin. Less blood means that less heat is lost from the skin's surface to the outside.

You leave the icy water but these mechanisms will continue until your body temperature is back up to 37°C.

Cooling down

You decide to sit inside a hot sauna. Now, your body temperature will start to increase. Changes in the skin help to prevent you from overheating.

Sweating

Sweat glands in the skin produce sweat and release it on to the skin's surface. Heat from the body evaporates the water in sweat, transferring heat away from the skin and cooling you down.

Lowering of body hair

Your body hair lying flat against the skin prevents a layer of air becoming trapped next to it.

Vasodilation

You are flushed red as more blood, warmed by body heat, flows through your blood vessels in the skin because the arterioles have widened.

Exam tip

It is not simply that having sweat on the skin makes you cooler: the sweat evaporates. To do this it needs heat energy, which it takes from the skin.

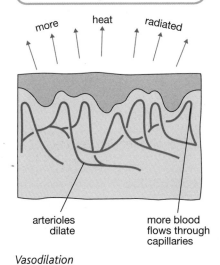

Vasodilation

Question

Explain how vasodilation cools down the body.

The nervous system

On your marks...

It's the 100 m sprint final. The starting gun fires and inside the athletes' bodies impulses are sent along nerves to the muscles, ordering them to move. It is important that this happens quickly.

Your learning aims:

A.1, B.2 Identify the main parts of the nervous system

B.3 Understand the difference between involuntary and voluntary responses

B.4, B.5 Describe the role of a reflex arc

Question

You pick up a hot pan and immediately drop it. You ease the burn by putting your hand under running cold water.

Name one involuntary and one voluntary response in this sentence.

Responding to stimuli

Imagine stepping on a drawing pin. The sharp point pricking your skin is the **stimulus** causing the response of pulling your foot away. You don't think about it; it's an **involuntary response** to protect your foot from even more damage.

Imagine your mobile is ringing. What do you do? You look to see who's ringing before answering it. This is a **voluntary response** because you thought about your action.

The nervous system

The function of the nervous system is to coordinate these responses. It is made up of two parts:

- the **central nervous system** (**CNS**) is the brain and spinal cord

- the **peripheral nervous system** (**PNS**) consists of the nerves connecting the central nervous system to all parts of the body.

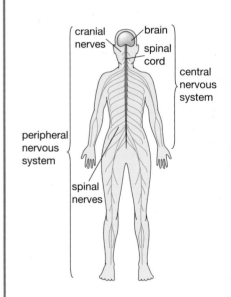

Neurones

Nerves are bundles of special cells called neurones. Neurones consist of a cell body and thin fibres that stretch out from it. Electrical **impulses** pass along the fibres. There are two main types of neurone, which send impulses in different directions.

- **Sensory neurones** send impulses from **receptors** to the central nervous system. Receptors detect stimuli. For example, you have receptors in your eyes that detect light.

- **Motor neurones** send impulses from the central nervous system to **effectors**. Effectors are muscles and glands.

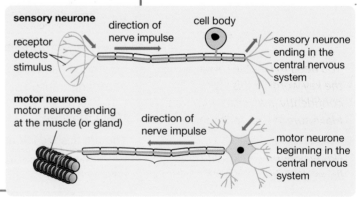

🔍 ...CNS ...sense organs

Question

Why do reflex actions need to be fast?

Exam tip

You may be shown a diagram of a reflex arc in an exam and be asked to name the parts. Take a look at the direction the nerve impulses are travelling. They always travel in the path: receptor → sensory neurone → relay neurone → motor neurone → effector.

The reflex arc

The involuntary behaviour of someone stepping on a pin is an example of a **reflex response**. It is automatic and quickly removes the foot from the pin.

Most reflex responses are fast, bypassing the brain, and helping to protect the body from damage.

A reflex response is brought about by a chain of nerves called a **reflex arc**:

- sensory neurones send nerve impulses from receptors to the spinal cord

- **relay neurones** in the spinal cord receive nerve impulses from sensory neurones and send them to motor neurones

- motor neurones send nerve impulses from the spinal cord to effectors, where a response happens.

The diagram shows how the reflex arc works; the numbers indicate the path of the nerve impulses.

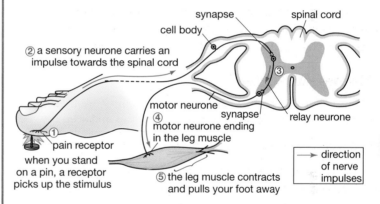

Synapses

Tiny gaps called **synapses** separate neurones.

The diagram below shows how impulses travel across a synapse using chemicals.

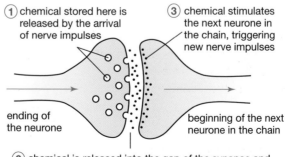

① chemical stored here is released by the arrival of nerve impulses

③ chemical stimulates the next neurone in the chain, triggering new nerve impulses

ending of the neurone

beginning of the next neurone in the chain

② chemical is released into the gap of the synapse and passes across the synapse

Exam tip

You need to be able to use the key words in this topic confidently in an exam question. Make sure you understand the difference between receptor and effector; neurone and nerve; sensory and motor.

...reflex arc ...neurotransmitters

Hormones at work

Fright: flight or fight?

Coming across this dog would cause you to experience rapid breathing and a racing heart. These responses cause extra glucose and oxygen carried in the bloodstream to reach your muscles quickly, enabling them to work hard. The hormone adrenaline is responsible for this. Your body is now ready for an important choice: do you stay or run away?

Your learning aims:

B.6, B.7 Understand how the endocrine system is used for communication and how its action differs from the nervous system

B.8 Describe how blood glucose concentration is regulated

The endocrine system

Hormones are chemicals produced by glands in the body and released into the blood. The glands that produce hormones are called **endocrine glands** and are part of the **endocrine system**.

Hormones travel in the bloodstream and affect their **target organs** and tissues. The sequence goes like this:

*   the endocrine gland produces...

*   a hormone, which circulates in...

*   the blood, where the hormone affects...

*   the target organ or tissue.

Hormones help to regulate the body's activities and keep the body's internal environment constant (**homeostasis**). Regulating body water content and blood glucose levels are examples.

The diagram shows some glands that produce hormones.

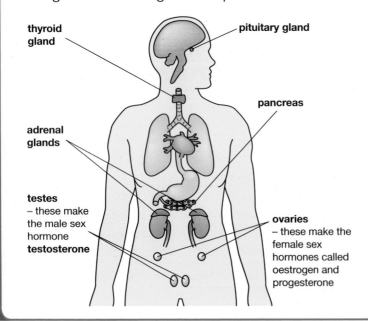

thyroid gland

pituitary gland

pancreas

adrenal glands

testes – these make the male sex hormone **testosterone**

ovaries – these make the female sex hormones called oestrogen and progesterone

Question

Name one target organ or tissue of the hormone adrenaline.

Exam tip

Remember, hormones travel in the blood so they will come into contact with all organs and tissues. However, they only affect their target organs and tissues.

🔍 ...flight or fight ...adrenaline

Exam tip

Be careful not to get the key words glucose, glycogen and glucagon mixed up. They are very similar but have different meanings.

Controlling blood glucose

An endocrine gland called the pancreas produces two hormones: **insulin** and **glucagon**. These hormones help to regulate blood glucose levels.

When blood glucose is too high:

- Insulin is released from the pancreas and travels in the blood to...
- its target tissues, the muscles and the liver.
- It decreases the level of blood glucose by...
- causing cells to take up glucose from the blood and store it as **glycogen**.

When blood glucose is too low:

- Glucagon is released from the pancreas and travels in the blood to...
- ts target organ, the liver.
- It increases the level of blood glucose by...
- causing the cells to turn glycogen back into glucose.

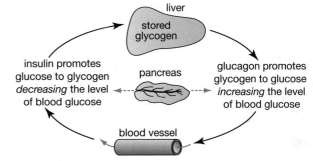

Control of blood glucose

Question

People with type 1 diabetes do not make insulin. Why is this dangerous if left untreated?

Differences in communication

Both the endocrine and nervous systems are responsible for sending messages around the body. The table below shows some differences between them.

	Nervous system	Endocrine system
How the 'message' is sent	by electrical impulses in neurones	by chemical hormones in the blood
Speed of the 'message'	very fast – milliseconds	slow – hours, days and even months (the exception is adrenaline)
How long the response lasts	stops quickly	remains active for a long time

The periodic table

Your learning aims:

C.1 Describe where metals and non-metals appear in the periodic table

C.8 Explain how elements are arranged in the periodic table according to their atomic number and properties

An accident waiting to happen

Hydrogen reacts explosively with oxygen. In 1937, the Hindenburg passenger airship caught fire as it landed in America after a flight from Germany. The airship was filled with hydrogen. Modern airships are filled with helium.

Scientists use the **periodic table** of the elements to see patterns in the properties of **elements** and in how they react.

Metals and non-metals in the periodic table

1	2											3	4	5	6	7	0
						1 H											2 He
3 Li	4 Be											5 B	6 C	7 N	8 O	9 F	10 Ne
11 Na	12 Mg											13 Al	14 Si	15 P	16 S	17 Cl	18 Ar
19 K	20 Ca	21 Sc	22 Ti	23 V	24 Cr	25 Mn	26 Fe	27 Co	28 Ni	29 Cu	30 Zn	31 Ga	32 Ge	33 As	34 Se	35 Br	36 Kr
37 Rb	38 Sr	39 Y	40 Zr	41 Nb	42 Mo	43 Tc	44 Ru	45 Rh	46 Pd	47 Ag	48 Cd	49 In	50 Sn	51 Sb	52 Te	53 I	54 Xe
55 Cs	56 Ba	57 La	72 Hf	73 Ta	74 W	75 Re	76 Os	77 Ir	78 Pt	79 Au	80 Hg	81 Tl	82 Pb	83 Bi	84 Po	85 At	86 Rn
87 Fr	88 Ra	89 Ac															

The simplified periodic table shows a large number of metals (coloured blue) and a small number of non-metals (coloured yellow).

...periodic table ...Hindenburg

Groups and periods

Each element has its own symbol. Hydrogen is H and gold is Au. The number of the element in the periodic table is called the **atomic number**.

The horizontal rows in the periodic table are called **periods**. All of the elements in the same period have the same number of electron shells in their atoms.

The vertical columns are called **groups**. All of the elements in a group have very similar properties.

Group 1 elements (on the left of the periodic table) are very reactive. Their reactivity increases down the group.

Question

Which element in group 1 is the most reactive?

Lithium (Li) is at the top of group 1. It reacts with water to form hydrogen and lithium hydroxide

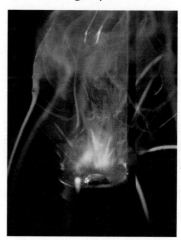

Potassium (K) is lower in group 1. It reacts with water to form hydrogen and potassium hydroxide

The reactivity of metals decreases across a period from group 1 to group 2 and to group 3.

Group 7 elements are non-metals that are also very reactive. Their reactivity decreases down the group.

This is what happens when the group 7 elements react with iron wool:

Question

Which element in group 7 is the most reactive?

Element	Symbol	Reaction with iron wool
fluorine	F	Iron wool bursts into flame as fluorine passes over it. No heating is required.
chlorine	Cl	Hot iron wool glows brightly when chlorine passes over it.
bromine	Br	Hot iron wool glows, but less brightly, when bromine vapour passes over it.
iodine	I	Hot iron wool shows a faint red glow when iodine vapour passes over it.

Exam tip

Remember that reactivity increases down group 1 but decreases down group 7.

...alkali metals video ...group 7 elements

Structure of the atom

Your learning aims:

C.2, C.3 Describe the structure of the atom as a very small nucleus containing protons and neutrons, surrounded by electrons in shells

C.4 Explain how atoms of a given element have the same number of protons in the nucleus and that this number is unique to that element

C.5–C.7 Understand the relationship between atomic number, mass number and the numbers of particles in an atom and its overall charge

Solid gold?

This gold ring contains more than 20 000 000 000 000 000 000 000 atoms. An atom is the smallest part of an element that can possibly exist. But most of an atom is empty space!

Atoms

Atoms are the building blocks of all matter, both living and non-living. They can join together in millions of different ways to make all the materials around us.

- Atoms are very small and have very little mass.

- An atom is made up of a **nucleus** that is surrounded by **electrons**.

- The nucleus is very small compared to the size of the atom. It is made up of **protons** and **neutrons**.

- Protons are positively charged and neutrons have no charge. This means that the nucleus has a positive charge.

- Electrons that surround the nucleus each carry a negative charge.

- The electrons orbit the nucleus in **shells**. These shells correspond to different energy levels.

- If an electron moves from a lower energy level to a higher energy level, energy is absorbed by the atom.

- If an electron moves from a higher to a lower energy level, energy is released (often as light).

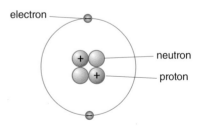

...atoms ...protons and neutrons

Particles in the atom

The relative mass of a proton is 1.

The relative mass of a neutron is also 1.

The relative mass of an electron is 0.0005, which is effectively zero.

	Charge	Mass (relative)
electron	−1	0.0005 (zero)
proton	+1	1
neutron	0	1

Atoms always have the same number of electrons as protons. This means that overall an atom has no charge.

Helium has two protons and two neutrons in its nucleus. The charge on the nucleus is +2.

Two electrons orbit helium's nucleus. This means that the total negative charge is −2.

Atomic number

Each atom has an **atomic number**. The atomic number is the number of protons in an atom. It is also the number of electrons.

If the atomic number of an element is known, it can be identified by looking on the periodic table.

The atomic number for helium is 2 because it has two protons.

Mass number

The **mass number** of an atom is the total number of protons and neutrons in the atom.

There are two neutrons and two protons in a helium nucleus. The mass number for helium is 4.

Relative atomic mass

Atoms of different elements have different masses. We compare their masses using the **relative atomic mass** scale. Hydrogen has a mass of 1 on this scale.

Other elements are heavier. For example, carbon has a relative atomic mass of 12.

Most versions of the periodic table include the relative atomic mass of the elements.

> 12
> C
> carbon
> 6

the relative atomic mass is always the larger of the two numbers by an element

> **Question**
>
> *Give two differences between an electron and a proton.*

> **Question**
>
> *What is the atomic number for gold?*

Isotopes

Your learning aims:

C.9 Describe an isotope of an element as having the same number of protons but a different number of neutrons

C.10 Explain why the existence of isotopes leads to relative atomic masses not being whole numbers

C.11 Explain how the relative atomic mass of an element can be calculated from the relative masses and abundances of its isotopes

What's stinging my eyes?

It's the chlorine used to disinfect swimming pools that can sting your eyes.

Chlorine is an element. Its atomic number is 17. Its relative atomic mass is 35.5. How can we explain the 'half'?

Chlorine

Chlorine is a yellow gas. It is very dangerous.

During World War 1, the German army were the first to use chlorine gas at the battle of Ypres in 1915. The gas causes a burning sensation in the throat and chest pains. It can lead to a painful death – you suffocate.

Chlorine occurs naturally in two different forms.

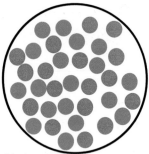

chlorine-35

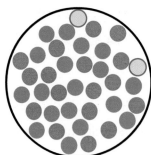

chlorine-37

All types of chlorine have 17 protons ● in the nucleus of the atom. This is because the atomic number is 17. There are also 17 electrons orbiting the nucleus.

Three-quarters of the naturally occurring chlorine atoms have 18 neutrons ● in the nucleus. This means the mass number is 35.

The remaining chlorine has two extra neutrons ◯ in the nucleus. This means the mass number is 37.

Chlorine gas

...chlorine isotopes

Isotopes

Every element can exist in different forms, with different numbers of neutrons in the atomic nuclei.

These forms are called **isotopes**.

When writing the symbols for isotopes, both the atomic number and the mass number are included, as shown in the table below.

Isotope	Protons	Electrons	Neutrons
$^{35}_{17}Cl$	17	17	35 − 17 = 18
$^{37}_{17}Cl$	17	17	37 − 17 = 20

Some elements have a large number of naturally occurring isotopes. Some have only two.

Other isotopes are produced artificially using nuclear reactors. Some isotopes are radioactive because their nuclei are unstable (see Unit 3).

Relative atomic mass

Because elements have different isotopes, a naturally occurring sample of an element has a relative atomic mass that is not necessarily a whole number.

- 75% of chlorine has an atomic number of 35.
- 25% of chlorine has an atomic number of 37.

Relative atomic mass of chlorine =
$$(0.75 \times 35) + (0.25 \times 37) = 35.5$$

- 49% of zinc has an atomic number of 64.
- 28% of zinc has an atomic number of 66.
- 4% of zinc has an atomic number of 67.
- 19% of zinc has an atomic number of 68.

Relative atomic mass of zinc =
$$(0.49 \times 64) + (0.28 \times 66) + (0.04 \times 67) + (0.19 \times 68) = 65.4$$

Exam tip

Remember the mass number is the larger of the two numbers and is at the top. The lower number is the atomic number.

Question

How many protons, electrons and neutrons are there in these isotopes of hydrogen, carbon, lead and sodium?

(a) $^{3}_{1}H$

(b) $^{14}_{6}C$

(c) $^{206}_{82}Pb$

(d) $^{24}_{11}Na$

...relative atomic mass isotopes

Electron shells

Your learning aims:

C.12 Describe the rules about the filling of electron shells and predict the electronic structure for the first 20 elements in the periodic table

C.13 Explain the relationship between the number of outer electrons and the position of an element in the periodic table

Silicon is a very useful element

This ant is holding a microchip. Microchips are used in computers and contain very many complex electronic circuits printed onto thin wafers of silicon. Silicon has an atomic number of 14. The nucleus of each atom contains 14 protons and 14 neutrons. There are 14 electrons that orbit the nucleus in shells of different energy levels.

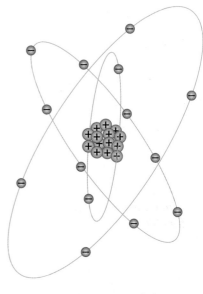

*How we imagine an atom of silicon (although the nucleus is **far** smaller)*

Schematic diagrams

Scientists usually represent an atom's electron shells by schematic two-dimensional diagrams. This is one for the silicon atom.

These show the nucleus at the centre with the electrons in circular orbits around it.

First shell

Electrons fill shells in a particular order depending on their energy levels.

The first shell can have a maximum of two electrons.

The atoms of hydrogen (H) and helium (He) only have electrons in this shell.

hydrogen

helium

... electron structure

Second shell

Once the first shell is complete, the second shell starts to fill from lithium (Li) until the shell is full at neon (Ne). The second shell can have a maximum of eight electrons.

Question

Draw the electron structure for nitrogen (N).

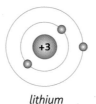

lithium

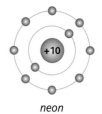

neon

Third shell

Once the second shell is complete, the third shell starts to fill from sodium (Na) until the shell is temporarily full with eight electrons at argon (Ar). The third shell can have a maximum of 18 electrons, but the rest of the shell is not filled yet.

Question

What is the electron structure for chlorine?

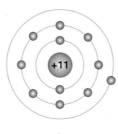

sodium

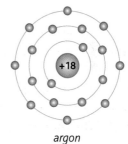

argon

Fourth shell

Once the third shell has eight electrons, the fourth shell starts to fill from potassium (K) to calcium (Ca). But then the *third* shell fills further, from scandium (Sc) to zinc (Zn). The fourth shell then fills to krypton (Kr).

Sometimes scientists simply use numbers to write down the arrangement of the electrons, or **electron structure**. Sodium would be written as 2.8.1 meaning 2 electrons in the first shell, 8 in the second and 1 in the third.

Electron structure and the periodic table

- Lithium, sodium and potassium all have one electron in their outer shell. They are all group 1 elements. They have similar properties.

- Beryllium, magnesium and calcium all have two electrons in their outer shell. They are all group 2 elements. They have similar properties.

Exam tip

You must be able to work out the electron structure for the first 20 elements in the periodic table – that's up to calcium.

Elements and compounds

Your learning aims:

D.1 Use information from the periodic table to recognise elements and the formulae of compounds

D.2 Recall the definitions of elements, compounds, mixtures and molecules

D.14 Recall the chemical formulae for all named reagents

Sodium chloride on that?

When sodium is dropped into water, there are flames from the violent reaction. Chlorine is a poisonous gas. But when sodium and chlorine react together, the product is used to flavour your chips!

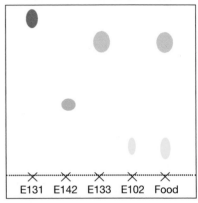

E131   E142   E133   E102   Food

A chromatograph of a food sample separates out the food colourings so they can be identified

Elements

An element is a substance that is made from only one type of atom.

There are over 100 elements. Most occur naturally but elements with high atomic numbers have been made artificially.

Mixtures

A mixture contains two or more substances that are not joined together. As they are not joined, they are fairly easy to separate.

To separate a mixture you need to know the properties of the substances in it.

Some of the ways in which mixtures can be separated include:

- dissolving, filtering and evaporating – salt can be separated from rock salt in this way

- chromatography – different colourings can be separated from food, paint or ink samples using this technique

- magnetism – iron, steel, nickel and cobalt are magnetic and can be separated from other substances that are not

- distillation – petrol, diesel, paraffin and other oils can be separated from crude oil using this method.

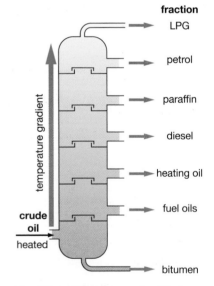

fraction
LPG
petrol
paraffin
diesel
heating oil
fuel oils
temperature gradient
crude oil
heated
bitumen

The different liquids in crude oil boil at different temperatures so can be separated by distillation

Question

How would you separate a mixture of salt and iron filings?

...chemical elements ...mixtures

Molecules

A molecule forms when two or more non-metal atoms have been combined chemically.

Some elements only occur naturally as molecules.

- Oxygen (O_2) and hydrogen (H_2) are examples of elements that occur as molecules. The molecules each contain two atoms.

Atoms of different elements also combine together to form molecules.

- Water (H_2O) and carbon dioxide (CO_2) are examples of different elements combining to form molecules. Water and carbon dioxide are both compounds.

Compounds

A compound is a substance that contains at least two different elements which have combined chemically.

The elements that have combined together to form the compound can be identified with the help of the periodic table.

Water has the chemical formula H_2O. A water molecule contains two hydrogen atoms and one oxygen atom.

Sulfuric acid has the chemical formula H_2SO_4. A sulfuric acid molecule contains two hydrogen atoms, one sulfur atom and four oxygen atoms.

Copper hydroxide has the chemical formula $Cu(OH)_2$. A copper hydroxide molecule contains one copper atom, two oxygen atoms and two hydrogen atoms.

Question

How many sulfur atoms are there in a molecule of S_6?

Exam tip

When working out how many atoms there are in a molecule, remember:

- *a subscript number shows how many atoms there are of the element before the number*
- *when elements are written in brackets, the subscript number refers to all elements inside the brackets.*

Acids, bases and metals

Your learning aims:

D.6 Recall the definitions of acids, bases and alkalis

D.3–D.5, D.7, D.13 Describe the reactions between acids and bases, write word and balanced chemical equations, and describe the uses of the reactions

D.3, D.8 Describe the reactions between acids and metals, and write word equations for the reactions

D.10, D.11 Describe the test for hydrogen, and for acids and alkalis

D.14 Recall the chemical formulae for all named reagents

What are acids?

Some acids are corrosive. They will cause burns to the skin.

But citrus fruits such as oranges, lemons and limes contain acid. There is also acid in your stomach to help break down food and kill bacteria.

Acids

The most common acids used in the laboratory are hydrochloric acid (HCl), sulfuric acid (H_2SO_4) and nitric acid (HNO_3). These are strong acids.

Weak acids include ascorbic acid (vitamin C) and ethanoic acid (found in vinegar). Weak acids in foods have a sour taste.

- Strong acids have a pH between 1 and 3.
- Weak acids have a pH between 4 and 6.

Acids turn litmus red.

Bases and alkalis

Bases are metal oxides or metal hydroxides. An **alkali** is a base that dissolves in water.

Sodium hydroxide (NaOH) is a strong base and, because it dissolves in water, it is also an alkali.

Copper oxide (CuO) and zinc oxide (ZnO) are weak bases. They do not dissolve in water.

- Strong alkalis have a pH between 11 and 14.
- Weak alkalis have a pH between 8 and 10.

Alkalis turn litmus blue.

Question

A solution of ascorbic acid turns universal indicator yellow. What is its pH?

pH scale

1	2	3	4	5	6	7	8	9	10	11	12	13	14

The pH of a solution can be found using universal indicator. This changes colour depending on the pH.

...acids ...bases ...alkalis

The acids used in school laboratories are irritants. They will make the skin turn red or blister.

Sodium hydroxide is corrosive.

If you use any chemical from a container marked with a hazard symbol, always wear goggles and wash any spills off your skin at once.

Question

What products are formed when zinc reacts with sulfuric acid?

Neutralisation reactions

When an acid reacts with a base, the products are a salt and water. The pH of any final solution is pH7. This means the solution is neutral. The reaction is called a **neutralisation** reaction:

$$acid + base \rightarrow salt + water$$

hydrochloric acid + copper oxide → copper chloride + water
$$2HCl + CuO \rightarrow CuCl_2 + H_2O$$

hydrochloric acid + zinc oxide → zinc chloride + water
$$2HCl + ZnO \rightarrow ZnCl_2 + H_2O$$

hydrochloric acid + sodium hydroxide → sodium chloride + water
$$HCl + NaOH \rightarrow NaCl + H_2O$$

sulfuric acid + copper oxide → copper sulfate + water
$$H_2SO_4 + CuO \rightarrow CuSO_4 + H_2O$$

sulfuric acid + zinc oxide → zinc sulfate + water
$$H_2SO_4 + ZnO \rightarrow ZnSO_4 + H_2O$$

sulfuric acid + sodium hydroxide → sodium sulfate + water
$$H_2SO_4 + 2NaOH \rightarrow Na_2SO_4 + 2H_2O$$

nitric acid + copper oxide → copper nitrate + water
$$2HNO_3 + CuO \rightarrow Cu(NO_3)_2 + H_2O$$

nitric acid + zinc oxide → zinc nitrate + water
$$2HNO_3 + ZnO \rightarrow Zn(NO_3)_2 + H_2O$$

nitric acid + sodium hydroxide → sodium nitrate + water
$$HNO_3 + NaOH \rightarrow NaNO_3 + H_2O$$

Neutralisation reactions are used to:

- cure indigestion if there is too much acid in the stomach
- reduce the acidity of soils to allow chosen plants to grow
- reduce the acidity of lakes polluted by acid rain.

Acids and metals

When a metal reacts with an acid, the products are a salt and hydrogen:

$$metal + acid \rightarrow salt + hydrogen$$

magnesium + hydrochloric acid → magnesium chloride + hydrogen
$$Mg + 2HCl \rightarrow MgCl_2 + H_2$$

Testing for hydrogen

In the laboratory, the test for hydrogen is to place a lighted splint into a test tube containing a sample of hydrogen. A squeaky pop indicates the presence of hydrogen.

Acids and carbonates

Your learning aims:

D.3, D.4 Write word and balanced chemical equations for reactions between acids and carbonates

D.9, D.13 Describe the reactions between acids and carbonates, and the uses of the reactions

D.10 Describe the test for carbon dioxide

D.14 Recall the chemical formulae for all named reagents

Getting rid of limescale

Washing soda is sodium carbonate. It acts as a water softener and helps to stop water pipes from clogging up with limescale.

Descalers contain an acid which reacts with the limescale to clear it.

Limescale's chemical name is calcium carbonate. The deposit can often be seen on the outlet of a tap

Hard and soft water

Hard water causes water pipes to clog up with limescale. It also makes it very difficult for soap to make bubbles. It will not lather easily. **Hardness** is caused by calcium or magnesium compounds dissolved in the water. The soap reacts with these to make a solid scum.

Once the soap has reacted, the rest of the soap works for washing. If you live in a hard-water area, most of the scum round the edge of your bath is not dirt, it is reacted soap! Soapless detergents do the same job as soap, but they are not affected by hardness in water.

One of the oldest water softeners of all is called washing soda, or soda crystals. The chemical name for washing soda is sodium carbonate. Soap powder used in washing machines contains washing soda. It precipitates out the compounds that cause hardness before they can react with the soap. The solid precipitate is washed out of the clothes along with the dirt.

Question

What is the advantage of using soft water?

...hard soft water

Acid–carbonate reactions

When an acid reacts with a carbonate, the products are a salt, water and carbon dioxide:

acid + carbonate → salt + water + carbon dioxide

hydrochloric acid + sodium carbonate → sodium chloride + water + carbon dioxide
$$2HCl + Na_2CO_3 \rightarrow 2NaCl + H_2O + CO_2$$

hydrochloric acid + copper carbonate → copper chloride + water + carbon dioxide
$$2HCl + CuCO_3 \rightarrow CuCl_2 + H_2O + CO_2$$

hydrochloric acid + calcium carbonate → calcium chloride + water + carbon dioxide
$$2HCl + CaCO_3 \rightarrow CaCl_2 + H_2O + CO_2$$

sulfuric acid + sodium carbonate → sodium sulfate + water + carbon dioxide
$$H_2SO_4 + Na_2CO_3 \rightarrow Na_2SO_4 + H_2O + CO_2$$

sulfuric acid + copper carbonate → copper sulfate + water + carbon dioxide
$$H_2SO_4 + CuCO_3 \rightarrow CuSO_4 + H_2O + CO_2$$

sulfuric acid + calcium carbonate → calcium sulfate + water + carbon dioxide
$$H_2SO_4 + CaCO_3 \rightarrow CaSO_4 + H_2O + CO_2$$

nitric acid + sodium carbonate → sodium nitrate + water + carbon dioxide
$$2HNO_3 + Na_2CO_3 \rightarrow 2NaNO_3 + H_2O + CO_2$$

nitric acid + copper carbonate → copper nitrate + water + carbon dioxide
$$2HNO_3 + CuCO_3 \rightarrow Cu(NO_3)_2 + H_2O + CO_2$$

nitric acid + calcium carbonate → calcium nitrate + water + carbon dioxide
$$2HNO_3 + CaCO_3 \rightarrow Ca(NO_3)_2 + H_2O + CO_2$$

Testing for carbon dioxide

In the laboratory, the test for carbon dioxide is to bubble the gas through lime water. The lime water changes from a clear solution to a milky white colour when carbon dioxide is bubbled through it.

Exam tip

You will need to recall the chemical formulae and balanced equations for all of the reactions described in this unit. To make sure an equation is balanced, count the numbers of each atom on each side of the reaction.

...carbonate acid reaction

Energy and energy stores

Energy makes things happen

The chemical energy in the fuel can lift a 2030-tonne spacecraft and its rockets off the launchpad.

Forms of energy and their uses

Thermal

Thermal energy is heat.

The energy can be stored in hot or warm bodies. Some homes have night storage radiators which store the energy in concrete blocks. They are heated up overnight and release the energy during the next day.

Electrical

Electrical energy is the most useful form of energy. It can be transferred into other forms of energy quite easily.

Most of the electrical energy we use comes from generators at power stations. Some comes from chemicals in a battery and some occurs naturally.

Light

Luminous objects such as the Sun, bulbs and flames produce their own light. We are able to see all other objects because light reflects from them into our eyes. Light transfers energy without moving the material it is passing through.

Question

Where else is heat stored in homes?

A natural release of electrical energy

...forms of energy

Loudspeakers produce sound by vibrations

Elastic potential energy is stored in stretched elastic material

An atomic bomb releases huge amounts of nuclear energy

Question

What is the difference between nuclear fission and nuclear fusion?

Sound

Sound transfers energy by vibrating the material it is passing through. Sound travels faster through solids than through gases.

People who work in noisy areas should protect their ears because loud sounds can damage hearing.

Mechanical

There are two types of mechanical energy.

- **Kinetic energy** is the energy of a moving object. The amount of energy depends on the mass of the object and the speed at which it travels.

  A bullet travelling at 450 m/s has the same kinetic energy as a typical teenager running at 5 m/s

- **Potential energy** is stored energy, ready to be released.

  Sometimes it is stored because an object is high up and ready to fall. This is called **gravitational potential energy**.

  The rope jumper has a lot of gravitational potential energy before he jumps. As he falls, he loses his gravitational potential energy and gains kinetic energy

  Sometimes it is stored in a spring or a stretched piece of elastic material. This is called **elastic potential energy**. When the spring or elastic material is released, something happens.

Nuclear

Radioactive elements, such as uranium, can split up into new elements. When they do this, a lot of energy is released from the nucleus of the atoms. The process is called **nuclear fission**.

The nuclear energy released can be used in a nuclear power station to generate electricity. It can also be used to make a nuclear bomb.

Other elements, such as hydrogen, release energy from the nucleus when they are joined together to make new elements. This is called **nuclear fusion**.

Transferring energy

Your learning aims:

E.3 Recall the different methods by which energy is transferred from one place to another

Working hard

Energy is transferred when a load is moved through a distance.

The amount of energy the strongman transfers when he pulls the two lorries depends on the weight of the lorries and the distance he moves them.

Energy transfer processes

Mechanical

Work is done when a force moves a certain distance. The amount of **work done** is equal to the amount of **energy transferred** by doing the work.

When you walk up a flight of stairs, you move your weight through a distance equal to the height of the stairs. You use energy when doing this.

Electrical

Electricity is used to transfer energy in a number of different ways.

- An element, in an electric fire or cooker, transfers energy as heat.

- A motor transfers energy as movement.

- A loudspeaker transfers energy as sound.

Conduction

Thermal energy is transferred by conduction between places or objects at different temperatures.

Solids are thermal conductors; metals are very good conductors but non-metals are poor conductors.

Question

What must you do to replace the energy you use every day?

Question

What device transfers energy as light?

The metal suacepan base transfers heat to the contents by conduction

...energy transfer examples

Question

Why do barbeque tools have wooden or plastic handles?

A hang glider uses the upward movement of warm air to obtain the lift needed to stay in the air

The temperature outside the spacesuit can be as hot as 120 °C because of radiation from the Sun

Conduction happens because particles in a solid vibrate and make the particles next to them vibrate. Particles do not move through the solid. Liquids and gases generally do not conduct.

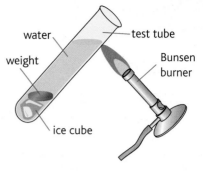

When the test tube is heated as shown, the water at the top boils but the ice does not melt

Convection

Convection transfers thermal energy in liquids and gases. Particles transfer the energy as they move.

A convection current is the bulk movement of particles through the liquid or gas. The warmer fluid rises and the cooler fluid falls.

This is how a radiator warms a room in your home

Radiation

The infrared **radiation** (heat) from the Sun and from fires transfers thermal energy to objects that absorb it. It does not need anything to travel through. There is no atmosphere in space but the energy from the Sun reaches all parts of the Solar System.

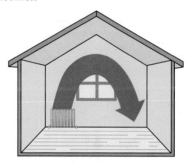

Sound

Sound travels as a wave. Energy from the source of sound transfers through the air as vibrations of the particles of the air.

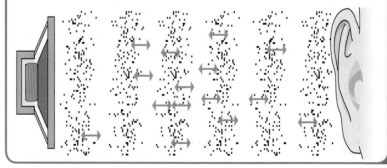

...conduction convection and radiation

Measuring energy

Your learning aims:

E.4 Recall that the joule is the unit of energy and the watt is a unit of power; perform calculations involving energy and power; interpret diagrams representing energy transfers

E.5 Understand the meaning of energy efficiency and calculate efficiency

Falling through the sky

At 4000 m, the skydiver has 2 800 000 joules (J) of gravitational potential energy. The energy is transferred into different forms as he falls, but the total amount is always the same.

Conserving energy

Gravitational potential energy depends on the height of an object above the ground. As the object falls, the gravitational potential energy is transferred into kinetic energy and some heat.

As an object hits the ground, it has lost all of its gravitational potential energy. Its kinetic energy is at a maximum. When the object hits the ground, all of the kinetic energy is transferred into other forms such as heat and sound.

Energy is **conserved**: it is never 'lost'.

Sankey diagrams

A kettle transfers 100 J of electrical energy into heat. 90 J is used to heat the water; the rest is wasted to the surroundings.

Scientists use diagrams to represent energy transfers. The width of the arrows in this **Sankey diagram** show the relative amounts of energy.

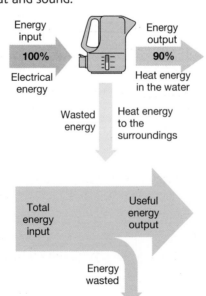

Energy input
100%
Electrical energy

Energy output
90%
Heat energy in the water

Wasted energy

Heat energy to the surroundings

Total energy input

Useful energy output

Energy wasted

During his honeymoon, James Joule asked his wife to help him show that water is warmer at the bottom of a waterfall than it is at the top: the kinetic energy of the falling water is transferred as heat

Question

What happens to the wasted energy?

...Sankey diagram

Question

The diagram shows where energy is transferred in a car engine. What is the efficiency of the car engine?

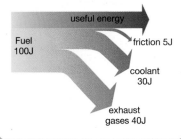

Energy efficiency

It is impossible to build an energy transfer device that is 100% efficient. Whenever an energy transfer takes place, some energy is always wasted as heat to the surroundings.

The **efficiency** of any transfer device is the proportion of energy that is transferred into useful forms:

$$\text{energy efficiency} = \frac{\text{useful energy}}{\text{total energy supplied}} \times 100\%$$

The kettle produced 90 J of useful energy for every 100 J of electrical energy supplied:

$$\text{energy efficiency} = \frac{90}{100} \times 100\% = 90\%$$

Measuring personal power

Power

Power is a measure of how quickly energy is transferred: how much energy is transferred per second.

Its unit is the watt (W) or kilowatt (kW). 1 kW = 1000 W

$$\text{power (W)} = \frac{\text{energy (J)}}{\text{time (s)}}$$

Asami is measuring the power in her legs by running up a flight of stairs. She uses 1500 J of energy. It takes her 4 s.
The equation can be used to work out how powerful her legs are: 1500 ÷ 4 = 375 W

A Sumo wrestler is stronger than Asami and is four times heavier. If it takes him longer than 16 s to get to the top of the stairs then Asami has more powerful legs!

Paying for electricity

Electrical appliances have a power rating. This shows how much energy they use each second.

A hairdryer has a power rating of 2400 W. This is 2.4 kW. The amount of electricity used depends on the power rating in kW and the time it is used for in hours:

$$\text{electrical energy used (kWh)} = \text{power (kW)} \times \text{time (h)}$$

The hairstylist uses the hairdryer for 4 hours a day. In 4 hours, the electrical energy used is 2.4 × 4 = 9.6 kWh. This is sometimes called 9.6 units of electricity.

The cost of using the electricity depends on how much the supply company charges for each unit.

Electricity is charged by the kilowatt-hour (kWh)

...energy efficiency ...fuel costs per kWh

Energy sources

We are running out of coal and oil

Wind farms are examples of alternative energy sources. Some people think that wind farms are unsightly and should not be built. But they provide 'clean energy' – they produce no pollution.

Non-renewable sources

Fossil fuels

Fossil fuels are formed from the remains of plants and animals that died millions of years ago. There is a finite supply – they are **non-renewable**.

Most power stations in the UK burn fossil fuels to produce electricity.

If we continue to use fossil fuels at the present rate, it is estimated that coal will run out in about 150 years and oil and gas will run out in between 50 and 75 years.

Nuclear fuels

Uranium is used in a nuclear reactor to generate electricity. Nuclear fuel such as uranium is non-renewable but there are enough reserves to last much longer than coal, oil and gas.

Nuclear power stations are cleaner than fossil-fuelled power stations. They do not produce smoke or carbon dioxide. This means they do not contribute to global warming.

The problem with nuclear power stations is that the waste remains radioactive for thousands of years. This waste has to be stored safely.

Coal-fired steam locomotives were replaced by diesels many years ago. But diesel may run out before coal. 'Tornado' is a newly built steam locomotive

Question

Is it possible that more coal-fired steam trains, like Tornado, will be built to replace diesel trains?

...fossil fuels

Renewable sources

Solar	 Panels of solar cells transfer light energy from the Sun into electricity.		Water-filled solar panels are heated by the Sun to provide hot water for the home.
Biomass	Biofuels are obtained from **biomass**. Biomass comes from many types of plant and animal waste including crop stalks, wood pellets and chicken manure. The fuel can be burned. It can also be fermented to make methane gas. When biomass is burned, the heat can be used to make steam in the same way as in a conventional power station. The biofuels ethanol and biodiesel are produced from crop plants. They are mixed with petrol or diesel for vehicle fuel.		

Some renewable energy sources use kinetic energy to drive turbines. The turbines turn generators which produce electricity.

Wind	The kinetic energy from the wind turns the blades. The blades turn a turbine. Many wind turbines are grouped together in a wind farm. Some wind farms are offshore.
Hydroelectric	The gravitational potential energy of the water in a reservoir is transferred into kinetic energy as the water falls through a dam. The falling water turns a turbine.
Wave	As the sea waves move up and down, the rocking motion turns a turbine.
Tidal	There are a few places in the world where a dam could be built across the mouth of a river. As the tide flows in and out, it could turn turbines built into the dam.
Geothermal	Beneath the surface of the Earth, the temperature of the rocks is very high. If water is pumped down into the rocks, it will come up at a higher temperature. Sometimes it comes up as steam. The steam can be used to turn a turbine. Hot water can be used in homes.

Energy stores

Batteries and fuel cells use the energy stored within chemicals to produce electricity.

Once the chemicals in a battery are used up, the battery is 'dead' and needs to be replaced or recharged.

A hydrogen **fuel cell** uses the chemicals hydrogen and oxygen. They react in the fuel cell to form water and produce electricity. A fuel cell can have a constant supply of hydrogen and oxygen so will continue to produce electricity.

Hot water can be stored in water tanks. The tanks should be well lagged to reduce energy conduction to the surroundings. Because we use so much energy and sources are running out, it is important that all energy is used and stored efficiently.

...renewable energy sources

Wave properties

Waves transfer energy

Some tsunami waves travel at speeds up to 1000 km/h. The height of the waves can be greater than 30 m. The energy they carry causes devastation.

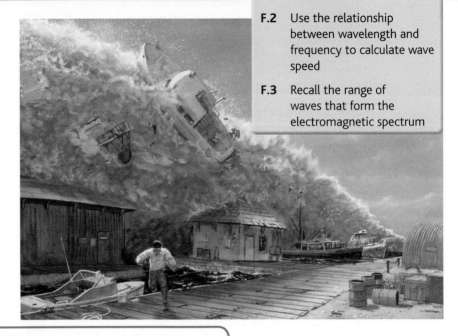

Wave characteristics

If you drop a pebble into water, water particles move up and down as a wave spreads out.

Water waves are transverse waves. The wave travels in a direction at right angles to the up and down movement.

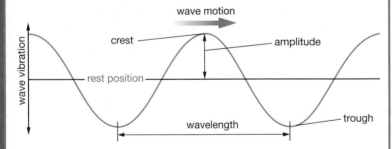

The water particles move up and down; the wave moves outwards

The **amplitude** of a wave is the maximum displacement of a particle from its rest position.

The **wavelength** of a wave is the distance between two adjacent points on the wave of similar displacement. The unit of wavelength is metres (m).

The **frequency** of a wave is the number of waves passing a point each second. The unit of frequency is hertz (Hz).

The **speed** of the wave is a measure of how fast the wave is travelling. The unit of speed is metres per second (m/s).

...wave characteristics

Wave speed

The speed of a wave depends on its frequency and wavelength:

wave speed (m/s) = wavelength (m) × frequency (Hz)

If a water wave has a wavelength of 0.1 m and a frequency of 5 Hz:

wave speed = 0.1 × 5 = 0.5 m/s

A radio station broadcasts with a wavelength of 3 m and a frequency of 100 000 000 (100×10^6) Hz:

speed of radio waves = $3 \times 100 \times 10^6 = 300 \times 10^6$ m/s

Radio waves are part of a group of waves that travel at the speed of light. They are known as **electromagnetic waves**.

The electromagnetic spectrum

A rainbow is one example of the visible spectrum, which is part of the electromagnetic spectrum

Electromagnetic waves with different names, such as radio waves and microwaves, are all members of the **electromagnetic spectrum**. They have a continuous range of frequencies and wavelengths. Wavelengths range from more than 3 km to less than 0.000 000 003 mm.

Question

What is the speed of light?

Exam tip

You will need to know the order of the electromagnetic spectrum. Remember radio waves are at the red end of the spectrum.

Question

What type of wave has a wavelength of 3 km?

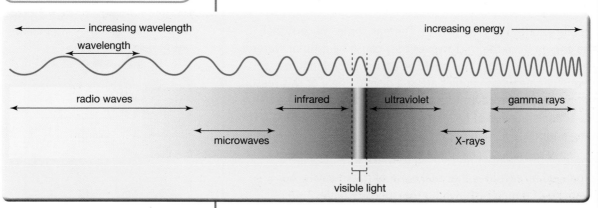

The electromagnetic spectrum

increasing wavelength

increasing energy

wavelength

radio waves

infrared

ultraviolet

gamma rays

microwaves

X-rays

visible light

Longer than light

Your learning aims:

F.4, F.5 Describe everyday uses of radio waves, microwaves and infrared radiation, explaining the risks associated with each

An infrared photo

A special type of camera detects the infrared radiated from the man on the running machine. The warmest areas shown here are bright pink. The temperature falls as the colours change through, red, orange, yellow, green, light blue, dark blue and black as the coldest.

Radio waves

Radio waves are used for communication.

Television and radio programmes are transmitted using radio signals.

Short-wavelength radio is used by the police and other organisations that want to communicate over relatively short distances.

Long-wavelength radio waves can travel around the world as a result of reflection by the atmosphere and large areas of water.

Microwaves

Microwave ovens are used to cook food quickly.

They work by the microwaves causing the water particles in the food to vibrate. This makes the water heat up. The energy is transferred to the rest of the food by conduction.

Microwaves are also used for communication. They are not reflected by the atmosphere so the transmitter and receiver must be in line of sight. This also means they can be used to send messages to satellites.

Mobile phones use microwaves. There is some concern that the energy from the microwaves may cause heating of water particles in the body. This could be particularly dangerous for young people whose bodies are still developing. For this reason, young people are advised to send text messages or use a hands-free phone, instead of holding the phone near to their brain for long periods.

Some of the weather maps used to make forecasts are produced by satellites that make use of microwaves. An example of a map is shown on the opposite page.

Question

Which radio station has the highest frequency: Radio 1 with a wavelength of 3.0 m or Radio 2 with a wavelength of 3.3 m?

...radio communication

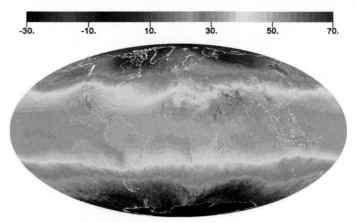

Sea surface temperatures in February 2012. If the temperature reaches 28 °C, there could be a tropical storm or hurricane

Infrared

Infrared radiation is emitted by warm and hot bodies. Hotter bodies emit more radiation.

Radiant heaters and fires emit infrared radiation to warm the home. Cooker elements are another source. When infrared radiation is absorbed it causes a rise in temperature.

Exposure to intense infrared radiation can cause burns on the skin.

Thermal imaging cameras detect infrared radiation and produce thermographs similar to the one of the running man shown on the opposite page. These can be used to search for criminals.

Modern communication systems use optical fibre cables to transmit data. Optical fibres are very fine glass fibres along which infrared radiation travels by continued reflection. Optical fibres are better than copper wires because they are cheaper, lighter and can carry much more data.

beam of infrared light

Infrared remote controllers mean that you don't have to leave the comfort of your chair to change the channel on your television.

Many homes, schools and workplaces are protected by infrared sensors. These detect the body heat of an intruder and sound an alarm.

An infrared sensor

...microwave weather map ...thermograph images

Shorter than light

Your learning aims:

F.4, F.5 Describe everyday uses of visible light, ultraviolet radiation, X-rays and gamma rays, explaining the risks associated with each

Using light

Visible light is the part of the electromagnetic spectrum that allows us to see.

A photographer uses light for illumination. The photograph he produces is a light (photo) picture (graph).

Bright light and laser light can be dangerous to the eyes. Some laser beams can cut through metal.

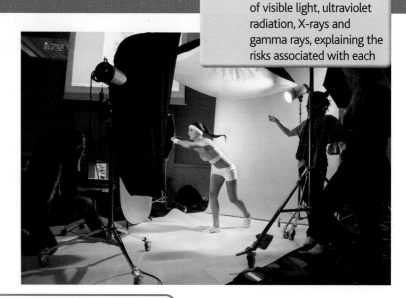

Ultraviolet

It is ultraviolet radiation that causes the skin to tan. The Sun is the main source of ultraviolet radiation, but lamps used in sun beds are also sources.

Ultraviolet is needed by the body to produce vitamin D, but too much exposure to ultraviolet radiation can cause sunburn or skin cancer. The eyes can also be damaged by over-exposure.

The best way to reduce the risks of sunburn and skin cancer is to reduce the amount of time the skin is exposed. In strong sunshine wear a wide-brimmed hat and pale, loose clothing; sit under a shade or use a high SPF sunscreen cream.

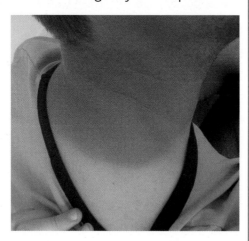

Sunglasses reduce the risk of ultraviolet radiation damaging the eyes

Ultraviolet radiation is used to detect forged bank notes. Genuine notes have a mark which only shows up under ultraviolet light.

Water treatment works use ultraviolet light to disinfect water. The treatment works because the ultraviolet radiation penetrates the cell wall of microorganisms. This disrupts the genetic material in the cell and makes reproduction impossible.

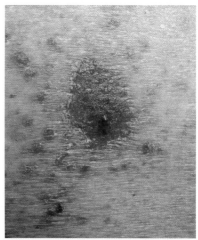

Skin cancer may start as a small, red shiny spot that may occasionally bleed. It may develop into an ulcer that doesn't heal

...sunsmart

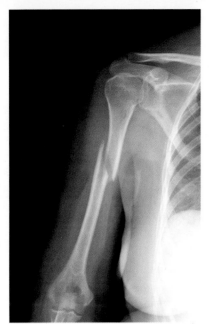

An X-ray image showing a broken arm bone

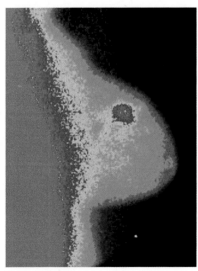

This gamma-ray image shows breast cancer (red blob)

X-rays and gamma rays

X-rays and gamma rays are both very high-energy, short-wavelength electromagnetic radiation. Their main difference is in the way they are produced.

X-rays are produced when high-speed electrons hit a metal target. Gamma rays come from the nucleus of a radioactive atom.

X-rays are used to detect broken bones. A doctor can find out what is wrong without having to operate. X-rays pass through soft tissue but are absorbed by bone. This means that no X-rays fall on the film if there is bone in the way. When the image is viewed, the area hit by X-rays appears black.

X-rays can also be used to see the internal structure of an object or the contents of a container.

Airport security staff use X-rays to examine the contents of luggage

Gamma rays are very energetic and very penetrating. They can destroy microorganisms and so are used to sterilise food and medical equipment.

They are also used as tracers in medicine. If a patient swallows or is injected with a liquid that emits gamma radiation, the path of the liquid through the body can be traced. A special camera is used to record an image. Cancer can be detected because a cancerous tumour absorbs more of the radioactive liquid than the healthy cells.

After a cancer is detected, gamma radiation can be used to treat it. Gamma rays (and X-rays) can kill body cells. A high dose of gamma radiation is directed at the cancer cells which destroys them. This is called radiotherapy.

As well as killing cells, gamma rays and X-rays can cause gene mutations (see page 15). These mutations can lead to cancer. Technicians who work with X-rays and gamma rays have to protect themselves from too much radiation.

...X-rays ...gamma rays

Exam-style questions

Biology

1 Conditions inside the body must be kept constant in order for organs to function.

    a What do we call the process of keeping internal conditions in the body constant? [1]

    b Name two conditions that are kept constant inside the body. [2]

    c Nisha went outside on a cold night with no coat on.

       i What will happen to her body temperature? [1]

      ii State one thing her body will do to reverse this change and explain how it works. [3]

                                        [Total 7]

2 Danny is playing in a football match. His body starts producing the hormone adrenaline, which increases his heart rate.

    a Is the production of adrenaline a voluntary or an involuntary response? [1]

    b Which organ system in the body is responsible for producing hormones? [1]

    c The heart is a target organ of adrenaline. What does this mean? [1]

    d Explain why a hormonal response rather than a nervous one is appropriate in this case. [2]

                                          [Total 5]

3 The allele for tongue rolling is dominant over the allele for non-tongue rolling.

Explain why Joe cannot roll his tongue although both his parents can. [3]

                                          [Total 3]

Chemistry

4 The diagram represents an atom of hydrogen with a mass number of 3.

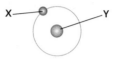

    a What is the charge of the particle labelled X? [1]

    b What is the name of the area of the atom labelled Y? [1]

    c How many protons are there inside Y? [1]

    d How many neutrons are there inside Y? [1]

                                          [Total 4]

5 Chemicals are represented by their chemical formulae.

Write down the chemical formulae for:

    a sulfuric acid [1]

    b copper nitrate [1]

    c calcium carbonate [1]

    d sodium hydroxide [1]

                                          [Total 4]

6 What is the difference between an element and a compound? [2]

                                          [Total 2]

7 The element aluminium has the electronic configuration 2.8.3. Draw a diagram to show how the electrons are arranged in the aluminium atom. [2]

                                          [Total 2]

8 Luke is testing some chemicals. He adds some universal indicator to a solution labelled **A**. The universal indicator changes colour to red.

  a What information does this give about solution **A**? [1]

He then adds a small amount of solution A to a powder labelled B. A gas is produced. Luke tests this by holding a lighted splint in the mouth of the tube. The splint is extinguished.

  b What gas was produced? [1]

  c What information does this give about powder **B**? [1]

[Total 3]

Physics

9 Jamie is lifting weights.

Each weight weighs 55 N. In one minute, each arm lifts a weight 80 times. The energy used in lifting each weight during that time is 3300 J.

Calculate the power developed by each arm. [2]

[Total 2]

10 Helen wants to get a sun tan.

  a Which part of the electromagnetic spectrum causes a sun tan? [1]

  b What are the dangers if Helen stays in strong sunshine for too long? [1]

  c Suggest how Helen can protect herself from sun damage. [2]

[Total 4]

11 The diagram represents the energy transfers for a coal fire.

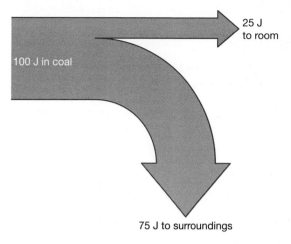

100 J in coal

25 J to room

75 J to surroundings

  a Calculate the efficiency of the coal fire. [2]

  b By what process is most of the energy from the coal fire transferred to the room? [1]

  c By what process is most of the energy transferred to the surroundings up the chimney? [1]

The room is also heated by a water-filled central heating radiator.

  d By what process is most of the energy from the radiator transferred to the room? [1]

[Total 5]

12 Microwaves are used for communication.

  a Explain why mobile phone masts have to be close together, but microwaves can be used to communicate with satellites. [2]

  b Write down one other use for microwaves. [1]

[Total 3]

Unit 2 **Chemistry and Our Earth**

LA

Be able to investigate chemical reactivity and bonding

- Lithium, sodium and potassium are so reactive we have to store them under oil

- Strong covalent bonds make diamond the hardest natural substance we know

- Conducting electricity depends on the type of bonding present

LA

Be able to investigate how the uses of chemical substances depend on their chemical and physical properties

- Your mobile phone contains small amounts of gold and platinum, as well as less valuable metals

- Chemical reactions inside airbags make them inflate when a vehicle has a collision

- Argon gas is so unreactive that we use it to blanket metal arc welding

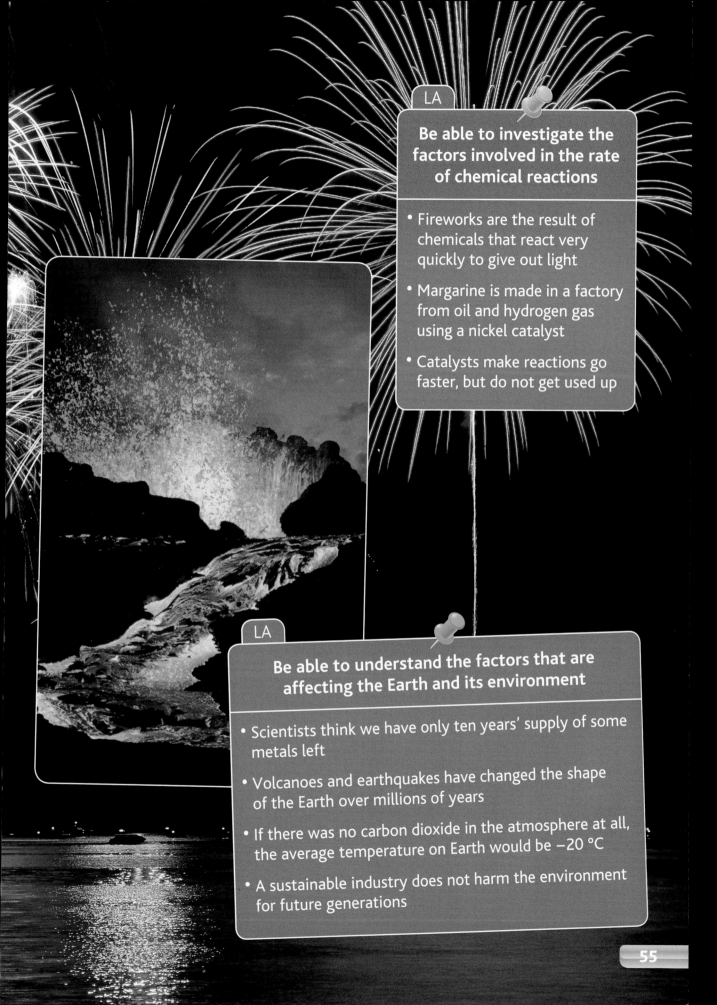

Be able to investigate the factors involved in the rate of chemical reactions

- Fireworks are the result of chemicals that react very quickly to give out light

- Margarine is made in a factory from oil and hydrogen gas using a nickel catalyst

- Catalysts make reactions go faster, but do not get used up

Be able to understand the factors that are affecting the Earth and its environment

- Scientists think we have only ten years' supply of some metals left

- Volcanoes and earthquakes have changed the shape of the Earth over millions of years

- If there was no carbon dioxide in the atmosphere at all, the average temperature on Earth would be −20 °C

- A sustainable industry does not harm the environment for future generations

Physical properties of group 1 and 7 elements

Your assessment criteria:

1A.1 Classify group 1 and 7 elements based on their physical properties

2A.P1 Describe the physical and chemical properties of group 1 and 7 elements

2A.M1 Describe trends in the physical and chemical properties of group 1 and 7 elements

Halogen lights

Major supermarkets sell a variety of energy-efficient lighting. Halogen bulbs get their name from the 'halogen' elements that they contain. Halogen bulbs burn hotter and give out more light than old-fashioned light bulbs. This saves electrical energy. They also last longer.

1A.1
2A.P1

About group 1

Group 1 elements are very reactive metals called **alkali metals**. They have similar physical and chemical properties to one another and are found on the left-hand side of the periodic table. They all have one electron in their outer shell. Group 1 metals are very different to the metals we commonly use in buildings, cars and everyday objects from cooking utensils to iPads. Group 1 metals:

- are soft and can be cut with a knife

- are grey and shiny when freshly cut, but corrode quickly

- have low melting points and boiling points

- have low densities.

But, like all metals, group 1 metals are good conductors of heat and electricity.

Some group 1 data:

Group 1 metal	Symbol	Atomic number	Melting point (°C)	Boiling point (°C)	Density (g/cm³)
lithium	Li	3	181	1347	0.53
sodium	Na	11	98	883	0.97
potassium	K	19	64	774	0.86
rubidium	Rb	37	39	688	1.48
caesium	Cs	55	29	679	1.87
francium	Fr	87	27	667	approx. 2?

Know more

Francium is radioactive and very rare. Radioactive elements break down to form subatomic particles and other elements, but francium is also formed when radioactive elements with larger atoms break down. There are only a few grams of francium on Earth at any one time.

Think about

The melting point of iron is 1535 °C and its density is 7.86 g/cm³. Why do we use iron (as steel) to make cars and not sodium?

Think about

The density of water is 1 g/cm³, so which group 1 metals float on water?

Think about

Why are scientists uncertain about the density of francium?

$\mathcal{P}$... alkali metals

Group 1 metals are so reactive they have to be stored under oil to keep water and oxygen away. Even so, they still corrode because a few oxygen molecules pass through the oil and react with the metal

1A.1
2A.P1

About group 7

Group 7 elements are colourful non-metals. They are called **halogens** and are found on the right-hand side of the periodic table. They all have seven electrons in their outer shell. Like group 1 metals, they have similar physical and chemical properties to one another. Group 7 elements:

- exist as solids, liquids and gases at room temperature
- have low melting and boiling points (they are typical non-metals)
- get darker in colour down the group.

Some group 7 data:

Group 7 non-metal	Symbol	Atomic number	Appearance (at room temperature)	Melting point (°C)	Boiling point (°C)
fluorine	F	9	pale yellow gas	−220	−188
chlorine	Cl	17	yellow/green gas	−101	−35
bromine	Br	35	dark red liquid	−7	59
iodine	I	53	shiny grey solid	113	184
astatine	At	85	black?	302	337

> **Know more**
>
> Astatine is also radioactive and very rare. There are only 25 g of astatine on the Earth at any one time.

> **Know more**
>
> Halogens help keep us healthy. Fluorine compounds in water supplies and toothpastes strengthen tooth enamel. Chlorine is used to disinfect our water supplies and swimming pools. Bromine can also be used to disinfect water supplies. Iodine is needed in our diet to make the hormone thyroxine, which controls growth.

At room temperature, chlorine is a gas, bromine is a liquid and iodine is a solid

> **Think about**
>
> What other trends can you find in groups 1 and 7?

Trends

2A.M1

A gradual change in properties is called a trend. In group 1, the melting and boiling points both decrease as you go down the group, but in group 7 the melting and boiling points increase as you go down the group.

🔍 ...uses of chlorine

Chemical properties of group 1 and 7 elements

Strange behaviour

Group 1 metals explode on contact with water. Metals so reactive that your teacher will only use pieces the size of half a pea. These are not everyday metals.

Sodium metal explodes with water

Your assessment criteria:

2A.P1 Describe the physical and chemical properties of group 1 and 7 elements

2A.M1 Describe trends in the physical and chemical properties of groups 1 and 7

2A.D1 Explain the trends in chemical properties of group 1 and 7 elements in terms of electronic structure

2A.P1

About group 1

Group 1 elements are very reactive. They have similar chemistry to one another, but some are more reactive than others. They react easily with water.

Group 1 element	How does it react with cold water?	Word equation	Symbol equation
lithium (Li)	fizzes	lithium + water → lithium hydroxide + hydrogen	$2Li(s) + 2H_2O(l) \rightarrow 2LiOH(aq) + H_2(g)$
sodium (Na)	fizzes and moves around violently	sodium + water → sodium hydroxide + hydrogen	$2Na(s) + 2H_2O(l) \rightarrow 2NaOH(aq) + H_2(g)$
potassium (K)	burns with a violet flame and moves around violently	potassium + water → potassium hydroxide + hydrogen	$2K(s) + 2H_2O(l) \rightarrow 2KOH(aq) + H_2(g)$

About group 7

Group 7 elements react with metals to make salts. Chlorine reacts with sodium to make the salt sodium chloride; bromine reacts with sodium to make sodium bromide; and iodine reacts with sodium to make sodium iodide. Some halogens are more reactive than others.

A more reactive halogen will displace a less reactive halogen from its salt. Adding chlorine gas to sodium iodide solution produces the following reaction:

chlorine + sodium iodide solution → iodine + sodium chloride solution

$Cl_2(aq) + 2NaI(aq) \rightarrow I_2(aq) + 2NaCl(aq)$

The chlorine and iodine have swapped places. The iodine produced makes a brown solution. This is called a **displacement reaction**.

> **Think about**
>
> *What similarities can you find between the reactions of different group 1 metals with water? Try to explain your similarities.*

...displacement reactions

2A.M1

Think about

Which halogens can displace bromine from potassium bromide solution? Write word and symbol equations for the reactions.

Trends

Group 1 and 7 elements also have trends in their chemical reactions. Group 1 elements react more violently with water as you go down the group, or as atomic number increases.

The most reactive group 7 element will displace other halogens from their salts. Fluorine is the most reactive halogen and displaces all other halogens. The reactivity decreases down group 7.

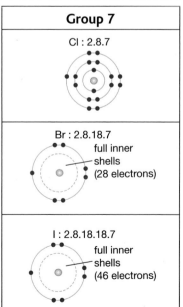

Group 1
Li : 2.1
Na : 2.8.1
K : 2.8.8.1

Group 7
Cl : 2.8.7
Br : 2.8.18.7 — full inner shells (28 electrons)
I : 2.8.18.18.7 — full inner shells (46 electrons)

2A.D1

Explaining the trends in reactivity

Atomic structure in groups 1 and 7

You can see in the tables that all group 1 elements have one electron in the outer shell. As you go down the group, each element has an extra full shell of electrons.

All group 7 elements have seven electrons in the outer shell. They also have an extra full shell of electrons as you go down the group.

Group 1

In an atom, the electrons and nucleus attract one another. When group 1 atoms react, they lose their outer electron. As you go down the group, there are more electron shells. These shield the nucleus. The outer electron is lost more easily.

So group 1 metals get more reactive as you go down the group.

Group 7

Group 7 elements gain one electron when they react. The new electron is attracted by the nucleus. Small atoms like fluorine have fewer electron shells to shield the nucleus. The nucleus can get up close and attract the new electron.

So group 7 non-metals get less reactive as you go down the group.

Think about

In a halogen bulb, bromine reacts with the tungsten filament. What compound is made?

Covalent bonding

The biggest diamond

The Golden Jubilee diamond is thought to be the biggest cut diamond in the world. South African miners discovered it in 1985. It is worth up to £9 million. Diamonds are made from carbon. So is soot. The difference lies in the bonding. The strong chemical bonds between the carbon atoms in diamond make it very hard, sparkly and very valuable.

1A.3 2A.P3

Making molecules

There are different types of chemical bond. The chemical bonds in diamonds are **covalent bonds**. The outer electrons of the atoms are rearranged when atoms join by making covalent bonds. Some of the electrons are shared between the two atoms. This bonds the atoms strongly together. Covalent bonds are very strong bonds.

In a hydrogen molecule, each hydrogen atom shares its electron with the other atom. This is called a **single covalent bond**. By sharing electrons, each hydrogen atom has a full outer shell. This makes it more stable.

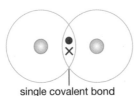

Covalent bonding in a hydrogen molecule, H

single covalent bond

We use dots and crosses to show how the electrons from each atom are arranged

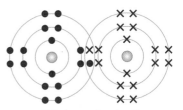

Chlorine molecule, Cl_2

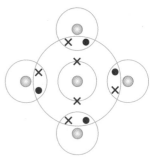

Methane molecule, CH_4

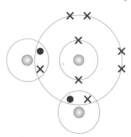

Water molecule, H_2O

φ ...covalent bonds

Know more

*Nitrogen (N₂) is the gas in crisp bags. It helps keep crisps fresh. Nitrogen molecules have a **triple covalent bond**. Each nitrogen atom shares three electrons with the other.*

Some molecules have **double covalent bonds**. Oxygen atoms each share two electrons with the other.

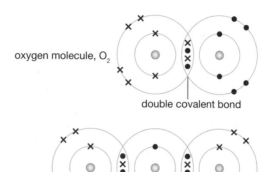

oxygen molecule, O₂

double covalent bond

carbon dioxide molecule, CO₂

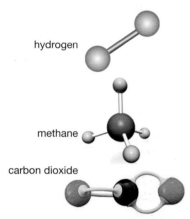

hydrogen

methane

carbon dioxide

Molecular models. Note the representation of double bonds in carbon dioxide

Covalent substances

A covalent bond forms when two non-metal atoms share a pair of electrons. So a covalent bond can form between two fluorine atoms, but not between a fluorine and a sodium atom. The electrons shared are from the outer shell. The charges on the atoms do not change because no electrons are lost or gained.

Covalent substances are either separate molecules, like water, or giant structures like diamond.

Think about

An electron is an electron. Does where it came from make a difference to the compound?

Carbon is a special case

A carbon atom has four electrons in its outer shell. It can make four single covalent bonds. This structure of bonded atoms can go on and on. In three dimensions, it makes a strong **tetrahedral structure**. This is diamond.

Discuss

Can you explain why diamond is the hardest natural substance we know?

Can you explain why diamonds take thousands of years to form?

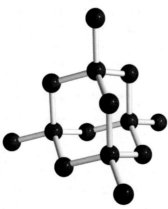

Diamond structure

...tetrahedral structure

Ionic bonding

Your assessment criteria:

1A.3 Classify substances as ionic or covalent

2A.P3 Draw dot-and-cross diagrams of simple ionic and covalent substances

2A.M3 Describe the formation of ionic and covalent substances

2A.D2 Relate applications of compounds to their properties and to their bonding and structure

Do you want salt on that?

We have been adding salt to our food for hundreds of years. It preserves food and gives that favourite salty taste. The salt we use is sodium chloride. This contains the group 1 element sodium and the group 7 element chlorine. They are chemically bonded together with ionic bonds.

1A.3
2A.P3

A reactive metal and a green gas

Sodium is a very reactive group 1 metal. Its atoms have one electron in their outer shell.

- The numbers 2.8.1 show the numbers of electrons in each shell.

Chlorine is a very reactive green gas. Its atoms have seven electrons in their outer shell.

- The numbers of electrons in each shell are 2.8.7.

When they bond together, sodium's one outer electron is transferred to chlorine. This gives both particles a full outer shell of electrons. It makes them very stable. The new particles do not have the right number of electrons to be atoms. They are called **ions**.

- Losing an electron gives the **sodium ion** a **positive charge**. We write it as Na^+.

- The **chloride ion** has gained an electron and has a negative charge. We write a chloride ion as Cl^-.

These opposite charges attract one another strongly by **electrostatic attraction**. Ionic bonds are strong bonds.

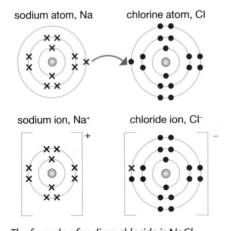

The formula of sodium chloride is NaCl

Fries with sodium chloride, commonly called salt

Know more

Electrons are negatively charged particles. Protons in the atom's nucleus are positively charged. Atoms have the same number of protons and electrons. The charges balance out. Losing or gaining electrons gives ions their charges.

Know more

It is a chlorine atom but a chloride ion.

...ions

magnesium ion, Mg^{2+} oxide ion, O^{2-}

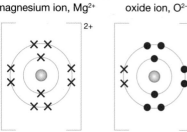

In the ionic compound magnesium oxide, two electrons are transferred from magnesium to oxygen

magnesium ion,   two chloride ions,
Mg^{2+} Cl^-

In magnesium chloride, the magnesium atom transfers one electron to each of two chlorine atoms. The formula is $MgCl_2$

Think about

Look at the sodium chloride lattice. Can you explain the shape of the sodium chloride crystals in the photo?

Think about

What does the formula NaCl tell us about sodium chloride?

Research

Find out how we use other ionic compounds found in the Earth's crust.

The word 'salt' to a chemist means a whole family of **ionic compounds**. Sodium chloride is just one of them.

1A.3
2A.P3

Does an NaCl 'molecule' exist?

2A.M3

The answer is 'No'. A positive sodium ion can surround itself with six chloride ions. Likewise, a chloride ion can surround itself with six sodium ions. It makes a **lattice**. Sodium chloride exists as a **giant ionic structure**.

○ Na⁺ (sodium ion)
● Cl⁻ (chloride ion)

NaCl lattice

Sodium chloride crystals

Useful ionic bonds

2A.D2

Most of the rocks in the Earth's crust have ionic bonds to bond the different atoms together. The strong ionic bonds make the rocks hard and durable. The Portland stone used to make St Paul's Cathedral and Buckingham Palace is a type of limestone containing mostly calcium carbonate. The calcium atoms formed ionic bonds with carbon and oxygen atoms millions of years ago.

Bonding and properties

Your assessment criteria:

1A.2 Describe properties of ionic and covalent substances

2A.P2 Compare properties of ionic and covalent substances

2A.M2 Explain the properties of ionic and covalent substances

2A.D2 Relate applications of compounds to their properties and to their bonding and structure

What's in our food?

Many of our foods contain **food additives**. They are listed on the label. Labelling must be accurate by law. Additives in food are regularly checked by the Food Standards Agency. Workers identify the additives and find out how much the food contains. Knowing how the atoms are bonded together is the first step in identifying an additive.

1A.2
2A.P2

Properties of ionic and covalent substances

Property	Covalent substances	Ionic substances
appearance	may be solid, liquid or gases at room temperature	most are solids at room temperature, many are crystalline
solubility	many dissolve in organic solvents, but not in water	many dissolve in water but not in organic solvents
melting and boiling points	most covalent substances have low melting and boiling points	ionic substances have high melting and boiling points
electrical conductivity	do not conduct electricity	conduct electricity when molten or (if soluble) when dissolved in water

Know more

Many ionic substances are soluble in water because their charged ions are attracted to small charges on the water molecules.

Discuss

Diamond and carbon dioxide are both covalent substances. Can you explain why the boiling point of diamond (3550 °C) is much higher than the boiling point of carbon dioxide (−78 °C)?

...food additive

2A.M2

Think about

The melting point of magnesium oxide is 2 852 °C. The melting point of oxygen is −218 °C. Can you explain these differences?

Property explanations

Melting and boiling points

When a covalent substance exists as simple molecules, the molecules are not strongly attracted to each other. Although covalent bonds are strong bonds, they do not have to break when the substance melts. Little energy is needed to melt many covalent substances. The melting point, and similarly the boiling point, is low. Hydrogen, chlorine and oxygen have covalent molecules which exist as gases at room temperature.

Ionic bonds are strong bonds, but since ionic compounds have giant ionic structures, some of the bonds have to be broken when the compound melts. This requires a lot of energy and the melting point is high.

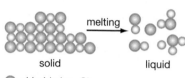

melting

solid   liquid

○ chloride ion, Cl^-

○ sodium ion, Na^+

When sodium chloride melts, the giant ionic structure has to break up. Bonds need to be broken

Electrical conductivity

Substances that conduct electricity must have charged particles that are free to move and carry the charge round the circuit. Covalent substances do not have charged particles so they cannot conduct electricity. The ions in ionic compounds have charges, but cannot move in a solid. Ionic solids do not conduct electricity. But if an ionic compound is melted or dissolved in water, the ions can move and conduct electricity.

Think about

Why does molten lead bromide conduct electricity when solid lead bromide does not?

Think about

Explain why graphite writes on paper easily.

Graphite is pencil 'lead'

Research

Find out what 'graphene' is, and what its special properties are.

Graphite, the exception

2A.D2

Like diamond, **graphite** is made from carbon atoms joined together by covalent bonds. Unlike diamond, each carbon atom makes three, not four, covalent bonds with other carbon atoms. The carbon atoms join up in hexagons forming flat sheets. Spare electrons make a layer between the sheets.

Electrons are negatively charged and these 'layer' electrons can move. Graphite conducts electricity and is used in electrical devices such as rechargeable lithium-ion batteries, the batteries used in laptops and mobile phones.

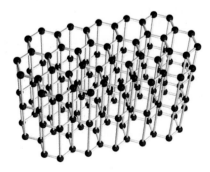

The structure of graphite

🔍 ...graphite ...graphene

Physical properties

Smart mobiles

The next generation of mobile phones could be made from 'smart' fabric. Smart materials react to something in the environment and change. A smart fabric mobile could be folded and put in your pocket without breaking.

1B.4
2B.P4

Testing physical properties

Materials must have the right properties to do their job.

Electrical conductivity

Some materials allow electricity to pass through them. These are **electrical conductors**. Other materials are **electrical insulators** and do not let electricity pass through. Metals are good electrical conductors. Non-metals usually make good insulators. In a mobile phone, electrical insulators surround the circuit.

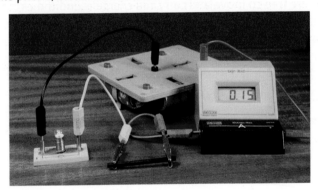

The material being tested makes up a section of the circuit. If it conducts electricity, the bulb lights up and the ammeter shows a current

Thermal conductivity

Good **thermal conductors** allow heat to pass through them efficiently. Metal kebab skewers are good thermal conductors. They take heat to the middle of the food and the kebab cooks quickly. Poor thermal conductors, such as the wooden handles of the skewers, are called **thermal insulators**.

Melting and boiling points

Each chemical substance has its own melting point and boiling point. These change if the substance has impurities. Scientists use melting and boiling points to check purity.

We use thermal insulators to keep our buildings warm

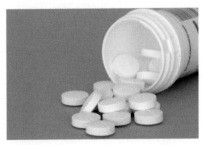

Aspirin has a melting point of 136°C. Batches of aspirin can be tested using melting point apparatus

...electrical conductors ...thermal conductors

Copper(II) sulfate is not soluble in ethanol, although it is soluble in water

'Multigrade' engine oils have polymers added. These stop the oil thinning too much when the engine is hot

Discuss

1 tonne of gold ore gives 5 g of gold metal.

1 tonne of mobile phones requires 150 g of gold metal.

What does this mean for our future gold supplies?

Think about

Use the data in the table to explain why these metals are used in mobile phones.

Research

Find out some physical properties of other metals used in mobile phones, such as palladium, platinum, aluminium and iron.

Solubility

Soluble substances (sometimes called **solutes**) dissolve in a **solvent** to make a **solution**. Water and ethanol are solvents. It is important that substances used in an everyday item like a mobile phone are not soluble in everyday solvents.

1B.4
2B.P4

Viscosity

Viscosity measures how easily a liquid flows. Thick liquids are more viscous and do not flow well. Thin liquids are less viscous.

Viscosity is an important property for engine oil. Engines need oil thin enough for a cold start and thick enough for when an engine is hot. The problem is that oil gets thinner when the engine is hot.

Mobile metals
2B.M4

Mobile phones contain many different metals.

- Copper is used for electric circuits because it is a good electrical conductor.

- Silver is used in switches on circuit boards and in the phone buttons because it is an even better electrical conductor. It lasts for millions of on/off cycles.

- Gold is used to plate the surfaces of the circuit board and the connectors. It is an excellent electrical conductor and does not corrode.

- Tantalum is used in the electronic components. It enables scientists to make mobile phones very small.

Which mobile metal?
2B.D3

The table shows some properties of metals used in your mobile phone. The values for hardness and electrical conductivity are based on special scales used to describe these properties.

Metal	Hardness	Electrical conductivity	Corrosion	Cost (£/kg)
copper	3.0	0.60	corrodes slowly	78
silver	2.5 to 4.0	0.63	corrodes slowly	650
gold	2.5	0.45	very corrosion resistant	32 990
tantalum	6.5	0.08	corrosion resistant below 300 °C	317

...smart materials

Chemical properties

Your assessment criteria:

1B.5 Describe chemical properties of chemical substances

2B.P5 Describe how chemical substances are used based on their chemical properties

2B. M4 Explain how physical and chemical properties of chemical substances make them suitable for their uses

2B.D3 Assess the suitability of different types of substance for a specified use

Airbags

Airbags are fitted as standard in most new cars. They inflate in a collision and protect the car's occupants. Road accident researchers have found that airbags reduce mortality on the roads by 63%. Only using seat belts has a greater effect with a 72% mortality reduction.

1B.5 2B.P5

Using chemicals

Sodium azide

Airbags inflate due to a chemical reaction. They contain sodium azide, NaN_3. Sodium azide is stable until heated, when it decomposes. The reaction is:

sodium azide → sodium + nitrogen

$$2NaN_3(s) \rightarrow 2Na(s) + 3N_2(g)$$

A handful of sodium azide produces $67\,dm^3$ of nitrogen gas, enough to fill an airbag.

Argon

Sometimes, chemicals are used because they don't react. Arc welding is used to join metals together. It produces a lot of heat to liquefy the metals at the joint. But welders don't want the metals to burn as well. They use argon gas to blanket the welding. Argon is very unreactive (**inert**) so the metals do not burn as they would in oxygen or air.

Silicon

Silicon (atomic number 14) is used to make computer chips because of its property as a **semiconductor**. This makes it easy to control the amount of electricity flowing. Some parts of the chip, however, need to be good insulators. A chemical reaction is used. Oxygen is added to the silicon and an **oxide** is formed, silicon(IV) oxide. This compound does not conduct electricity.

Think about

Why is it important that airbags also contain chemicals that react safely with sodium metal and produce non-toxic products?

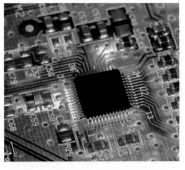

Silicon is ideal for electronic circuitry

Know more

*Silicon is a semiconductor and this is a **physical property**. Silicon reacting with oxygen is a **chemical property**.*

1B.5
2B.P5

Think about

Sodium hydrogen carbonate is $NaHCO_3$. Write word and symbol equations to show how it decomposes when heated.

Research

Find out how argon gas is obtained. Why is it cheap?

Think about

Traditional light bulbs are filled with argon gas. Why is air not used?

argon : 2.8.8

Electron shell structure of argon

Research

Which other elements have full outer shells of electrons?

Argon gas has been pumped over the metals to be joined, to stop them reacting

Carbon dioxide

Carbon dioxide is used in fire extinguishers. Fires need oxygen to burn. Although oxygen atoms make up part of the carbon dioxide molecule, the double covalent bonds are very strong and carbon dioxide does not decompose easily. So carbon dioxide does not let things burn. It is also heavier than oxygen and air. Smothering a fire with carbon dioxide gas will extinguish it. Some fire extinguishers contain compressed carbon dioxide gas and other contains solid powders like sodium hydrogen carbonate that decompose on heating and produce carbon dioxide.

Aiming the carbon dioxide foam at the base of the fire extinguishes it

Why is argon unreactive?

2B.M4

An argon atom has a full outer shell of electrons, as shown on the left. This makes it very stable. Atoms that do not have full outer shells of electrons undergo chemical reactions in order to become more stable. The products often have full outer shells.

Is argon the best gas to use in welding?

2B.D3

Argon is a noble gas in group 0 in the periodic table. All noble gases have full outer shells of electrons. The table shows some of their physical and chemical properties.

Noble gas	Atomic number	Percentage in Earth's atmosphere	Density (g/dm^3)	Chemical reactivity
helium	2	0.000 524	0.18	very unreactive
neon	10	0.0018	0.90	very unreactive
argon	18	0.94	1.78	very unreactive
krypton	36	0.000 114 5	3.73	very unreactive
xenon	54	0.000 008 6	5.79	very unreactive

The density of air at 20 °C is $1.20 \, g/dm^3$. A gas used in blanket welding must be denser than air, so helium and neon are not suitable. Argon is the commonest noble gas in the Earth's atmosphere. This makes it more readily available and cheaper.

...inert gas

Describing chemical reactions

An explosive reaction

Sodium metal (group 1) reacts with chlorine gas (group 7) to make sodium chloride. The reaction is spectacular. Chemistry is happening. Scientists need a way to describe what is happening.

Sodium burning in chlorine

1C.7
2C.P7

Chemical equations

Chemical equations tell us about a reaction. They use chemical symbols to represent the chemicals used and made.

A chemical equation:

- describes a real event
- tells you which chemicals are reacting, the **reactants**
- tells you which chemicals are made, the **products**
- uses chemical shorthand to describe the reaction
- tells you how many particles are involved.

The first step is to write a word equation:

sodium + chlorine → sodium chloride

Now use symbols and formulae for the substances:

$Na + Cl_2 \rightarrow NaCl$

You must now balance the equation. List the number of each type of atom:

$Na + Cl_2 \rightarrow NaCl$

1   2   1 1

You must have the same number of each type of atom on each side of the equation. There is 1 sodium on each side, so sodium balances. There are 2 chlorines on the left-hand side and 1 on the right. Cl_2 can make two NaCl. We write this as 2NaCl.

$Na + Cl_2 \rightarrow 2NaCl$

But there is now 1 sodium on the left and 2 on the right. 2Na are needed to make 2NaCl. So the **balanced equation** is:

$2Na + Cl_2 \rightarrow 2NaCl$

> **Know more**
>
> *Chemical equations are used in every country in the world. Scientists use equations to talk to each other.*

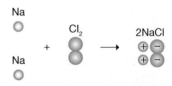

Diagrammatic representation of a balanced chemical equation. Each side of the equation must have the same number of each type of atom

...reactants and products

Potassium reacting with water

Remember:

- Cl_2 means there are two atoms of chlorine, chemically bonded together.

- $2Cl$ means there are two separate atoms of chlorine. They are not bonded together.

Balancing equations

Potassium reacts with water to make potassium hydroxide and hydrogen gas. The gas is given off and the potassium hydroxide dissolves in the water. The word equation is:

potassium + water → potassium hydroxide + hydrogen

Using symbols:

$K + H_2O \rightarrow KOH + H_2$

Balancing:

$K + H_2O \rightarrow KOH + H_2$
1   2 1   1 1 1   2

There is 1 potassium on the left and 1 on the right. Potassium balances.

There are 2 hydrogens on the left and 3 on the right. $2H_2O$ will give enough hydrogen (and oxygen) to make 2KOH. But this needs 2K on the left. The balanced equation is:

$2K + 2H_2O \rightarrow 2KOH + H_2$

Adding state symbols:

$2K(s) + 2H_2O(l) \rightarrow 2KOH(aq) + H_2(g)$

What equations tell us

Symbol equations give us more information than word equations. We can get hints about what the reaction will look like.

Calcium carbonate reacts with dilute hydrochloric acid:

$CaCO_3(s) + 2HCl(aq) \rightarrow CaCl_2(aq) + CO_2(g) + H_2O(l)$

An acid solution (HCl) is added to a solid ($CaCO_3$). It will probably fizz, as gas is given off (CO_2). The calcium chloride made will dissolve in the water.

Know more

State symbols *in equations tell us more. They are added after each substance.*

(s) means solid

(l) means liquid

(g) means gas

(aq) means aqueous (dissolved in water)

Think about

Lithium and sodium are also in group 1. They have similar reactions with water. Can you write word and symbol equations for these reactions?

Think about

What do equations not tell us about a reaction?

Useful reaction types

A clean-up job

Industry uses millions of cubic decimetres of water every day. Most of it is eventually returned to the environment, but it often needs to be cleaned up so that it does not harm wildlife or damage the ecosystem. That's the law. This may involve removing acids, alkalis or heavy metals, such as lead, from the water.

Your assessment criteria:

1C.7 Identify reactants and products, including state symbols in chemical equations and whether reactions are reversible or irreversible

2C.P7 Identify the number and types of atoms in balanced chemical equations

1C.7 2C.P7

Neutralisation reactions

The pH of water supplies should be between 6.5 and 9.5. Industrial processes often produce acid waste which ends up in the waste water. **Neutralisation** reactions can be used to increase the pH (reduce the acidity) and produce neutral waste water. Water containing sulfuric acid as waste can be neutralised with sodium hydroxide solution. The chemistry is:

sulfuric acid + sodium hydroxide → sodium sulfate + water

$$H_2SO_4(aq) + 2NaOH(aq) \rightarrow Na_2SO_4(aq) + 2H_2O(l)$$

What the equation tells us:

- this is a neutralisation reaction because the reactants are an acid and a base (or alkali) and the products are a salt and water
- one sulfuric acid unit reacts with two sodium hydroxide units
- one sodium sulfate unit is produced and two water molecules
- the reaction happens when all the reactants are in solution.

Some industries remove excess sulfuric acid by reacting it with local limestone (calcium carbonate). The chemistry is:

$$H_2SO_4(aq) + CaCO_3(s) \rightarrow CaSO_4(s) + H_2O(l) + CO_2(g)$$

What this equation tells us:

- solid calcium carbonate is added to the sulfuric acid solution
- the salt formed is calcium sulfate
- solid calcium sulfate is made (it is insoluble); the mixture will go cloudy
- water and carbon dioxide gas are produced; the mixture will fizz.

Know more

Producing calcium sulfate from excess sulfuric acid is good economics. Calcium sulfate is the plaster in plaster board, which is used extensively in the building industry. The waste sulfuric acid can be turned into a profit-making business.

Think about

There are seven atoms in a unit of sulfuric acid and five in a unit of calcium carbonate. The total number of atoms on the left-hand side of the equation is 7 + 5 = 12. How many atoms will be on the right-hand side?

Think about

Equations for other neutralisation reactions are:

$HCl(aq) + NaOH(aq) \rightarrow$
$\qquad NaCl(aq) + H_2O(l)$

$HNO_3(aq) + NaOH(aq) \rightarrow$
$\qquad NaNO_3(aq) + H_2O(l)$

$H_2SO_4 + CuO(s) \rightarrow$
$\qquad CuSO_4(aq) + H_2O(l)$

How are these equations similar?

...symbol equations

Think about

Equations for other displacement reactions are:

$Fe(s) + CuSO_4(aq) \rightarrow FeSO_4(aq) + Cu(s)$

$Cu(s) + 2AgNO_3(aq) \rightarrow Cu(NO_3)_2(aq) + 2Ag(s)$

If copper sulfate solution is blue, iron sulfate solution green, silver nitrate solution colourless and copper nitrate solution blue, what would you see happening? (Copper metal is reddish brown, iron and silver are grey.)

Think about

Other displacement reactions involving halogens are:

$2NaI(aq) + Cl_2(aq) \rightarrow 2NaCl(aq) + I_2(aq)$

$2NaI(aq) + Br_2(aq) \rightarrow 2NaBr(aq) + I_2(aq)$

What do these equations have in common?

Think about

Another combustion reaction is:

$2C_2H_6(g) + 7O_2(g) \rightarrow 4CO_2(g) + 6H_2O(g)$

What do combustion reactions have in common?

Know more

Ammonia gas is used to make fertilisers. Ammonium fertilisers provide food for 50% of the world's population.

Discuss

Why do scientists use chemical equations?

Displacement reactions

Lead is toxic in water supplies. Several methods are used to remove lead from industrial waste water. **Displacement reactions** can be used to swap the lead ions for safer metal ions such as zinc. A more reactive metal will displace a less reactive metal from its salt. The equation shows the chemistry:

$Pb(NO_3)_2(aq) + 2Zn(s) \rightarrow Pb(s) + Zn(NO_3)_2(aq)$

The solid lead metal produced can be removed by filtering. The other product, zinc nitrate, stays dissolved in the water and is less harmful than lead nitrate.

Halogens also have displacement reactions. A more reactive halogen will displace a less reactive halogen from its salt. Bromide in water supplies can form harmful products. Large amounts of bromide can be removed from industrial waste water by treating it with chlorine gas. The chemistry is:

$2NaBr(aq) + Cl_2(aq) \rightarrow 2NaCl(aq) + Br_2(aq)$

The bromine can be separated and sold to other industries.

Reversible or irreversible reactions

Neutralisation and displacement reactions can be used to clean up contaminated water because they are not reversible. That means that all the reactants react to make the products and the reaction does not go backwards. We use the arrow sign ($\rightarrow$) to show this. **Combustion** reactions are other examples of **irreversible reactions**. Methane, CH_4, is the chemical in the gas we burn to keep warm and cook food. The chemistry is:

$CH_4(g) + 2O_2(g) \rightarrow CO_2(g) + 2H_2O(g)$

The reactants in combustion reactions are the fuel and oxygen gas. Carbon dioxide and water cannot be made to produce methane and oxygen. The reaction is irreversible.

Some reactions are **reversible**. Nitrogen gas reacts with hydrogen to make ammonia gas. The chemistry is:

$N_2(g) + 3H_2(g) \rightleftharpoons 2NH_3(g)$

But, ammonia also breaks down to form nitrogen gas and hydrogen gas. We never get 100% ammonia and the reaction never finishes. This is what the double arrow sign ($\rightleftharpoons$) means.

The ammonium fertiliser used to produce these tomatoes was made in a reversible reaction

Rates of reaction

The food additive business

Calcium chloride is a widely used food additive. It is E509. It makes food taste salty, keeps canned vegetables firm and is added to foods to increase their calcium content. It is also used to stop the caramel in chocolate bars going hard.

1C.6
2C.P6

Controlling the reaction

Dynamite and TNT react explosively – the reaction is very fast. The rusting of iron is a very slow reaction. We use the words **rate of reaction** to describe how fast a reaction is. It measures how much product is made in a second.

There are three ways of manufacturing calcium chloride. One way is using limestone (calcium carbonate, $CaCO_3$) and hydrochloric acid (HCl). Calcium chloride manufacturers need to control the reaction. If the reaction is too fast, there may be a dangerous explosion. If it is too slow, they will lose money.

The equation for the reaction is:

REACTANTS		PRODUCTS
calcium carbonate + hydrochloric acid	→	calcium chloride + carbon dioxide + water

$$CaCO_3(s) + 2HCl(aq) \rightarrow CaCl_2(aq) + CO_2(g) + H_2O(aq)$$

In the school lab, we can follow the rate of a reaction by two methods.

Limestone, marble and chalk are all different forms of calcium carbonate. They all have the formula $CaCO_3$

Method 1

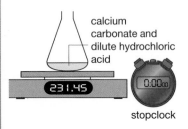

calcium carbonate and dilute hydrochloric acid

231.45

stopclock

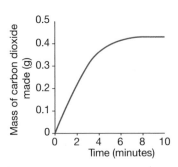

The calcium carbonate and dilute hydrochloric acid are in the flask. The mass on the balance decreases as the reaction takes place. This is because carbon dioxide gas is escaping.

...calcium chloride food additive

The graph plots the mass of carbon dioxide made against time. The reaction is fastest when the graph is steepest. It is slowest when the graph is least steep. When the graph is flat, the reaction has stopped.

Method 2

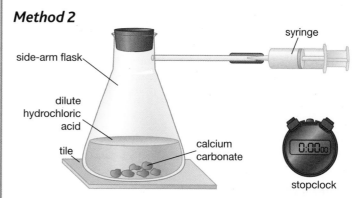

The carbon dioxide gas produced is collected in a syringe. This measures its volume. A graph can be plotted of volume of carbon dioxide against time.

Changing the rate of reaction

The manufacturers can control the reaction by:

1 changing the concentration of the reactants

2 changing the size of the reactant particles

3 changing the temperature of the reactants, or

4 using a **catalyst**.

1 Changing the concentration of the reactants

The concentration of the hydrochloric acid used can be changed. The same amount of a more concentrated acid has more acid particles to react with the limestone. The reaction will be faster. The reaction can be followed using either of the two methods described above.

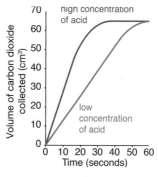

Graph to show how the rate of reaction changes when the concentration of the acid changes. You can tell that the reaction is faster with the higher concentration because the graph is steeper

> ### Know more
>
> *As the reaction progresses, the rate of reaction decreases. This is because the reactants are being used up.*

> ### Know more
>
> #### The collision theory
>
> *Manufacturers know that a reaction will only take place when particles collide. They must be moving very fast – have lots of **kinetic energy**. Only particles with enough energy will react. These are the **successful collisions**.*
>
>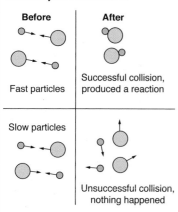
>
> *Successful and unsuccessful collisions*

> ### Know more
>
> #### Concentration
>
>
>
> low concentration   high concentration
>
> ● Reacting particle of substance A
> ● Reacting particle of substance B
>
> *At high concentration, the particles are more crowded. Collisions are more frequent. The rate of reaction increases.*

1C.6
2C.P6

2 Changing the size of the reactant particles

Limestone can have any size of particles, from large lumps to fine powder. The smaller the particles, the faster the reaction with hydrochloric acid. Powdered limestone reacts fastest.

3 Changing the temperature of the reactants

Consider a different reaction: sodium thiosulfate reacting with dilute hydrochloric acid. Small particles of sulfur form. These make the reaction mixture go cloudy. You can tell how long the reaction takes by timing how long it takes for a cross drawn under the flask to disappear.

This reaction can be carried out at different temperatures. Most reactions are faster at higher temperatures.

4 Using a catalyst

A catalyst is a substance added to a chemical reaction to make it go faster. It is not used up in the chemical reaction.

Manufacturers find catalysts very useful. They can make the product more quickly and the catalyst can be used over and over again.

Consider the reaction of hydrogen peroxide, H_2O_2. Left on its own, it slowly breaks down into oxygen gas and water. A catalyst will make this happen quicker because it lowers the energy needed for the reaction to happen.

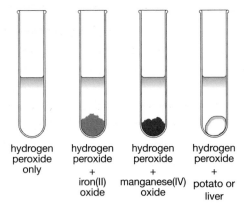

| hydrogen peroxide only | hydrogen peroxide + iron(II) oxide | hydrogen peroxide + manganese(IV) oxide | hydrogen peroxide + potato or liver |

All the test tubes contain hydrogen peroxide. The other substances act as catalysts. Some are better catalysts than others

Know more

Particle size

When a substance is broken into small pieces, there are more places for collisions to happen. The rate of reaction increases.

1 g of powdered limestone has a larger total surface area than a 1 g lump of limestone. There are more places for the reaction to happen and so the reaction is faster.

Know more

Temperature

low temperature   high temperature

⚪ Reacting particle of substance A
⚫ Reacting particle of substance B

Particles move faster at higher temperatures. Collisions are more frequent. The rate of reaction increases.

Think about

If colliding particles do not have enough energy to react, what happens to them?

🔍 ...catalyst

By controlling the reaction conditions in the factory, margarine manufacturers can produce hard or soft margarines

Research

Hydrogenation produces a white semi-solid fat. How do manufacturers make their margarine resemble butter? How do they make it a healthy option?

Products such as detergents and air fresheners usually contain perfumes made in a lab. Perfumes made from natural ingredients are usually used in cosmetic products

Think about

The reaction to make methanol is reversible. What does this mean for the manufacturers?

Research

How do catalytic converters remove unburnt petrol from exhaust fumes?

Research

Research other industrial reactions that use catalysts.

Rates and industry

2C.M5

Making margarine

Margarine is made in food factories from vegetable or fish oils. Hydrogen gas is bubbled through the oil. When the hydrogen molecules react with the oil molecules (hydrogenation), the oil hardens to a more solid fat; the basis of margarine.

At room temperature, there is no reaction. But the reaction can happen at a profitable rate by using:

- a nickel catalyst
- a temperature of 175 °C to 190 °C
- a high pressure to concentrate the hydrogen gas.

The higher temperature, higher pressure and catalyst increase the reaction rate.

Making smells

Methanol is CH_3OH. It is used to make the compounds responsible for apple, pineapple and ylang-ylang smells. The chemistry used to make methanol is:

carbon monoxide + hydrogen $\rightleftharpoons$ methanol

$$CO(g) + 2H_2(g) \rightleftharpoons CH_3OH(l)$$

Making methanol production a profitable business requires choosing the best conditions to give the optimum rate of reaction. The reaction also has to be safe for the workers.

Manufacturers use these conditions to make methanol:

- a temperature of 250 °C – a higher temperature increases the rate of reaction and more methanol can be made per day
- a pressure of 50–100 atmospheres (50–100 times atmospheric pressure) – this increases the concentration of the reactants by forcing the molecules closer together; a higher concentration means a faster reaction
- a catalyst made from copper, zinc oxide and aluminium oxide – this also increases the rate of reaction.

Catalytic converters

The high temperatures in car engines produce toxic gases – carbon monoxide and nitrogen oxide. Catalytic converters fitted in exhaust pipes turn these gases into substances naturally found in air:

carbon monoxide + nitrogen oxide $\rightarrow$ nitrogen + carbon dioxide

$$2CO(g) + 2NO(g) \rightarrow N_2(g) + 2CO_2(g)$$

The exhaust gases are hot from the engine and the converter contains a catalyst made from rhodium, palladium and platinum metals. The reaction rate increases.

Industrial processes

Green chemistry

Chemical manufacturers must make money. Managers must consider the rate of reaction and the yield of products. These days they must also use 'green chemistry'. Green chemistry produces as little environmental harm as possible. Ibuprofen is now made in three steps instead of six. There is less waste and less pollution.

Green Chemistry
Centre of Excellence

2C.M6

Yield

Industrial chemists use raw materials (the reactants) to make new products. Making a good profit means making the maximum amount of product possible. Chemists can use relative atomic masses and balanced equations to calculate the maximum mass of product possible. This is called the **theoretical yield**. We use this to calculate the actual **yield** or **percentage yield**:

$$\text{yield (\%)} = \frac{\text{mass of product actually made}}{\text{theoretical yield}} \times 100$$

Calcium oxide is made in chemical factories by heating calcium carbonate (limestone) in large kilns. The equation is:

$$CaCO_3(s) \rightarrow CaO(s) + CO_2(g).$$

Chemists can calculate that 100 kg of calcium carbonate can produce a maximum of 56 kg of calcium oxide. If they only obtain 42 kg, the yield is: $42 \div 56 \times 100 = 75\%$

So 25% of the product is not made or is lost in the process.

Atom economy

Yields tell chemists how efficient their process is, but not how much waste they are producing. Calcium carbonate ($CaCO_3$) contains these atoms:

- one calcium
- one carbon
- three oxygen

When it is heated in a lime kiln, only one calcium atom and one oxygen atom are used to make the product. The rest of the atoms make waste carbon dioxide.

The amount of wasted atoms in an industrial process is measured by its **atom economy**. It can also be calculated from the balanced equation and relative atomic masses.

These lime kilns are used to produce calcium oxide. Calcium oxide has many uses including making cement and mortar

Think about

Industrial chemists calculate that a batch of iron ore can produce 112 tonnes of iron. They obtain 72.8 tonnes. What yield are they getting?

Know more

A yield of 100% is rarely obtained because:

- *other chemical reactions happen*
- *some product is lost in the apparatus*
- *not all the reactants react*
- *the reaction may be reversible.*

🔍 ...green chemistry principles

Think about

What can industrial chemists do about a process that has a low atom economy?

Think about

What will an equation look like if the atom economy is 100%?

2A.P1

$$\text{Atom economy (\%)} = \frac{\text{mass of atoms in desired product}}{\text{total mass of atoms in all products}} \times 100$$

For the reaction $CaCO_3(s) \rightarrow CaO(s) + CO_2(g)$

mass of atoms in calcium oxide = 40 + 16 = 56 (add up relative atomic masses for each atom)

total mass of atoms in all products = 40 + 16 + 12 + (2 × 16) = 100 (add up relative atomic masses for all atoms in products)

$$\text{Atom economy} = \frac{56}{100} \times 100 = 56\%$$

This means that of the reacting atoms 56% (by mass) are made into the useful product and 44% make waste products.

Careful control of the conditions inside the lime kiln ensures the highest possible percentage yield

Discuss

How can calcium oxide manufacturers make their process more environmentally friendly? [Hint: think about the energy needed for the process and the problems created by carbon dioxide gas in the atmosphere.]

Calcium oxide production

2C.D4

Calcium carbonate decomposes at temperatures over 900 °C. The kilns used are packed with crushed calcium carbonate and heated. Industrial chemists control the conditions to get the best rate and yield.

Using small even-sized particles of limestone so that the kiln heats evenly. Heat cannot penetrate larger particles and the yield is reduced.

Using temperatures between 950 and 1300 °C, depending on the type of limestone. The temperature can be uneven inside the kiln. This makes sure all the contents reach the minimum temperature.

Conditions used to get the highest yield

Continually flushing out the carbon dioxide produced. The reaction to make calcium oxide is reversible. Removing carbon dioxide stops it going backwards.

Carefully choosing which fuel is used to heat the kiln. Coal and oil both contain sulfur. This reacts with oxygen as the fuel burns: $S(s) + O_2(g) \rightarrow SO_2(g)$. Sulfur dioxide does unwanted chemistry with calcium oxide and reduces the yield.

Some calcium oxide manufacturers are finding commercial uses for the carbon dioxide product. This increases the atom economy as some of the waste atoms become useful products.

...uses of calcium oxide

Human activity and the environment

It's not rocket science

But we may need rocket science to get materials from the Moon. We are using up Earth's materials faster than ever before. We still have large deposits of iron and titanium but other metals are running out. Indium is used in 'touch screens' and television screens. We have about ten years' supply left in known deposits. Is it worth developing new technologies if we haven't got the metals needed?

1D.8
2D.P8

Materials from the Earth

From the sea

Sea water contains dissolved salts. We evaporate it to get sea salt. Salt ponds can be found along the coasts of warmer countries. We also process sea water to take out the bromine. Bromine is used in many medicines and in flame-proofing.

From the land

We get some **fossil fuels** from the land. **Coal** deposits are found underground and on the surface. Coal formed naturally 300 million years ago. It is fossilised plant material.

Crude oil and **natural gas** are found together, underground and under the ocean floor. They are also fossil fuels, the remains of plants and animals that lived in the oceans 100 million years ago.

Few metals are found naturally as elements. Most are in compounds. Iron is found as iron oxide. This iron **ore** is mined and the iron is extracted in a **blast furnace**. We take millions of tonnes of metal ore from the Earth every year.

Quarries are places where ore or building stone is dug out. All of our buildings and roads are made from different types of rock. The city of Aberdeen is often called 'the granite city' because of its many buildings built from local granite. The tarmac on our roads is a mixture of crushed rock and tar (from oil). Slate is quarried for roofing material.

Know more

*Fossil fuels are finite, or **non-renewable**. There is only so much in the Earth. Once we have used that up, we can't replace it.*

Oil is extracted from deep beneath the ocean floor

Know more

Gold, silver and platinum are found as elements in the Earth's crust.

🔍 ...coal formation

1D.8
2D.P8

Research

Find out how iron is extracted from iron ore. What are the waste materials and what happens to them?

From the air

We have many uses for the gases in air (see the table). We separate them out from the mixture of gases using **fractional distillation**. Air is cooled until it becomes liquid. As it slowly warms up, gases boil off at different temperatures.

Gas	How do we use it?
oxygen	Breathing apparatus, welding.
nitrogen	Making fertilisers, explosives, modified atmosphere packaging of food.
argon	In light bulbs, plasma globes, blue laser lights, arc welding.
helium	Diving gas (mixed with oxygen for divers to breathe), filling balloons, helium-neon lasers.

2D.M7

Chemical processing

Most of the substances we take from the Earth have to be processed to make them useful. This can involve **physical changes** and **chemical changes**, which need energy. We obtain most of our energy from fossil fuels. When we burn these, carbon dioxide and pollutants are given off.

Metal extraction processes often have low atom economies. This means a lot of waste is produced. This may be piled in slag heaps, changing the landscape. It can be **toxic**.

Waste heaps are unpleasant to look at and can be toxic

Think about

How will green chemistry help reduce slag heaps?

Think about

Platinum is a very expensive metal. It is used in catalytic converters. Small amounts may be lost in car exhaust systems. Should we recycle dust from road sweepers?

2D.D5

Solutions

In the UK we have local planning regulations and government bodies to control material extraction and building. Mining licences have to be obtained before companies can start digging. Planning permission must be obtained to put up new buildings. The Environment Agency keeps a close watch on possible environmental impacts.

...oil formation

The changing Earth

The Thames barrier

The Thames barrier protects central London from flooding due to high tides. Its floodgates have been used increasingly often since 1990. This is because the sea level is rising by 3 mm per year. Global warming is blamed for this rise. The sea level is expected to rise one metre by 2100. Plans are underway to improve the barrier to cope with this.

1D.8
2D.P8

Human activity problems

Global warming

Scientists agree that the Earth is getting warmer. Most think this is because we are burning large amounts of fossil fuels. Fossil fuels contain carbon. When they burn, carbon dioxide is made. Carbon dioxide is a **greenhouse gas**. It absorbs heat energy in the atmosphere. The Earth gets hotter.

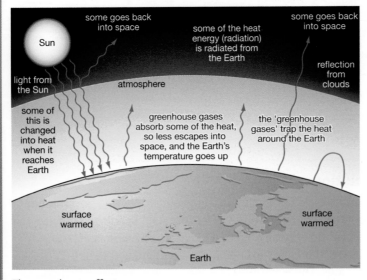

The greenhouse effect

Know more

There are several greenhouse gases. Water vapour and methane are also greenhouse gases. We need some greenhouse gas in the atmosphere. Without carbon dioxide, the average temperature round the Earth would be −20 °C.

... greenhouse gases

Know more

Most countries now use different chemicals (not CFCs) in aerosols and refrigerators. But some of these replacement chemicals act as greenhouse gases.

Ozone issues

There is a layer of **ozone** gas high in the atmosphere. This absorbs some of the harmful UV radiation from the Sun. UV radiation can cause skin cancer. Chemicals called **CFCs** were used in aerosols and refrigerators. These break down the ozone high in the atmosphere. When ozone is destroyed more harmful UV radiation can reach the Earth.

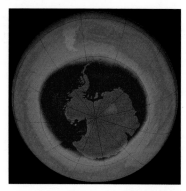

There are now holes in the ozone layer over the South Pole; ozone layer thickness is colour coded from purple (lowest) to green (highest)

Acid rain

Many fuels contain sulfur impurities. The sulfur makes sulfur dioxide when the fuel burns. Sulfur dioxide in the air reacts with water and oxygen producing sulfuric acid. This makes rain water acidic.

Oxides of nitrogen are made in car engines and escape in the exhaust. These also make **acid rain**.

Acid rain changes the chemistry of lakes and rivers. Fish are killed. It damages trees, other plants and buildings.

Know more

Unpolluted rain is pH 5 to 6. Acid rain is pH 2 to 4.

Know more

Power stations making electricity from fossil fuels have been the major sulfur dioxide producers.

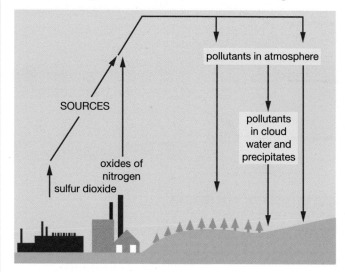

How acid rain is formed

2D.M7

Natural changes

The Earth formed over 4.5 billion years ago and has been changing ever since. We can't be absolutely sure how today's environment came about, but most scientist agree on this sequence of events.

Time (billions of years ago)

4.5 — The Earth formed. The early atmosphere contained gases from the intense volcanic activity: mostly carbon dioxide and water vapour with smaller amounts of methane (CH_4) and ammonia (NH_3).

4 —

3.5 — The Earth cooled and the water vapour condensed to form the oceans. Some carbon dioxide dissolved in the new oceans.

3 —

2.5 — Green plants evolved. **Photosynthesis** used up some of the carbon dioxide in the atmosphere and released oxygen. Fossil fuels started to form and lock up carbon in the Earth's crust. The amount of carbon dioxide in the atmosphere started to fall as the amount of oxygen increased.

2 —

1.5 — There was enough oxygen in the Earth's atmosphere for respiring animal life to evolve.

1 —

0.5 — Photosynthesis and **respiration** keep the amounts of carbon dioxide and oxygen in the atmosphere constant. Nitrogen = 78% and oxygen = 21%. Carbon dioxide in the atmosphere is currently 0.039%. In 2000, this was 0.037%. This change from human activity is faster than at any other time in Earth's history.

0 — (present day)

Adverse effects of chemicals

An inherited problem – land contamination

In some areas of the UK, 200 years of industry has left many chemicals in the soil. Some of these **contaminants** are hazardous. Many sites such as old chemical factories, disused

Think about

Which human activities are increasing in the percentage of carbon dioxide in the atmosphere?

...photosynthesis and respiration

mines and places where waste was tipped are now classed as contaminated sites. The Government now requires developers to clean up land before they build on it.

A current problem – sheep dips

Sheep farmers regularly wash their sheep in an insecticide solution called 'sheep dip'. The dip kills the parasites in the wool. But the used dip can end up in rivers and streams, where it kills invertebrates and fish. Sheep dip chemicals also cause health problems for some users. Organic farmers are developing alternative methods to deal with parasites.

A success story

Acid rain was discovered in the 1960s. Since then:

- many governments have made energy producers clean up the smoke from their tall chimneys
- money has been provided to restore ecosystems damaged by acid rain
- use of clean, **renewable** energy has been encouraged.

Sulfur dioxide emissions from industry in the UK have now fallen by 80%. Environmentalists say our wildlife is recovering.

Research

What are the alternatives to using sheep dip?

Think about

How does using renewable energy sources to produce electricity help reduce sulfur dioxide in the air?

Discuss

Is the problem of acid rain over? Can we now write about it in the history books?

Carbon capture and storage

The carbon in a fuel produces carbon dioxide when the fuel burns. 'Carbon capture and storage', or CCS, involves capturing this carbon dioxide before it gets to the atmosphere and then storing it safely, so it can't act as a greenhouse gas. Old oil and gas fields are good places for storing the carbon dioxide. They are large enough to store millions of tonnes. The carbon dioxide is injected underground. With less carbon entering the air as carbon dioxide, global warming is reduced.

Think about

Capturing carbon dioxide from power stations is possible. But what about car exhausts?

Research

What are the problems of storing carbon dioxide underground?

ONSHORE   OFFSHORE

CO_2 CO_2

— unmineable coal seams

— depleted oil and gas reservoirs

— deep saline (salty) formations

Storing carbon dioxide underground

🔍 ... greenhouse gases

The Earth's natural activity

The Earth is moving

Mount Etna is in Italy. It is the largest active volcano in Europe. It is always active. Mount Etna regularly spews out molten rock or lava, hundreds of metres into the air. Its lava flows threaten and sometimes cover small villages. But the volcanic ash makes rich soil. People take a chance living near the volcano to farm the fertile soil.

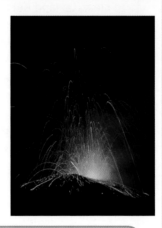

1D.9
2D.P9

Why do we have volcanoes?

We live on the thin rocky **crust** of the Earth. Beneath us is the **mantle** and at the centre an **iron core**. The mantle is semi-liquid and moves slowly.

The Earth's crust is made up of **tectonic plates**. They float on the mantle and move very slowly. At plate boundaries the movements of the plates cause **earthquakes** and **volcanoes**. The map shows where they occur.

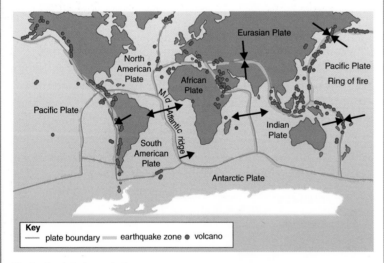

Key
— plate boundary — earthquake zone • volcano

Tectonic plate boundaries

What happens in a volcano?

Molten rock (**magma**) can work its way through weak spots in the Earth's crust. When it reaches the surface, it erupts as **lava**. This then cools and solidifies. Layers of lava build up and make the volcano mountain. Volcanoes can erupt many times.

The Earth's layers

Know more

The Earth's crust is between 10 and 50 km thick. The thinnest parts are under the oceans.

...tectonic plates

1D.9
2D.P9

Know more

The city of Pompeii was buried by 20 m of volcanic ash and rock when Mount Vesuvius erupted in AD79. Few survived.

The ground literally moves during an earthquake

As well as lava, volcanoes spew out rock fragments, ash and volcanic gases. These gases may cause explosions. The common gases given off are water vapour, carbon dioxide and sulfur dioxide. Carbon dioxide and sulfur dioxide are heavy gases. They can form a suffocating blanket over living things. Chlorine and fluorine can also be produced.

How do earthquakes happen?

Tectonic plates move slowly. Some move apart, others move together, some slide past each other. If the plates get stuck, pressure builds up. An earthquake occurs when the plates move again.

crust

mantle

Inside a volcano

Research

Find out how Iceland was made from volcanoes on the ocean floor.

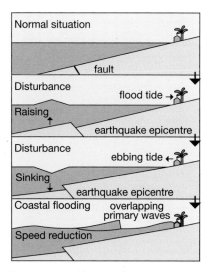

How a tsunami is caused

Volcanic effects

2D.M7

Volcanoes and earthquakes change the environment.

Good changes	Bad changes
Volcanic ash and lava make very fertile soil.	Lava flows destroy crops.
Volcanoes on the ocean floor eventually make new islands.	Volcanic gases are harmful. Sulfur dioxide makes acid rain. Carbon dioxide is a greenhouse gas. These are both heavy gases that can suffocate living things. Chlorine and fluorine are poisonous.
Volcanic mountains can give rise to beautiful landscapes.	Gases dissolve in rivers, lakes and oceans. This makes the water more acidic. Wildlife can be harmed.
	Earthquakes destroy buildings, roads and power supplies.
	Earthquakes on the ocean floor cause **tsunamis** (large waves able to destroy coastal areas).

Early warnings

2D.D5

Geologists study volcanoes and tectonic plate movements to try to predict activity. They use **seismographs** to detect vibrations in the Earth. Satellites look for changes in the shape of volcanoes, which may mean that magma is getting nearer the surface.

🔍 ...tsunami

Choices and solutions

Making cement

Making cement can be a messy business. It uses rocks from quarries. Quarries leave scars on the landscape. It needs a lot of energy, mostly produced from fossil fuels. These produce carbon dioxide and sulfur dioxide. But the company **Castle Cement** has cleaned up its act. It is becoming a sustainable industry.

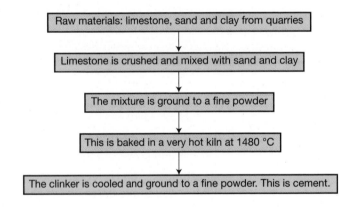

2D.M7

A case study: how cement is made

Raw materials: limestone, sand and clay from quarries

↓

Limestone is crushed and mixed with sand and clay

↓

The mixture is ground to a fine powder

↓

This is baked in a very hot kiln at 1480 °C

↓

The clinker is cooled and ground to a fine powder. This is cement.

Being sustainable

- **Castle Cement** recycles waste from other industries as raw materials. They use ash from burning coal, and old plaster moulds from the pottery industries. This saves on quarrying.
- They are using alternative fuels. They have swapped 160 000 tonnes of coal for 195 000 tonnes of scrap tyres, waste chemicals, paper and plastic to heat the kilns. They also use **biomass** fuel made from abattoir waste. This cuts the sulfur dioxide emissions and also produces less carbon dioxide.

Know more

Crushing the limestone, mixing and grinding the materials and baking all use energy.

Know more

A sustainable industry is one that:
- *is successful*
- *does not harm the environment for future generations.*

Fuel pellets are made from plastics and paper that cannot be recycled

Know more

Recycling 1 tonne of aluminium saves 9 tonnes of carbon dioxide.

The aluminium smelter extracts new aluminium. Note the mining waste in the foreground

Research

How are paper and glass recycled?

- The kiln is carefully controlled to prevent heat loss.
- The cement produced by **Castle Cement** is whiter. It needs less dye to get it the right colour.
- They have planted 18 000 trees. Trees use carbon dioxide in photosynthesis. This helps to balance out the carbon dioxide made.

Other choices

Recycling

Most local authorities have schemes to collect and recycle some of our household waste. The rest ends up in landfill tips that are eventually covered over and the land returned to its former use.

Reasons for recycling:

- We are running out of landfill sites. We currently have landfill sites for nine years of waste only. Public opinion issues include landfill sites are environmentally unfriendly; no one wants one where they live; they may contain toxic material which causes problems for future land use.

- The Earth's resources are limited and we need to recycle materials to ensure a future supply.

- Recycling usually uses less energy than preparing the product from its raw materials. This may mean that less fossil fuel is used and less carbon dioxide produced.

- Recycling is usually cheaper than making the product from its raw materials.

These reasons make recycling a sustainable option.

What can be recycled?

Paper and card, glass, some plastics and most metals can be recycled. Aluminium cans are often collected in schools.

These cans can be recycled and made into new cans in just six weeks

... landfills

2D.M7

Recycled aluminium versus extracted aluminium

	Extracting aluminium from its ore, bauxite	Recycling aluminium
process	The ore has to be mined and the metal extracted by **electrolysis**. Mining scars the landscape and can cause environmental problems.	Scrap aluminium is melted, cooled into thin sheets and used to make new products. No raw materials are used.
energy use	Electrolysis is energy intensive. The ore has to be melted first.	Recycling uses only 5% of the energy used to extract the metal from its ore. There are lower carbon dioxide emissions.
waste products	Mining produces waste rock. Aluminium cans not recycled end up in landfill sites.	Less waste is sent to landfill sites.
facts and figures	Electric power makes up 40% of the cost of extracting aluminium.	55% of all aluminium cans in the UK are recycled and 42% of aluminium products. Aluminium products can be recycled many times.

Fuels for the future

There are other fuels and energy sources we can use to replace fossil fuels. We can use **biofuels** in vehicles. **Bioethanol** is made from sugar cane or corn. **Biodiesel** is made from rape seed. Cars can be powered by **hydrogen fuel cells** or by electricity produced from renewable sources. **Nuclear power** is another option for electricity production.

> ### Research
>
> Find out
> - how bioethanol is made
> - what a fuel cell is.

2D.D5

Renewable energy

Renewable energy sources are replenished naturally. We can get energy from sunlight, wind and moving water, and we can get geothermal heat from the Earth. Using renewable energy does not produce carbon dioxide. Global warming is reduced.

Solar energy

Energy from the Sun can be used in different ways:

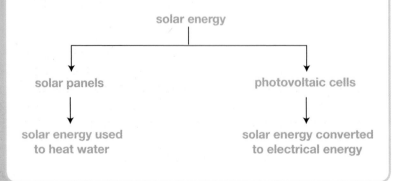

solar energy
- solar panels → solar energy used to heat water
- photovoltaic cells → solar energy converted to electrical energy

Energy from the Sun can produce electricity directly in photovoltaic cells

 ...fuel cells

Wind turbines are non-polluting

Discuss

Why are volcanic areas, such as Iceland, good places to make use of geothermal energy?

Discuss

Oil and gas supplies will run out one day. We need to have alternative energy sources in place. How will we make enough electricity in the future?

Wind energy

Energy from the wind is used to turn the blades on a wind turbine. These are connected to a generator which produces electricity.

Energy from water and tides

Water turbines work in a similar way to wind turbines. Fast-moving streams of water, or the changing sea level as the tide ebbs and flows, are used to turn paddles that are connected to an electricity generator. We have very high tidal ranges in the UK. When technical problems have been overcome, tidal turbines just offshore could provide a major part of the UK's electricity.

Geothermal energy

The deeper you go inside the Earth, the hotter it gets. **Geothermal energy** plants use some of this heat energy to heat water and make steam. The steam can drive turbines and generate electricity.

Nuclear power

A lot of energy is released when nuclei in atoms react. We can harness the energy from some types of nuclear reactions.

Nuclear fission happens when nuclei split. Nuclear fission fuels are used in controlled reactions in nuclear reactors. The heat produced can be used to generate electricity in nuclear power stations.

There are advantages and disadvantages of nuclear power.

People in favour of nuclear power say:

- no carbon dioxide is made, so there is no contribution to global warming
- modern nuclear reactors are very safe
- there is no reliance on imported oil and gas.

People against nuclear power say:

- radioactive waste needs to be stored safely for a long time
- nuclear power stations could be terrorist targets.

Nuclear fusion happens when two small atoms join to make one larger one. Nuclear fusion reactions are constantly happening in the Sun. They give out huge amounts of energy. Scientists think that the energy from controlled fusion reactions will be an important energy source in the future. The main drawback with using nuclear fusion is attaining the high temperature needed for the process to occur and capturing the energy released.

...fission and fusion

To achieve a Pass grade, my portfolio of evidence must show that I can:

Assessment Criteria	Description	✓
2A.P1	Describe the physical and chemical properties of group 1 and 7 elements	
2A.P2	Compare properties of ionic and covalent substances	
2A.P3	Draw dot-and-cross diagrams of simple ionic and covalent substances	
2B.P4	Describe how chemical substances are used based on their physical properties	
2B.P5	Describe how chemical substances are used based on their chemical properties	
2C.P6	Describe the factors that can affect the rates of chemical reactions	
2C.P7	Identify the number and types of atoms in balanced chemical equations	
2D.P8	Describe the human activities that affect the Earth and its environment	
2D.P9	Describe natural factors that have changed the surface and atmosphere of the Earth	

If you do not meet all the Level 2 Pass criteria for this Unit then your work will be assessed against these Level 1 criteria. If your work meets all these criteria you will achieve a Level 1 Pass for this Unit. If you do not achieve all these Level 1 criteria you will get a U (Unclassified) for this Unit.

Assessment Criteria	Description	✓
1A.1	Classify group 1 and 7 elements based on their physical properties	
1A.2	Describe properties of ionic and covalent substances	
1A.3	Classify substances as ionic or covalent	
1B.4	Describe physical properties of chemical substances	
1B.5	Describe chemical properties of chemical substances	
1C.6	Identify the factors that can affect the rates of chemical reactions	
1C.7	Identify reactants and products, including state symbols in chemical equations, and whether reactions are reversible or irreversible	
1D.8	Identify the human activities that affect the Earth and its environment	
1D.9	Identify natural factors that have changed the surface and atmosphere of the Earth	

To achieve a Merit grade, my portfolio of evidence must also show that I can:

Assessment Criteria	Description	✓
2A.M1	Describe trends in the physical and chemical properties of group 1 and 7 elements	
2A.M2	Explain the properties of ionic and covalent substances	
2A.M3	Describe the formation of ionic and covalent substances	
2B.M4	Explain how physical and chemical properties of chemical substances make them suitable for their uses	
2C.M5	Explain how different factors affect the rate of industrial reactions	
2C.M6	Explain the terms 'yield' and 'atom economy' in relation to specific chemical reactions	
2D.M7	Discuss the extent to which human activity has changed the environment, in comparison to natural activity	

To achieve a Distinction grade, my portfolio of evidence must also show that I can:

Assessment Criteria	Description	✓
2A.D1	Explain the trends in chemical properties of group 1 and 7 elements in terms of electronic structure	
2A.D2	Relate applications of compounds to their properties and to their bonding and structure	
2B.D3	Assess the suitability of different types of substance for a specified use	
2C.D4	Analyse how different factors affect the rate and yield of an industrial reaction	
2D.D5	Evaluate possible solutions to changes in the environment, occurring from natural or human activity	

Unit 3 **Energy and Our Universe**

LA

Understand ionising radiation, its uses and sources

- Our biggest exposure to ionising radiation is from our surroundings; people living in regions where granite is found are likely to have higher rates of lung cancer due to radioactive radon gas seeping from the rock

- For fusion reactors to work on Earth, they must create temperatures of 150 million °C, ten times hotter than the Sun's core

- If all the nuclear power stations in Europe were replaced by fossil fuel power stations, an extra 700 million tonnes of CO_2 would be emitted each year – the same amount produced by all the private cars in Europe

LA

Know the components of the Solar System, the way the Universe is changing and the methods we use to explore space

- Our Solar System has 8 planets and 4 dwarf planets – Pluto, Ceres, Eris and Makemake

- Most of the mass of the Solar System is the Sun – 99.86%

- The future of the Universe depends on how much matter is in it; too little matter and it will keep expanding, or too much and it will start to contract again and we will have the Big Crunch

- The Cassini–Huygens space probe took 7 years to reach Saturn. Instructions and information sent between computers on Earth and the space probe take hours to arrive because of the huge distances

Know how electrical energy produced from different sources can be transferred through the National Grid to homes and industry

- Pacemakers contain tiny electrical circuits that send a signal to the heart to keep it beating in the correct rhythm

- Abergeirw in Wales was the last village in the UK to get a supply of mains electricity in 2008; before then they used noisy diesel generators that could not be left on all the time

- During the day there are surges in demand for electricity; people controlling the National Grid anticipate these surges and shut down or start up power stations to match the demand with the supply

- Energy can't be created or destroyed, but is transferred between different energy stores when things happen. The Earth receives energy from the Sun, as well as losing some energy to its surroundings

- Sources of renewable energy include cow dung and peat cut from bogs and dried

- The Three Gorges Dam in China will be the world's largest hydroelectricity scheme; its reservoirs will destroy towns, forests and habitats of native animals, and disrupt the flow of water above and below the dam; however, flooding from the river, which has killed thousands in previous years, will be easier to control

Radioactive decay and half-life

Dating ancient scrolls

How can scientists tell if scraps of paper found in caves near the Dead Sea are really 2000 years old? The age of ancient objects made from plants is measured using carbon dating. Our surroundings contain different types of carbon atoms (isotopes). When a plant dies, the ratio of two isotopes of carbon in the plant starts changing. Measuring this ratio tells us roughly when the plant died.

1A.1 2A.P1

What's in an atom?

All atoms are made from the same basic particles. They have a central nucleus that contains **protons** and **neutrons**. Protons and neutrons are called **nucleons**. The nucleus is surrounded by electrons in shells (energy levels).

Different elements have different numbers of protons and electrons in their atoms. Each element has an **atomic number**. This is the number of protons, and also the number of electrons. You can find this number on a periodic table.

Sodium (Na) has atomic number 11, so a sodium atom has 11 protons and 11 electrons.

Each element also has a **mass number**. This is the total number of nucleons. We can use the mass number to find out how many neutrons an atom has:

number of neutrons = mass number − atomic number

Sodium's mass number is 23. So sodium has:

23 − 11 = 12 neutrons

Radioactive decay

Some atoms have unstable nuclei. They randomly emit radiation from their nucleus. Their atomic number changes and a different element forms. This is called **radioactive decay**.

The time taken for half the unstable nuclei in a sample to decay is called the **half-life**. The half-life of a sample only depends on the type of nucleus that is decaying. Half-lives vary between a fraction of a second to thousands of years.

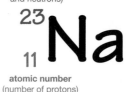

- ⊖ electron
- ⊕ proton
- ◯ neutron

The structure of an atom

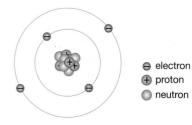

mass number
(total number of protons and neutrons)

$^{23}_{11}$Na

atomic number
(number of protons)

The nuclear structure of sodium shown in symbol notation

Know more

Isotopes of an element have the same proton number. They have different mass numbers because their nucleus has a different number of neutrons.

...proton ...neutron

Showing half-life on a graph

The **activity** or count rate is the number of nuclei decaying in a certain time. This depends on:

*   the half-life of the sample

*   the original number of undecayed nuclei.

All half-life graphs have the same shape, but the time scale and count rates are different. This graph shows a sample with a half-life of 20 days:

*   at 0 days, the count rate is 1600

*   after 20 days the count rate is 800 (it has halved)

*   after 40 days, the count rate is 400 (it is a quarter of the original value).

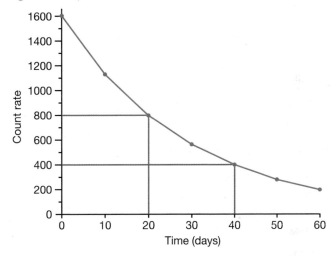

Know more

A graph showing the amount of radioactive material against time shows the same pattern, with the same half-life .

Calculating half-life

The half-life of radioactive isotopes can be calculated in different ways:

*   using a graph to find the average time for the count rate or activity to halve

*   measuring the ratio of different isotopes in a sample.

The second method relies on the fact that the amount of a radioactive isotope halves in one half-life, falls to a quarter in two half-lives, to one-eighth after three half-lives, and so on. Measuring the proportion of the original isotope left after a certain time enables its half-life to be calculated.

Some rocks can be dated by comparing the amount of uranium and lead they contain. Uranium changes to lead, with a half-life of 4.5 billion years.

Know more

Radiometric dating is reliable because the half-life stays the same even if the physical or chemical conditions of the sample change.

...calculate half-life

Ionising radiation

Radiation and cancer

Cancers are caused when damaged cells in the body replicate rapidly, forming a tumour. Exposure to ionising radiation is one factor that increases the risk of developing cancer.

But often, people with cancer have radiotherapy – ionising radiation is used to treat the cancer it may have caused. How is that possible?

1A.2
2A.P2
1A.3
2A.P3

Types of ionising radiation

Atoms have a central **nucleus** surrounded by tiny **electrons**. Radioactive elements have an unstable nucleus. They give out **ionising radiation** when the nucleus decays. This happens randomly. Ionising radiation affects other atoms by knocking electrons from them, forming **ions**.

The following types of ionising radiation are given out by radioactive elements.

Alpha particles are the same as helium nuclei – two protons and two neutrons:

* They are very ionising.
* They travel only a short distance in air.
* They cannot pass through skin or paper.

Beta particles are electrons:

* They are less ionising than alpha radiation.
* They have high penetrating power and pass through skin.
* 5 mm of aluminium sheet will stop them.

Gamma rays are high-energy (high-frequency) electromagnetic waves:

* They are not as ionising as beta or alpha radiation.
* They can penetrate almost everything.
* A block of lead about 10 cm thick will stop only half of them.

Radioactive isotopes have saved many lives in homes, workplaces and hospitals. However, ionising radiation can damage living cells. Exposure may cause cell death (radiation burns and sickness), some cancers or cell mutations. Workers and users must be protected from strong radioactive sources. They must not be exposed to radiation over a long period of time. Used sources from equipment must be disposed of safely.

Your assessment criteria:

1A.2	Identify the types of ionising radiation
2A.P2	Describe the different types of ionising radiation
1A.3	Identify the problems associated with the use of radioactive isotopes
2A.P3	Describe the problems associated with the use of radioactive isotopes
2A.M2	Compare the benefits and drawbacks of using radioactive isotopes in the home or workplace
2A.D2	Justify the selection of a radioactive isotope for a given use within the home or workplace

Know more

The Earth has always been naturally radioactive. 'Background' ionising radiation surrounding us from natural, medical and industrial sources usually causes no problems. But some parts of the UK are built on granite which is more radioactive; lung cancer rates are higher in these places.

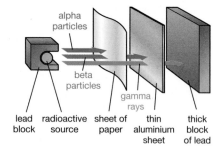

The three radiations and their penetrating abilities

Know more

X-rays and ultraviolet rays also cause ionisation, but are less energetic than gamma rays so are less harmful. See Unit 1.

🔍...ionising gamma rays

Uses and problems of ionising radiation

2A.M2

Use	Benefits	Drawbacks
smoke detectors (alpha)	Smoke absorbs alpha radiation in a smoke detector and sets off the alarm. Small amounts of smoke are detected quickly.	No risk unless the smoke detector is damaged.
paper thickness monitoring (beta)	Beta radiation passes through paper being produced on rollers. The rollers adjust the thickness if too much or too little radiation is detected.	Workers must be shielded from the radioactive source.
treating cancer (gamma)	Gamma radiation aimed at the tumour kills cancer cells.	Surrounding healthy cells may be damaged.
tracking moving liquids (gamma)	A tracer containing a gamma source is injected into a fluid. The flow of fluid inside a patient's bloodstream, in an engine or in pipes is traced by detecting the gamma radiation.	A short-half life is needed so the radioactivity dies away and healthy cells are not damaged.
sterilisation (gamma)	Harmful bacteria on surgical equipment or in food is killed by gamma radiation.	Workers must be shielded from the radioactive source.

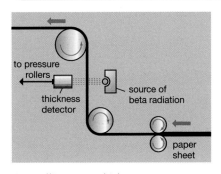

Controlling paper thickness

Discuss

Should we worry about radioactivity and cancer? Find out the main causes of cancer. Is radioactivity the main risk factor? Which causes can you control with lifestyle choices?

Choosing a radioactive isotope

2A.D2

Exposure to radiation must be kept as low as possible, although lifestyle choices such as smoking or diet cause a much higher cancer risk.

The damage to cells from radiation depends on:

* how strong the source is
* how much time a person is exposed
* the type of radiation.

Low doses, or higher doses for very short times, are unlikely to cause problems.

Gamma radiation is less damaging to living cells than alpha or beta radiation but is more penetrating, so sources outside the body can damage cells inside the body.

Alpha radiation is not very penetrating, so is only damaging when breathed in, swallowed or injected.

A short half-life radioisotope is used in tracers because its radioactivity dies away quickly and reduces the exposure of living cells to radiation.

Sources with a long half-life are used in equipment that supplies a constant level of radioactivity such as a smoke detector or radiotherapy equipment.

...radiation uses

Nuclear fission and fusion

Recycled stardust

You, and everything around you, are made from recycled stardust. Nuclear fusion reactions in stars billions of years ago combined hydrogen, helium and other elements into heavier elements. These massive stars exploded in a supernova, forming even more new elements and flinging them across the galaxy. Some of this stardust formed our Solar System and everything in it.

Supernova

1A.4
2A.P4

Nuclear fission and fusion

Nuclear fusion takes place in the Sun and other stars. Small light nuclei are crushed together and form a heavier nucleus of a different element, releasing energy. Nuclear fusion reactors built on Earth have not yet produced controlled nuclear fusion reactions. The longest reaction to date lasted only half a second.

Nuclear fission happens naturally in elements found in the Earth's crust. Heavy nuclei split in to two or more smaller nuclei of different elements, releasing energy. In nuclear power stations, controlled fission reactions take place. The main nuclear fuels are uranium and plutonium. The heat produced from nuclear fission is used to generate electricity. Control rods are raised and lowered in the reactor to control the speed of the reaction. When they are lowered, the control rods absorb neutrons that are needed for the fission reactions, so less heat is produced.

Know more

Nuclear fusion reactions need temperatures as high as those in the core of the Sun. The main fusion reaction in the Sun is hydrogen nuclei fusing to form helium nuclei. This produces all the energy emitted by the Sun that sustains life on Earth.

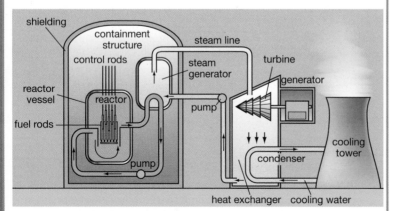

The essential parts of a nuclear power station

...fission and fusion

Environmental impact of nuclear power

2A.M3

In normal use, nuclear power stations do not release radioactive material into the surroundings. However, they do produce radioactive nuclear waste, which needs very careful disposal. About 1% of this waste is highly radioactive and is vitrified (changed to glass) before it is stored underground.

A major nuclear accident may release radioactive material to the surroundings but safety procedures limit the chance of this happening. If an accident happens, there are ways of reducing the effect on people and the environment.

There have been two major nuclear accidents in the past 25 years. In 2011 in Japan, a 15-metre tsunami followed a major earthquake. The tsunami damaged the cooling systems in the Fukushima nuclear power station. The reactors overheated, releasing radioactive materials. No deaths or radiation sickness have occurred amongst the public, but the surrounding area was evacuated to reduce the risk to health.

Research

Find out about the safety features built into nuclear power stations. Explain what a fail-safe feature is.

Half-life and the impact of radiation

2A.D3

The effect on the surroundings after a nuclear accident depends on the isotopes that are released:

- People working at the nuclear power station when an accident happens receive the most radiation. Some may develop radiation sickness.

- Radioactive iodine may cause thyroid cancer in people living nearby, developing over several years. Iodine's half-life is 8 days, so the radioactivity dies down in a few weeks. Of the people with thyroid cancer, 99% survive. Giving people iodine tablets straightaway prevents it developing.

- Caesium has a 30-year half-life and spreads further from the power station , contaminating food supplies. However, it is not as dangerous as iodine, and is not thought to cause cancer. It is excreted in urine within a few weeks.

...Fukushima

Comparing sources of energy

Can we get energy for free?

Windmills, water mills and the heat of the Sun once provided all our energy needs. Now billions of people live on Earth and more of us than ever before want to live in comfort. It's time to make decisions about where our energy is coming from.

1B.5
2B.P5

There are different ways to obtain the electricity we use.

Using batteries

Batteries change chemical energy to electrical energy using chemical reactions. Batteries provide a steady current called **direct current (d.c.)**.

- Once the chemical reaction is completed in a **non-rechargeable** battery, it needs to be disposed of and cannot be reused. Most batteries we use are non-rechargeable.

- **Rechargeable** batteries can be used many times before they run out. They are plugged into a mains supply of electricity using a recharger. The chemical reaction is reversed using electrical energy from the mains.

Using solar cells

Solar cells (or 'photovoltaic' cells) convert sunlight and other forms of light directly into electricity. Solar cells are made from special materials that capture energy from light to produce a voltage.

Using mains electricity

Electricity is generated in power stations using **renewable** and **non-renewable** sources of energy.

- Non-renewable sources of energy include fossil fuels (coal, oil and gas) and nuclear fuels (uranium and plutonium). These are used to produce heat from which electricity can be generated.

- Renewable sources of energy include wind energy and hydroelectricity, which use wind or falling water to spin a generator. Biomass is waste wood and other natural materials, which can be burned in power stations instead of fossil fuels.

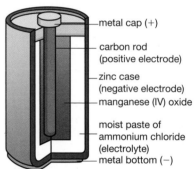

metal cap (+)

carbon rod (positive electrode)

zinc case (negative electrode)

manganese (IV) oxide

moist paste of ammonium chloride (electrolyte)

metal bottom (−)

Structure of one type of battery

Know more

Batteries contain heavy metals which are poisonous if they leak into the ground or rivers. Almost all batteries can be recycled safely and yet most people don't bother. Many retailers need to provide places for people to recycle their used batteries, to improve the recycling rate.

Know more

Non-renewable energy sources are fuels that took millions of years to form. Once they are used up, they cannot be replaced.

...non-renewable energy

Power stations are needed to generate large amounts of electricity at all times, whatever the weather

Discuss

Sources of fossil fuels are likely to run out during your lifetime. It will then become very expensive to generate electricity on today's scale. How much are you prepared to pay for electricity? Would you prefer to change your lifestyle? Are you prepared for power cuts?

Using solar energy

Think about

Why is it of concern that most wind farms are in remote places?

Think about

Suggest how your school or college could reduce its use of energy.

Which sources should we use?

2B.M4

All forms of energy used to generate electricity have advantages and disadvantages.

Type of energy source	Advantages	Disadvantages
fossil fuels	Generate large amounts of electricity when needed.	Release greenhouse gases which lead to global warming. Will run out in the future.
nuclear power	Generates large amounts of electricity when needed. No greenhouse gases emitted.	Radioactive waste needs safe disposal. High costs involved. Will run out in the future, but not as soon as fossil fuels.
solar energy	Will not run out. Useful in remote places. No greenhouse gases emitted.	No use at night. Each panel generates only a small amount of electricity.
wind energy	Will not run out. Useful in remote places. No greenhouse gases emitted.	No use if there is too much or too little wind. Wind turbines need to be in large 'farms' for sizeable output
biofuels	Will not run out.	Release greenhouse gases which lead to global warming. Biofuel crops can reduce the land available for growing food crops.
hydroelectricity	Generates electricity when needed. Large-scale schemes can provide large amounts of electricity.	Causes flooding behind the dams. Affects the normal flow of rivers and habitats.

Know more

Electricity can also be generated from tides. A large barrage in an estuary traps seawater, which is released through pipes to spin turbines.

Geothermal energy in volcanic regions uses hot underground rocks to produce steam for generating electricity.

🔍 ...renewable energy

Producing electricity

Your assessment criteria:

2B.P5 Describe methods of producing a.c. and d.c. electricity

2B.M4 Compare the efficiency and environmental impact of electricity generated by different sources

Where our electricity comes from

Over 150 years ago, a scientist called Michael Faraday discovered that moving a magnet near a coil of wire created an electrical voltage in the wire. Today, this simple idea is used in every power station, generator and dynamo to generate the electricity we take for granted.

2B.P5

Generating electricity

Magnetism, electric current and movement of a conductor always go together. Wherever you find two of them, you will find the third as well.

Push a magnet into a coil of wire and a voltage is created in the wire. The same thing happens if the magnet is pulled out of the coil or if it spins inside it.

If the coil is part of a circuit, then the voltage forces a current to flow in the wire. The current can be measured using an ammeter, or used to light a bulb.

A larger voltage is created if:

- the magnet moves more quickly
- a stronger magnet is used
- there are more turns on the wire coil.

It doesn't have to be the magnet that moves – a voltage is also created if the coil moves towards or away from the magnet.

The generator

A **generator** is designed to create electricity by spinning a coil of wire or a magnet. In the simple generator shown on the right:

- the magnets are fixed
- a handle or wheel spins the coil of wire
- slip rings are used so that the wires don't get tangled as the coil spins
- carbon brushes are conductors that connect the rest of circuit to the generator.

This produces a varying current called **alternating current (a.c.)**.

Faraday's work changed our world

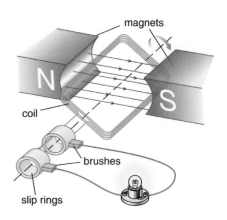

This generator can easily be made in a school lab, but the same ideas are used in power stations

...how a generator works

How to make generators spin

All power stations use a **turbine** to spin a generator. A turbine has blades (like a windmill). The turbine spins when jets of steam, moving water or wind pass over its blades. Turning the turbine turns **electromagnets** in a generator.

The difference between different types of power station is what makes the turbine spin.

In power stations fuelled by non-renewable energy sources, fossil fuels or nuclear reactions create heat. This changes water to steam which passes through a turbine making it spin.

In generators powered by renewable energy sources:

- wind turns the blades of a wind turbine directly

- moving water in hydroelectric schemes and tidal schemes turns turbines directly

- burning biomass or biofuels heats water in a boiler, and the steam produced spins a turbine.

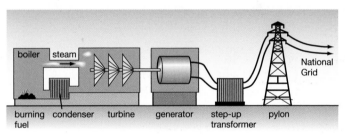

Different stages in a power station

Know more

Recently built gas-powered generating stations have two stages:

- *gas is burned, producing jets of hot gas which spin a turbine*

- *the hot gases also heat water, producing steam which turns another turbine.*

This improves the efficiency of electricity generation.

Think about

What would you look for if you were choosing an energy source? Rank these in order of importance: cost of fuel; cost of the generating equipment and buildings; reliability; efficiency; pollution caused; how easily available or transportable the energy source is.

Know more

Biomass is material from living matter. It includes wood waste, crops and manure. A biofuel is produced from processed biomass, for example biogas from animal waste.

Comparing the efficiency of power stations

Remember that efficiency is the proportion of energy input that is transformed into useful energy, in this case electrical energy. Different methods of electricity generation have different levels of efficiency.

Type of power generation	Efficiency
fossil fuel (coal, oil or gas)	35%
recent 'combined cycle' gas turbines	60%
nuclear	35%
hydroelectric	80%
wind	20%
biofuel	20%
biomass	35%

Circuits

Circuits all around us

All around us electrical equipment entertains and informs us, communicates, makes decisions, carries out work and does a whole range of different jobs. Battery-operated equipment has a complete circuit inside it. Plugs are used to join mains-operated equipment to a circuit linking the home to the power station where electricity is generated.

Your assessment criteria:

1B.6 Demonstrate building simple series and parallel circuits

2B.P6 Use $V = IR$ to predict values in electric circuit investigations

2B.D4 Assess, in quantitative terms, ways to minimise energy losses either when transmitting electricity or when transforming electricity into other forms for consumer applications

1B.6
2B.P6

Series and parallel circuits

All electrical equipment contains circuits. A circuit needs a **power source** (battery or mains electricity), a continuous loop of electrical **conductors** (usually plastic-covered wire) and **components** to change electrical energy into different forms (e.g. a bulb).

Circuit diagrams use symbols to represent these different parts.

An electric **current** is a flow of charge round a circuit. Current is measured in **amps** (A) or milliamps (mA) using an ammeter connected in series. In metal wires the moving charges are electrons.

Voltage measures the energy carried by the current betwen two points. It is measured in **volts** (V) or millivolts (mV) using a voltmeter connected in parallel with a component.

A **series circuit** is a single loop of conductors. The current is the same in all places in a series circuit because the electrons have only one path they can take. The voltage is shared between the different components.

A **parallel circuit** has more than one loop, forming separate paths that the electrons can go through. Each loop links back to the battery. The current is shared between the loops of a parallel circuit because the electrons have a choice of paths. The voltage is the same in each loop because each loop links to the battery.

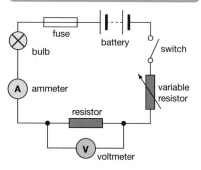

Circuit symbols

Know more

Electrical conductors are materials that let electricity flow through easily, for example metals and graphite. Electrical insulators, like plastic and wood, have a high resistance to current.

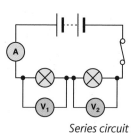

Series circuit

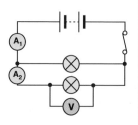

Parallel circuit

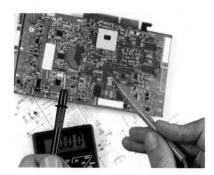

Measuring current and voltage in a circuit

...circuit symbol charts

Know more

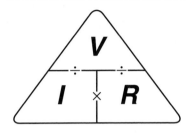

You can use this triangle if you are asked for the resistance or current. Cover up the quantity you need to find and the rest of the triangle shows you how to calculate it

Resistance

2B.P6

Resistance measures how hard it is for a current to pass through a material. Resistance is measured in **ohms** (Ω) or kilohms (kΩ). It is calculated by measuring the current that flows when different voltages are applied in the circuit.

For many materials, doubling the voltage doubles the current. These materials obey Ohm's law, which states:

voltage (volts, V) = current (amps, A) × resistance (ohms, Ω)

Here is an example using Ohm's law.

The resistance of a bulb is 30 ohms. If a current of 0.2 amps flows through it, what is the voltage across it?

Resistance = 30 Ω   Current = 0.2 A

Voltage = current × resistance

= 0.2 × 30

= 6 V

Minimising energy losses

2B.D4

Current passes easily through some wires but not others. More energy is used in pushing electrons through:

- longer wires

- thinner wires

- wires made from materials that are not such good conductors

because they all have higher resistance. Copper is used in circuits throughout the home because it has a low resistance. This means that, compared with wires that are not such good conductors:

- a larger current flows through copper wires

- more energy is available for equipment that is plugged in.

Think about

Why is it important to use highly conducting copper for electrical wiring? What would be the effects of using material of a higher resistance? Why are copper wires coated with plastic?

...electrical circuits

Electrical energy and power

Getting electrical energy to where we need it

Over 700 million batteries are bought in the UK each year. Batteries are useful because they provide a portable source of electrical energy. The choice ranges from tiny batteries for hearing aids to very large batteries for cars, with 'AA' batteries one of the most popular types. It is likely that in every room in your house there is at least one battery-operated item. But some appliances need more power than a battery can provide.

Your assessment criteria:

1B.7 Describe electrical power in terms of voltage and current

2B.P7 Describe how electricity is transmitted to the home or industry

2B.M5 Assess, in qualitative terms, ways to minimise energy losses when transmitting electricity

2B.D4 Assess, in quantitative terms, ways to minimise energy losses either when transmitting electricity or when transforming electricity into other forms for consumer applications

1B.7
2B.P7

Power

Power measures how quickly equipment transfers energy. A 1000 watt electric fire transfers 1000 joules of energy each second to its surroundings. Electrical power can be calculated using this equation:

Power (watts, W) = voltage (volts, V) × current (amps, A)

Here is an example: a kettle uses mains electricity (supplied at 230 V). A current of 10 A flows when it is switched on.

The power of the kettle is 230 × 10 = 2300 W

Using mains electricity

Electricity is generated in power stations. Then it has to get from the power stations to our homes along a network of cables, pylons and transformers called the **National Grid**.

Mains electricity is **alternating current (a.c.)**. It isn't a one-way flow, like direct current from a battery, but changes direction repeatedly, 50 times a second. Alternating current is easier to generate and can be transmitted more efficiently over long distances.

Know more

*What you are used to calling a 'battery' is actually an electric **cell**. A battery is, strictly, a series of cells in a circuit.*

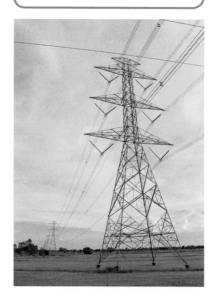

🔍 ...recycling batteries

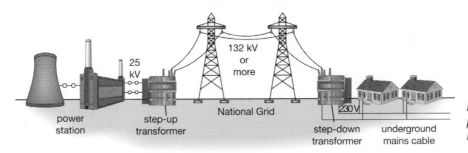

Electrical energy from power stations reaches our homes via the National Grid

Transmitting electricity efficiently

2B.M5

Transmitting electricity over long distances causes energy losses as the cables heat up.

Transformers are used to increase, or **step up**, the voltage to many thousands of volts before the generated electricity is output to the National Grid. This reduces the current, so the wires do not heat up as much. This means less energy is lost as thermal energy.

Near our homes, transformers in **substations** reduce, or **step down**, the voltage to 230 volts so it is at a suitable level for our appliances and a safer level for us to use.

Another way to reduce energy losses when transmitting electricity is to reduce the distance over which it is transmitted.

Transformers at a substation change the voltage in the cables

Research

Try to find out what percentage of energy is lost in the National Grid.

Reducing energy losses in the National Grid

2B.D4

Electricity is transmitted long distances at very high voltages to reduce the current in the cables. High currents heat up cables. Energy losses in the National Grid are reduced because the cables heat up less.

If the power of two cables is the same, the current in a cable at 1000 V is 100 times larger than the current in a cable at 100 000 V. The power lost goes up by 10 000 times.

...the National Grid

Our Solar System

Shooting stars

At certain times of the year, showers of 'shooting stars' can be seen in the night sky. Fast-moving intense streaks of light are caused by pieces of rock burning as they race through the night sky, so bright they look like stars. These 'shooting stars' are meteors. Sometimes they hit the ground as rocks called meteorites.

1C.8
1C.10
2C.P8

The Solar System

Our Solar System contains these parts.

- The Sun is the **star** at the centre of the Solar System. The heat and light from the Sun is caused by nuclear fusion reactions in its centre.

- **Planets** are large balls of rock or gas that travel around the Sun in nearly circular orbits. There are eight planets in our Solar System, and Earth is one of them.

- **Dwarf planets** also orbit the Sun, but are smaller than planets. They have less effect on their surroundings than planets. Pluto is a dwarf planet.

- **Moons** are smaller lumps of rock that travel around planets – they are 'natural satellites'. Some planets have several moons.

- **Comets** travel through space and are formed from small lumps of rock and ice. Some orbit the Sun in long, stretched-out orbits, so that the comet is sometimes far from the Sun and at other times much closer to the Sun. When it is close, the comet appears to have a tail streaking out from behind it.

- **Asteroids** behave like planets and dwarf planets, but are much smaller. Most are found orbiting between Mars and Jupiter.

- **Meteors** are seen when rocks burn up as they pass through the Earth's atmosphere.

Know more

The four inner planets have a rocky surface you could walk on. The four outer planets, called the gas giants, are very massive and formed from gases – you would sink into them if you tried to walk on them. The rocky planets are much closer to one another than the gas giants.

The planets Mercury, Venus, Earth, Mars, Saturn, Jupiter, Uranus and Neptune travel around the Sun, which is at the centre of the Solar System

...Solar System

A nebula where new stars are forming

How was our Solar System formed?

Stars like the Sun form from swirling clouds of dust and gases in space called **nebulae**.

- Gravity makes the centre of the cloud clump together.
- This clump is so massive that gravity crushes the particles very, very tightly.
- The centre heats up to millions of degrees.
- This is hot enough for nuclear fusion reactions to ignite.
- The star starts to shine and gives out heat.

As the star forms, the outer edges of the cloud are still swirling around the centre. These particles of dust and gas may clump together, attracting other nearby particles. Their gravity is not strong enough for nuclear reactions to ignite, but it is strong enough to hold the particles together. This is how planets are formed. Their movement means that they orbit the star, and the Solar System is complete.

During a star's lifetime, it changes size and colour as different reactions take place in its core. Eventually, some stars explode in a supernova, flinging out elements that have formed in the nuclear reactions in their core. These particles will form part of nebulae, where new stars will form.

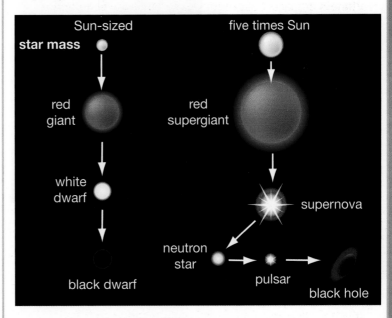

How stars change during their lifetime

Research

Have you heard of a red giant, and a white dwarf? Research the main stages in the life cycle of a star and find out what these names mean.

The changing Universe

Investigating starlight

When different chemicals burn, the flames change colour. An instrument called a spectroscope is used to analyse the light coming from different elements when they are heated. Each element has its own special

The spectral pattern for hydrogen

spectrum made up of lines of different colours. If scientists look at light coming from far-away stars, they can tell what elements are in the star, giving out light in its hot core.

2C.P8
1C.9
2C.P9
1C.10
2C.P10

What shows us the Universe is changing?

The **Universe** is the whole of space and includes billions of groups of stars called **galaxies**, each with billions of stars, many with a solar system. Our own galaxy is called the Milky Way.

Making observations

Telescopes based on Earth and in space detect electromagnetic radiation (radio waves, infrared, light, ultraviolet, X-rays and gamma rays). This gives scientists information about the appearance, temperature and make-up of objects in space. Telescopes obtain information from very distant objects in the Universe but cannot collect samples.

We can see very distant galaxies with the Hubble Space Telescope

Space probes and robots can travel to planets in the Solar System, and take direct measurements and samples. It takes too long for space probes to travel out of our Solar System.

Red shift

The Universe does not have a centre or edge but there is evidence it is expanding. Light from distant galaxies appears redder than expected. This is called the **red shift** and shows that all galaxies are moving apart.

Your assessment criteria:

2C.P8 Describe the structure of the Universe and our Solar System

1C.9 Identify methods of observing the Universe

2C.P9 Describe the suitability of different methods for observing the Universe

1C.10 Describe the dynamic nature of our Solar System and Universe

2C.P10 Identify evidence that shows the dynamic nature of the Universe

2C.M6 Describe how the Universe and the Solar System were formed

2C.M7 Explain how evidence shows that the Universe is changing

2C.D5 Evaluate the evidence leading to the Big Bang theory of how the Universe was formed

Know more

Reflecting telescopes are used to observe space. They are cheaper and easier to build than telescopes using lenses. They use a mirror instead of a lens. This gives a clear, undistorted image of faint objects.

...red shift theory

2C.M6
2C.M7

Discuss

What will happen to the Universe in the future? Current evidence suggests that the expansion of the Universe is speeding up. Scientists had thought it might slow down and the Universe would reach a fixed size, or even contract to a 'Big Crunch'. Discuss how certain it is that our current ideas are right.

What does the evidence tell us about the origin of the Universe?

Scientists believe that the red shift evidence tells us that at some point in time, billions of years ago, all the matter and energy in the Universe was concentrated in the same place. A massive explosion took place, called the Big Bang. It flung all the matter and energy apart. As the new Universe cooled, particles formed and clumped together, making stars and galaxies. Ever since then, the Universe has been expanding and cooling down.

If there had been such an explosion billions of years ago, scientists knew they should be able to detect an 'echo' of it today. This would be very faint radiation coming from all directions. That is why the discovery of this **cosmic background radiation** was so exciting and important.

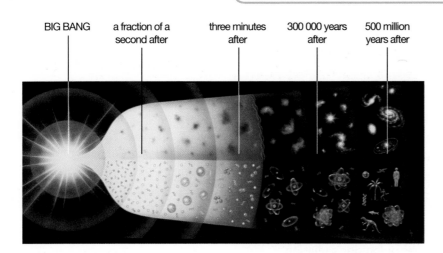

BIG BANG   a fraction of a second after   three minutes after   300 000 years after   500 million years after

The Big Bang theory suggests that before the Universe existed, everything was concentrated in a space smaller than a pin head

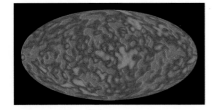

Scientists have detected cosmic background radiation

Is the theory right?

2C.D5

The startling discoveries of the red shift of distant galaxies and the cosmic background radiation suggest that the Big Bang theory is right. There is no strong counter-evidence to say it is wrong. It cannot be proved, but most scientists believe the Big Bang took place. What we probably will never know is what happened before the Big Bang or what caused it.

The evidence that the Universe is still changing is strong. Photographs and other detection equipment can record the changes clearly. They can not only tell us what is happening now, but what happened in the past. Light from stars takes years to reach us. Light from stars in the next galaxy takes thousands of years to reach us, and we have even detected light from stars formed soon after the Big Bang that has taken 14 billion years to reach us. We can literally see the evolution of the Universe.

...big bang

To achieve a Pass grade, my portfolio of evidence must show that I can:

Assessment Criteria	Description	✓
2A.P1	Describe half-life in terms of radioactive decay	
2A.P2	Describe the different types of ionising radiation	
2A.P3	Describe the problems associated with the use of radioactive isotopes	
2A.P4	Describe how controllable nuclear fission and fusion reactions are	
2B.P5	Describe methods of producing a.c. and d.c. electricity	
2B.P6	Use $V = IR$ to predict values in electric circuit investigations	
2B.P7	Describe how electricity is transmitted to the home or industry	
2C.P8	Describe the structure of the Universe and our Solar System	
2C.P9	Describe the suitability of different methods for observing the Universe	
2C.P10	Identify evidence that shows the dynamic nature of the Universe	

If you do not meet all the Level 2 Pass criteria for this Unit then your work will be assessed against these Level 1 criteria. If your work meets all these criteria you will achieve a Level 1 Pass for this Unit. If you do not achieve all these Level 1 criteria you will get a U (Unclassified) for this Unit.

Assessment Criteria	Description	✓
1A.1	Describe the structure of atomic nuclei	
1A.2	Identify the types of ionising radiation	
1A.3	Identify the problems associated with the use of radioactive isotopes	
1A.4	Describe nuclear fission and fusion	
1B.5	Identify methods of producing electricity from different sources	
1B.6	Demonstrate building simple series and parallel circuits	
1B.7	Describe electrical power in terms of voltage and current	
1C.8	Identify the components of our Solar System	
1C.9	Identify methods of observing the Universe	
1C.10	Describe the dynamic nature of our Solar System and Universe	

To achieve a Merit grade, my portfolio of evidence must also show that I can:

Assessment Criteria	Description	✓
2A.M1	Use graphs to explain radioactive decay and half-life	
2A.M2	Compare the benefits and drawbacks of using radioactive isotopes in the home or workplace	
2A.M3	Describe the environmental impact of radioactive material from nuclear fission reactors released into the environment	
2B.M4	Compare the efficiency and environmental impact of electricity generated by different sources	
2B.M5	Assess, in qualitative terms, ways to minimise energy losses when transmitting electricity	
2C.M6	Describe how the Universe and the Solar System were formed	
2C.M7	Explain how evidence shows that the Universe is changing	

To achieve a Distinction grade, my portfolio of evidence must also show that I can:

Assessment Criteria	Description	✓
2A.D1	Calculate the half-life of radioactive isotopes	
2A.D2	Justify the selection of a radioactive isotope for a given use within the home or workplace	
2A.D3	Evaluate the environmental impacts of a nuclear fission reactor accident, in terms of half-life	
2B.D4	Assess, in quantitative terms, ways to minimise energy losses either when transmitting electricity or when transforming electricity into other forms for consumer applications	
2C.D5	Evaluate the evidence leading to the Big Bang theory of how the Universe was formed	

LA

Be able to investigate the relationships that different organisms have with each other and with their environment

- We vary genetically from one another and from other species, yet we share around 98% of our DNA with chimpanzees and bonobos

- Antibiotic-resistant bacteria and poison-resistant rats are examples of natural selection at work

- All of the two million different types of known living organisms, no matter how large or how small, interact in some way with others

- It's estimated that about one-third of plants that provide us with food are dependent on bees for pollination

Be able to explore the factors that affect human health

- Our immunisation programme helps to reduce diseases caused by microorganisms

- Estimates suggest that antibiotics may have saved 200 million lives since their discovery, but now, resistance to 'last-line' antibiotics is found in many hospitals

- Infectious diseases are caused by micro-organisms, but many other human conditions are inherited

- It is estimated that 13 million deaths across the world each year have preventable, environmental causes

Be able to demonstrate an understanding of the effects of human activity on the environment and how these effects can be measured

- With the major growth of industry in the last 50 years, some scientists believe that we may have reached a 'tipping point', where even if we reduce pollution, it will be too late to stop climate change

- Farmers in the UK are introducing methods to reduce the loss of habitats and species of animals and plants

- The 10 million tonnes of rubbish we recycle every year reduces pollution of the environment by these wastes and helps to preserve natural resources

Variation and adaptation

Your assessment criteria:

1A.1 Distinguish between variation due to genes and variation due to environmental factors

2A.P1 Describe the role of genes and the environment in variation

2A.M1 Explain the role of genes and the environment in evolution

2A.D1 Evaluate the impact of genes and the environment on the survival or extinction of organisms

Two sisters

Harriett and Imogen are sisters. Their differences in appearance are the result of genetic and environmental variation.

Harriett and Imogen

1A.1
2A.P1

Genetic and environmental variation

The sisters inherited **genes** from their parents, so they're similar in appearance to, but not identical to, each parent. They also have certain features that make them resemble each other.

Individuals of every organism on the planet (with a few exceptions) are different. This is because of **genetic variation**. With the exception of identical twins, we all have different sets of genes. Our genes give us a unique set of characteristics by controlling the proteins our bodies produce.

But some of the sisters' features have nothing to do with genetics. Imogen has dyed her hair. Harriett wears spectacles. Both use make-up to change their appearance. The effects of injuries, such as scars, can also affect our appearance. These differences are part of **environmental variation**.

Some of our characteristics, e.g. our body weight and skin colour, are controlled by a combination of genetic and environmental factors.

Features in humans affected by...		
our genetics	the environment	a combination of both
blood group	hair colour and length	height
eye colour	language	skin colour
	scars	weight
	tattoos	

Know more

Some environmental influences on us are under our control; others are not.

...genetic variation ...environmental variation

2A.M1

Variation and survival

Genetic and environmental variation in individuals certainly make life more interesting. But variation is also essential to survival. Scientists studying populations of organisms can also see how this variation has led to changes in these populations. We can also suggest how, eventually, variation has led to the **evolution** of new species.

Brown bears and polar bears

Scientists studying polar bears think that they first appeared around 200 000 years ago. They suggest that a few brown bears became isolated from their group by glaciers (ice flows). Over a long time, the bears' fur colour became paler. They also developed other features to help them to live and catch food on the ice.

2A.D1

How did the bears adapt to their environment?

In modern-day brown bears, scientists have observed a lot of genetic variation. The colour of the bears' coats shows a wide variation of shades from dark to pale. In their new environment (the Arctic ice), the bears with the palest coats would have been better camouflaged. This would have made them better hunters of seals for food. These bears would have survived while others would have starved. They would have passed on their genes for their pale coat colour.

This is called **genetic adaptation**.

> **Think about**
>
> *Make a list of environmental influences we can control, and those we can't.*

🔍 ... genetic adaptation

Natural selection and evolution

Rats are good at survival

Gary is a pest controller. One of his jobs is to kill rats. He says, 'Warfarin and similar poisons have been used for over 50 years to kill rats. But in recent years, some populations of rats have become resistant to them'.

There are now thought to be over 80 million rats in the UK

2A.M1

Natural selection

This resistance to poison is evidence of natural selection, which was first identified by naturalist Charles Darwin.

In his 1859 book *The Origin of Species*, Darwin wrote that a 'struggle for existence' was going on all the time in a population of organisms. Because of genetic variation, some individuals have characteristics that give them a better chance of survival than others. For animals, this would be those best able to catch food and to escape predators, and those most resistant to disease. In the case of these rats, it's the animals that are not killed by the poison.

These survivors, when they breed, then pass on these characteristics. The genes that helped these organisms to survive are passed on to the next generation. 'Unfavourable' genes would disappear over a number of generations. Darwin called this process **natural selection**.

Darwin, along with another biologist called Alfred Russel Wallace, thought about the possibility of a changing environment. They suggested that, if the environment changed, over time the characteristics of an organism would change. This could eventually lead to the development of a new species. We call this process **evolution**.

What evidence is there for natural selection?

More evidence that natural selection takes place has come from studies of the peppered moth. The wings of this moth are white and 'peppered' with black spots. But sometimes completely black peppered moths occur. This is called the **melanic form** of the moth. This melanic form appears when there's a change in the gene for the production of the black pigment melanin. This change is called a **gene mutation** (see Unit 1).

Research

Much of the evidence for Darwin's theory of evolution by natural selection came from his expedition to the Galapagos Islands, 600 miles off the coast of South America. Research Darwin's observations of the organisms that lived on the different islands, and those on mainland South America, which led to his ideas.

Think about

You may have heard of a 'killer bug' in hospitals, called MRSA. This is a bacterium that has become resistant to certain antibiotics. Bacteria reproduce very rapidly by dividing into two. Using your knowledge of natural selection, explain how bacteria can become resistant to antibiotics.

...genetic variation

2A.M1

A hundred years ago, in the countryside, the melanic form was very rare. But studies in the 1950s suggested that the melanic form was spreading throughout peppered moth populations.

Peppered moths are eaten by birds. Scientists suggested that in rural areas, normal peppered moths resting on trees would be well camouflaged. These trees had organisms called lichens growing on their bark, and were pale in colour. In urban areas, which were becoming more and more polluted in the 1950s, lichens on trees were sensitive to pollution and were killed. Trees became covered in soot. The black melanic moths therefore had a selective advantage and were found in greater numbers.

The melanic peppered moth

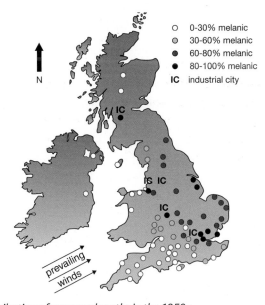

The distribution of peppered moths in the 1950s

Natural selection is operating as rats become resistant to poison. Eight gene mutations are involved, but the rats remain the same species

The driving forces of evolution

2A.D1

Sexual reproduction leads to genetic variation. And movement of genes as one population of a species mixes with another is an important source of genetic variation.

Mutations are accidental, random changes to genetic material. These can occur at chromosome level, or by changes to the bases in DNA. Most mutations that occur are harmful. Occasionally, however, mutations produce characteristics that are beneficial. These mutated genes will spread through a population. A single mutation can have a large effect on a species, as we can see with the peppered moth. But evolutionary change requires the accumulation of many mutations.

It is this variation, together with environmental change, that leads to natural selection and evolution.

The interdependence of living organisms

Your assessment criteria:

1A.3 Construct food chains and food webs

2A.P3 Describe the different ways in which organisms show interdependence

2A.M2 Discuss the factors that affect the relationship between different organisms

Relationships in danger

Simon is an ecologist working for a conservation organisation. He is studying the interaction between species of animals and plants in British woodlands. He is concerned that, as our environment changes, these relationships will change.

1A.3
2A.P3

Organisms depend on one another

Every organism on the planet interacts with its physical environment. All organisms, however large or small, also interact with, and depend on, other organisms. Ecologists use the term **ecosystem** to describe a habitat and all the organisms that live in it.

The main way that plants, animals and microorganisms depend on one another is for food. Many animals eat plants; others eat animals that have eaten plants. Most microorganisms, which include bacteria and fungi, feed on dead or living plants and animals.

Food chains and webs

Ecologists show which organisms feed on each other using types of flow charts called **food chains** and **food webs**. These show how food (and therefore energy) moves from organism to organism.

Feeding relationships between organisms are usually complex. Not many organisms eat just one type of organism. In reality food chains in most ecosystems interconnect as food webs.

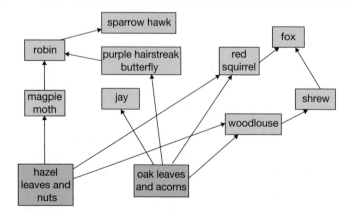

Part of a food web in an oak woodland ecosystem

Energy enters the food web as plants photosynthesise. Energy is transferred from organism to organism. Arrows show the direction of flow. Some energy is wasted as it goes from one level to the next.

...food chains ...food webs

Ticks and tapeworms are parasites

Both organisms that make up a lichen benefit

The lynx hunts the snowshoe hare

Think about

What would happen to a predator–prey cycle if the prey became diseased and died?

Research

Large predators once lived in Britain. The bear and the lynx were probably hunted to extinction in Roman times, and the wolf in the 1600s. Conservationists are thinking about re-introducing these animals in some wild areas of Britain. Find out more about these proposals, and list reasons for and against them.

Research

Some foreign species have been introduced into countries to control pests. Find out the effect this change in the environment has on native species.

Relationships between organisms

2A.P3

Food has a major influence on how organisms interact with each other. Feeding relationships are of several types. A polar bear is a **predator** that hunts, kills and eats seals. The seal is called the **prey**. An animal can sometimes act as both predator and prey: a seal eats fish.

A **parasite** lives on, or inside, the body of another organism, which is called the **host**. The parasite takes food from its host. Some parasites kill their host. Others cause disease or weaken the host. For instance, the parasite that causes malaria kills at least one million people per year. The tapeworm lives in the human gut. It can cause ill health but rarely death.

Commensal organisms live together and benefit each other, for example the fungus and alga that live together to make up an organism called a lichen.

Predator–prey relationships

2A.M2

The relationship between predator and prey is one of high interdependence. One of the best known studies is that between the Canadian lynx and the snowshoe hare. Fur trappers in Canada kept detailed records of the numbers of the animal skins traded. In some parts of North America, the snowshoe hare is the only prey of the lynx, and the lynx is one of the main predators of the hare.

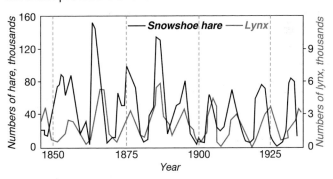

Cycles of hare and lynx numbers over 90 years

As numbers of hares increase, there will be more prey. → The number of lynxes increases. → More prey will be eaten, so numbers of hares will fall. → Food for the lynxes becomes scarce, so their numbers will fall. → The numbers of hares will increase, and the cycle will continue.

For organisms to survive, their interrelationships are finely balanced. Upsetting this balance could lead to the **extinction** of one or both organisms.

The variety of life

Discovering new organisms

New species of plants and animals are being discovered every day.

In 2010, the Louisiana pancake batfish was one of around 15 000 species discovered that year. It is as flat as a pancake, covered in spikes, has huge bulging eyes and hops on its fins.

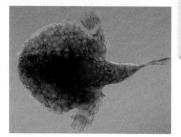

The fish was discovered just before the oil spill in the Gulf of Mexico in 2010

1A.2
2A.P2

Identifying organisms

If a species that is thought to be new to science is discovered, scientists check to see if it has been described already. Identification of species is also important when studying organisms living in a habitat. Biologists could work through textbooks or pocket guides with photographs or drawings until they make a correct identification. But most use an **identification key**, especially when the organism is difficult to identify.

An identification key is a simple pathway to identifying an organism. There are questions that give you two choices. You must decide which of these choices matches your organism. Then you go to the next question. You continue until you identify the organism. There is an example below.

Know more

So far, scientists have identified and named almost 2 million species of organisms. But they estimate that there may be anything from 10 million to 100 million different species on the planet. Over half of these are likely to be different types of insect.

1 Is the animal's body divided into
parts called segments? _____ go to question 2

Is the animal's body not divided into
parts called segments? _____ go to question 3

2 Do the animal's legs have joints? _____ crab
Do the animal's legs have no joints? _____ marine worm

3 Has the animal a shell?_____ go to question 4
Has the animal no shell? _____ go to question 5

4 Is the shell in two parts?_____ cockle
Is the shell in one piece?_____ top shell

5 Has the animal tentacles? _____ sea anemone
Has the animal five arms? _____ starfish

You can identify these organisms using the key alongside

...identification keys for organisms

Know more

The classification system we use is based on the one devised by Carl von Linné in the 1700s. It gives all organisms a name in two parts. Humans have the scientific name Homo sapiens; 'Homo' is the **genus** (shared with some of our fossil ancestors), 'sapiens' the **species** (specific to us).

Classifying organisms

When a new species is discovered, scientists **classify** it. They look for distinctive features of the organism. They aim to place it in a group along with other organisms having similar features.

All living organisms are grouped into five large groups called **kingdoms**. The kingdoms are subdivided into smaller groups, and these groups into smaller groups still.

Kingdom
Phylum
Class
Order
Family
Genus
Species

Kingdoms are divided into smaller groups

2A.P2

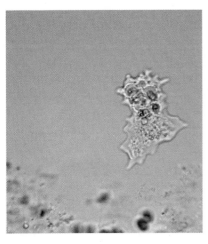

Protists are small single-celled organisms. Sometimes, these are grouped together. They include Amoeba and certain algae

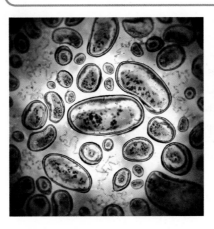

Bacteria are very small, simple cells. They have a cell wall. Their DNA is not enclosed in a nucleus

Some fungi are single-celled, like yeast. Others, such as moulds, mushrooms and toadstools, are made up of tiny threads of cells called hyphae

The FIVE KINGDOMS are protists, bacteria, fungi, plants and animals

Plants are multicellular. Their cells have walls made from cellulose. The cells above ground contain chlorophyll. Non-flowering plants reproduce using spores or cones. Flowering plants produce flowers

Animals are multicellular. Their cells do not have walls. Most feed using a mouth. **Invertebrates** are animals without backbones. **Vertebrates** are animals with backbones: fishes, amphibians, reptiles, birds and mammals

...classification of organisms

125

Human impact on ecosystems

A world in balance

Georgina is an environmental campaigner. She is protesting against a high-speed rail route that is being built across England. She says, 'The environmental impact of building the line will be massive. The rail track and building work will destroy unique natural habitats, including ancient forests and woodlands, nature reserves and lakes. This will affect many rare species that live there'.

1B.4
2B.P4

How do humans affect the environment?

New transport links such as new railways, new roads and new airports and runways can affect or even destroy ecosystems.

Human activity often affects either the living or the non-living part of many ecosystems. Ecosystems are affected by any activities that involve clearing land. We chop down trees to provide timber for building houses, or to make way for agriculture. This is called **deforestation**. Our demand for food means that huge areas of land have been converted into farmland.

Ecosystems in the way of these activities can be destroyed or changed forever.

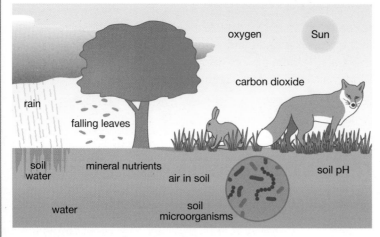

An ecosystem is the combination of all the organisms and physical factors in a particular habitat

Think about

What other effects do new roads or railways have on organisms in a location? Can you think of any positive effects these might have?

🔍 ...ecosystems

Soil erosion has been caused by deforestation

2B.P4

Deforestation

Deforestation contributes to climate change because it leads to increased levels of carbon dioxide in the atmosphere. The removal of trees decreases **biodiversity** (the range of different organisms in a habitat) because it destroys habitats. It can also lead to **soil erosion**. Without the protective trees and their roots, heavy rains can wash away soil leading to landslides.

Farming in the UK

After the Second World War, farmers were encouraged to increase their yields of crops. Hedgerows were removed so that farmers could grow a single crop in huge fields. This is called **monoculture**. It is much easier to move agricultural machinery around larger fields.

Hedgerows are rich in wildlife, so their removal has a serious effect on the numbers and types of plant and animal species living in the area. A single plant crop in a large field will lead to lower biodiversity than smaller fields surrounded by hedgerows.

Transport

In addition to clearing areas to create transport links, increased travel means burning more fuels. This will produce more pollutant gases. These cause short- and long-term effects on ecosystems.

2B.M3

Acidification

Many of the pollutant gases, such as carbon dioxide, nitrogen oxides and sulfur dioxide, react with water to form acids. The gases dissolve in rain, which then falls as **acid rain** (see Unit 2). Evidence from dying trees has shown that acid rain is affecting many parts of Europe.

Carbon dioxide is very soluble in water. The gas dissolves easily in the sea, lakes and ponds. Measurements have shown that these are becoming more acidic. Many organisms will die and food chains will be seriously affected.

Trees in this forest have been killed by acid rain

Coral reefs are dying because seawater has become more acidic and warmer. Coral reefs are an important part of the world's food webs

...deforestation

The effects of agricultural pollutants on ecosystems

Your assessment criteria:

2B.M3 Analyse the effects of pollutants on ecosystems

2B.D2 Explain the long-term effects of pollutants on living organisms and ecosystems

Our changing environment

Sam works for the Environment Agency. He is one of the many scientists across all disciplines – biologists, chemists and physicists – who are investigating our changing environment. Sam believes that if we don't do things to try to prevent the changes he's observing, it could have serious effects on all the organisms on the planet.

2B.M3

Using chemicals to improve production causes pollution

To obtain improved yields of crops, farmers use **fertilisers** and **pesticides**. Fertilisers provide extra minerals for plant crops and increase their yields. But chemicals from the fertilisers can get washed into lakes and ponds. These become enriched with nutrients. This process is called **eutrophication**. Microscopic algae grow in huge numbers and use up the oxygen in the water. All the organisms in the water will eventually die.

Pesticides may be **insecticides**, **fungicides** or **herbicides**. Insecticides kill insects that are pests of the crops. Herbicides kill weeds that compete with the crops for light and minerals. Fungicides kill fungi that are parasites of crop plants.

Many pesticides previously in use have now been found to be toxic to other organisms. Some pesticides **bioaccumulate** as they are passed from one organism to another along food chains. In low concentrations the pesticides may be non-toxic, but in high concentrations they may be highly toxic.

Climate change

Carbon dioxide is also a **greenhouse gas**. It is present in very low concentrations in the air (0.04%), but this level has been increasing rapidly during the last 50 years. The huge quantities of carbon dioxide that are being produced by human activities surround the Earth like a blanket. This reduces the amount of heat that the Earth radiates into space. We call this the greenhouse effect (see Unit 2). As a result, the Earth is becoming warmer and this drives climate change.

Know more

An insecticide called DDT was widely used for many years. In the 1960s, researchers found that it accumulated in aquatic food chains to toxic levels. DDT was banned in the UK in 1984. But it is very slow to break down and is still present in food chains – even in you.

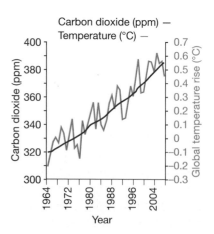

Scientists' analyses show a correlation between atmospheric carbon dioxide concentration and global temperature

$\mathcal{P}$ ...greenhouse gas

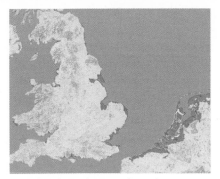

If sea levels rise by 2 m, the red areas would be under water

The long-term effects of climate change

2B.D2

The rise in average global temperature is causing the world's climate to become more unstable. We can expect periods of very wet or very dry weather, with the likelihood of severe storms. Ice in the polar regions and in mountain glaciers is melting, causing sea levels to rise. The map shows how parts of the UK and mainland Europe would be affected by a 2 metre rise in sea levels.

These changes affect the lives of plants and animals. Biologists monitor these effects. In the 1960s, hazel trees produced catkins in mid-February. You can now often see them in mid-December. Oak trees show a similar change as the graph shows.

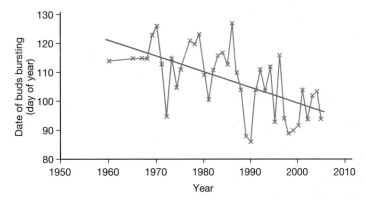

Oak trees are coming into leaf two weeks earlier than they did in the 1950s.

As temperatures rise, many of our woodland trees may be unable to cope with long, dry summers. Such changes will seriously affect the relationships between organisms. Life cycles of plants and animals are carefully synchronised. Food and shelter have to be available at the appropriate times of year.

The **distribution** of organisms is also changing – many are moving northwards as the temperatures rise.

Birds are nesting 1 to 3 weeks earlier than they did 25 years ago

The comma butterfly is spreading northwards

...climate change

Discuss

Life cycles of interdependent plants and animals have to be synchronised. What would happen to butterfly caterpillars if they hatched before trees were in leaf? What effect would this then have on birds that ate the caterpillars?

Monitoring change

Measuring pollution

Sam, along with members of similar monitoring organisations, uses various methods to measure and monitor pollutants.

Your assessment criteria:

1B.5 Identify living and non-living indicators and the type of pollution they measure

2B.P5 Describe how living and non-living indicators can be used to measure levels of pollutants

1B.5 2B.P5

Using living and non-living indicators

Scientists need to look for pollution, and monitor the effects of pollution in water, in the air and on the land. They use **indicators** to detect pollutants.

Living organisms used as indicators

Indicator	Pollution in:	Indicates:
algae	water	phosphate and nitrate pollutants
caddis fly larva	water	very low levels of pollution; very high levels of oxygen
freshwater shrimp	water	low levels of pollution; high levels of oxygen
lichens	air	level of sulfur dioxide

Non-living indicators

Indicator	Pollution in:	Indicates:
limestone (buildings)	air/rain	level of sulfur dioxide
nitrates	water	levels of fertilisers in water
dissolved oxygen	water	levels of organic pollutants, such as sewage

Think about

The lives of many organisms are affected by pollution, but what makes them good indicators of pollution?

⌕...pollution indicators

The common orange lichen can live in highly polluted environments. The beard lichen can only live in very clean air

Concentrations of algae in water are proportional to the concentration of nitrates in the water

Detailed studies are being made of the rate of erosion of the limestone that was used to build York Minster

Using lichens to monitor pollution

2B.P5

Sulfur dioxide is produced when fossil fuels are burned. Many organisms are sensitive to sulfur dioxide in the air. Lichens are good indicators because different types vary in their sensitivity to the gas. They can be used to indicate levels of sulfur dioxide in the air.

Using biological indicator species

Animals need oxygen to live. Oxygen dissolves in water and aquatic organisms use this oxygen to live. Many, however, have ways of tolerating very low oxygen concentrations. Other organisms are very sensitive to small changes in oxygen concentration.

Environmental scientists look for the presence of certain organisms in water, called **biological indicators**, to assess how polluted the water is. The types of organism in the water give a very good indication of the levels of dissolved oxygen. Numbers of algae and water plants such as duckweed are good indicators of levels of nitrates in water. These have run off farmland.

Caddis fly larvae are good biological indicators. They need clean water to live

Non-living indicators

Levels of oxygen and nitrates can also be measured using instrumental or chemical methods.

When exposed to acidic gases in moist air, or acid rain, limestone reacts and 'dissolves'. The rate at which limestone erodes as it reacts with acid rain provides a very good measure of the levels of sulfur dioxide in the air.

...indicator species

Halting and reversing change

Your assessment criteria:

1B.6 Describe how recycling and reusing materials can reduce the impact that human activities have on an ecosystem

2B.P6 Describe the different methods used to help reduce the impact of human activities on ecosystems

2B.M4 Discuss the advantages and disadvantages of methods used to reduce the impact of human activity on ecosystems

2B.D3 Evaluate the success of methods to reduce the impact of human activity on an ecosystem, for a given scenario

The Heart of England Forest Project

The project aims to create typical English broadleaf forest in south Warwickshire, in the heart of England. So far, around 770 hectares have been planted. That's an area around five times the size of Hyde Park.

The forest covers part of the area once written about by Shakespeare – the ancient Forest of Arden

1B.6 2B.P6

Reuse and recycle

Scientists are trying to halt human effects on the environment in a number of ways. These include conservation, organic farming and using renewable resources. But measures can begin with you, in your home.

We can all recycle paper products, glass, metals and plastics to conserve natural resources. This may reduce exploration for, and mining of, natural resources. We should also re-use items where we can. This will cut down on the energy required – and the resulting pollution – to make new products.

Conservation

In recent years, governments, conservationists, farmers and other organisations have been attempting to conserve habitats and species.

Research

Make a list of the items in your home that you can recycle or reuse. How will these reduce the impact on ecosystems?

 ...recycling

2B.P6

Reforestation and replacement planting

As they photosynthesise, plants remove carbon dioxide from the air and give out oxygen. Trees and other plants therefore act as **carbon sinks** and can help to reduce carbon dioxide released into the air by the burning of fossil fuels. **Reforestation** programmes – like the Heart of England Forest Project – are helping to replace ancient forests, long-since removed. **Replacement planting** is an initiative designed to plant a tree for every one removed.

Breeding programmes

Many zoos and other organisations do valuable work in breeding species of animals that are at risk of extinction in the wild. Many of these organisations work in collaboration across the world. Today, some species owe their existence to these breeding programmes.

The Arabian oryx became extinct in the wild in 1972. It was reintroduced after breeding programmes in zoos

Farming methods

Some farmers now use organic farming methods, without harmful chemicals, to control pests. 'Skylark strips' (edges of crop fields left uncultivated) and 'beetle banks' have been created in some fields of monoculture crops. These provide new habitats for predators that will feed on insect pests.

Organic fertilisers include manure, composted waste and hops from the brewing industry. These are all natural products, and don't require energy to produce them.

Research

A technique called 'bioremediation' uses living organisms to remove toxic chemicals, such as heavy metals and petroleum products, from land or water. Research a bioremediation project that has been successful.

Know more

Hedgerows removed to create huge fields for crops are now being replaced. Over 600 different species of plant, 1500 species of insect, 65 species of birds and 20 species of mammals have been recorded, at some time, living in British hedgerows.

...reforestation ...organic farming

2B.P6

Using renewable resources

A renewable resource is something that can be renewed or replaced.

We can use renewable energy resources such as biomass, tidal, solar, wave and wind energies, which are all dependent on the Sun, and alternative energy technologies.

Elephant grass is being grown as a biomass energy plant to heat buildings

More and more, we are running vehicles on **biofuels**. Biofuels are made using plants or microorganisms, and are therefore renewable as more organisms can be grown. Very often, we can produce biofuels from wastes produced by industrial processes. When a biofuel plant crop is grown, it absorbs carbon dioxide from the air. This is released when the plant is burned for fuel. So there is no overall, or 'net', output of carbon dioxide. The biofuel is said to be a **carbon-neutral** fuel. This is in contrast to the burning of fossil fuels, where it's carbon dioxide that was locked away millions of years ago that is being released today. This has a huge impact on the world's carbon balance.

Biofuel is carbon-neutral

Research

Elephant grass, or Miscanthus, is native to Africa and Asia but grows very well in the UK. What steps have British scientists taken to stop it spreading into the wild?

Discuss

The generation of electricity from nuclear fuel produces no carbon dioxide emissions. But building the power stations does. Uranium ore must be mined, transported and processed. And there's the problem of dealing safely with radioactive waste. What is your view on nuclear power?

...biofuels

Advantages and disadvantages

2B.M4

There are advantages and disadvantages to all of these initiatives. We must be sure that the advantages outweigh any disadvantages.

Recycling requires an input of energy to carry out the process. Sometimes, this is more than we'd need to produce more new material. But we have to remember that by recycling, we're conserving raw materials. And as time goes by, recycling processes are becoming more efficient.

There are also disadvantages to renewable energy sources, not least the set-up costs. Some of them may even impact negatively on the environment (see Unit 3).

And conservation projects cost money. In times of economic or political instability, governments may be reluctant to invest money in such projects. They then depend on the goodwill of the public to finance and carry out charitable work.

Think about

Make a list of conservation projects, farming methods, recycling initiatives and renewable resources designed to reduce the impact of human activity on ecosystems. For each, give the advantages and disadvantages.

Success, failure, or a bit of both?

2B.D3

Scientists must review and evaluate the success of these efforts to reduce the impact of human activity on ecosystems. And if there is an element of failure, they must put forward some suggestions for improvement.

The large copper butterfly died out in Britain in 1851 as fenlands were drained for agriculture. Several attempts to reintroduce the species have all failed

The larvae of the large blue butterfly depend on ants for their survival. It died out in Britain in 1979 as habitats became unsuitable for the ants. It has been reintroduced successfully in Devon and Somerset

Research

Research a project local to you that is involved in reducing human impact on the environment. Evaluate its success.

Microorganisms and disease

Measles, mumps and rubella

Measles, mumps and rubella used to be common childhood illnesses. The symptoms of these were often quite mild. But sometimes there were complications and the illness became much more serious. Now children are immunised against these diseases with the MMR vaccine.

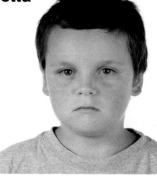

1C.7
2C.P7
1C.8
2C.P8

What factors affect our health?

Measles, mumps and rubella are caused by **viruses**. All viruses cause disease. Other **infectious** diseases in humans are caused by another group of microorganisms called **bacteria**. Organisms that cause disease are called **pathogens**.

But we can also inherit some diseases. These are **non-infectious** diseases.

Other human conditions are caused by our lifestyle or the environment. Risk factors include alcohol, cigarettes, recreational drugs, poor diet and too much exposure to intense sunlight.

Virus infections

Some viruses, such as the common cold virus, cause only minor diseases. We soon get over them. But others are much more serious. AIDS is caused by the human immunodeficiency virus (HIV). The virus attacks cells in the body's immune system. HIV now kills more women of reproductive age worldwide than any other disease.

Long-term virus infections

In many cases, after infection, the viruses do not leave our bodies. If you've had a cold sore, after the infection has cleared up, the virus lies dormant in your nerves. If you're under stress, or spend too long in strong sunlight, the cold sore returns.

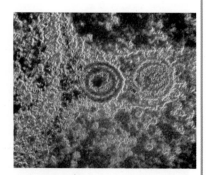

A cold sore virus

...immunisation

An HPV vaccination programme started in the UK in September 2008 to help protect girls from cervical cancer

Think about

Some people say that as the incidence of a disease falls, the risk of contracting it becomes small. So why vaccinate?

Research

In 2000, two studies (now known to be flawed scientifically) suggested that the MMR vaccine might be responsible for the increase of a complex condition called autism in children. For several years, some parents refused to allow their children to have the MMR vaccine. What effect did this have on the numbers of cases of measles, mumps and rubella?

Research

Evaluate the use of vaccinations in controlling disease. Remember to include negative as well as positive points. Try to include and process some data.

We now know that many viruses can affect the DNA in our cells and lead to cancer. Nearly all women who develop cervical cancer (cancer of the neck of the womb, or cervix) show signs of having had an infection of the human papilloma virus (HPV).

1C.7
2C.P7
1C.8
2C.P8

Vaccines and immunisation

When you get a mild illness, such as a cold, you usually get better on your own. But with many diseases, such as measles, mumps and rubella, it's better to prevent them by being vaccinated.

Vaccines contain microorganisms that have been weakened or killed so that they won't cause disease.

When the vaccine is injected, the body produces proteins called **antibodies**. The antibodies help the white blood cells to destroy the weakened microorganisms.

After the vaccination, cells called 'memory cells' stay in the body. These will produce antibodies very quickly if the person is ever exposed to the virus. The person has been **immunised** against the infection, and will be immune for some years. Vaccines are an important measure in disease prevention.

Vaccination programmes

2C.M5
2C.M7

Antibodies produced by the body are always specific to one type of bacterium or virus. So different vaccines are required for different diseases.

In the UK, a vaccination programme helps protect our children against serious diseases. The vaccines may have to be topped-up in later life. It's difficult to vaccinate everyone. And some parents are discouraged from having their child vaccinated because there's always a slight risk from any medical procedure. Very few children have a severe reaction when a vaccination is given to them.

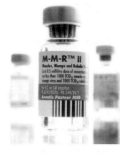

MMR vaccine

The success of vaccination programmes

2C.D4

Smallpox is a disease that has been eradicated from the world because of vaccination programmes. And a recent global vaccination programme means that we're also quite close to getting rid of polio.

But for some diseases, such as AIDS, we may be many years from having a successful vaccine. Some viruses can also change genetically, so this makes vaccine production very difficult.

 ...vaccination

Bacterial diseases

Your assessment criteria:

1C.7 List the different biological, social and inherited factors that affect human health

2C.P7 Describe how pathogens affect human health

1C.8 Identify measures that can be taken to prevent and treat infectious disease

2C.P8 Describe two different treatment regimes: one used to prevent a disease and one used to treat a disease

2C.M5 Explain how bacteria can become resistant to antibiotics

2C.D4 Evaluate the use of antibiotics, pedigree analysis and vaccination programmes in the treatment and prevention of childhood illnesses

A very rare case of diphtheria

A child has died from what is suspected to be diphtheria. The child had not been vaccinated against the disease. The family had been on holiday in a country where the disease is still common. Parents are urged to have their children vaccinated against the disease.

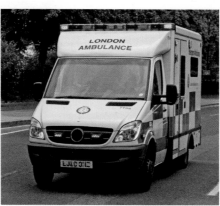

1C.7
2C.P7
1C.8
2C.8

Diseases caused by bacteria

Diphtheria is caused by a bacterium. Many diseases familiar to us are also caused by bacteria, including some sore throats, bronchitis, food poisoning, pneumonia and tuberculosis (TB).

Some diseases can be prevented by good hygiene. Food poisoning can be prevented by careful handling of food, keeping it away from flies and ensuring that it's well-cooked.

Because of our immune system, we often get better on our own. But sometimes we need drugs called **antibiotics**. These only work against bacteria – for diseases caused by viruses, we use **antivirals**.

The cause of diphtheria

Cases of diphtheria in the UK are very rare. The bacterium is transferred from person to person by very close physical contact and by droplets of mucus from the respiratory system.

Diphtheria affects the throat and the tonsils. The early symptoms are a sore throat, swollen lymph glands, fever and loss of appetite. After a few days, severe problems with breathing can develop. The person may become extremely weak and die.

Bacteria cause disease by producing toxins

Many bacteria cause disease by producing poisons, or **toxins**. The toxins harm living cells in the human body. The toxins produced by the diphtheria bacterium are proteins. The proteins enter body cells and stop the cells synthesising their own proteins.

Know more

Bacterial toxins are the most powerful poisons known. The botulinum toxin, which paralyses the nervous system, is lethal at a concentration of 8×10^{-9} mg in mice. But some people decide to be injected with the toxin. The paralysis caused smooths out wrinkles. It's a lifestyle choice most of us decide not to take! Would you use Botox®?

Antibiotic treatment

2C.M5

Diphtheria can be treated with a course of antibiotics, which kill bacteria. An antitoxin, which neutralises the toxin, is also given. There are around 100 different types of antibiotics. Their use is essential for treating disease such as diphtheria, or patients would die. But in the past 50 years, antibiotics have often been prescribed for minor illnesses. Some bacteria – 'superbugs' – have developed a resistance to the most widely used antibiotics. These bacteria are no longer killed by common antibiotics.

How does antibiotic resistance develop?

Antibiotic resistance in bacteria is an example of natural selection (page 120). In any population of bacteria, because of genetic variation, a few may be resistant to the antibiotic. These will survive the antibiotic and reproduce. Bacteria reproduce very quickly. The genes for antibiotic resistance will quickly spread throughout the population.

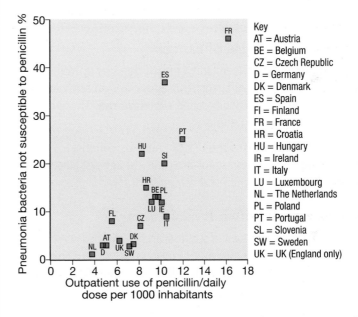

This scattergraph shows the correlation between antibiotic resistance and use of antibiotics in different countries

The overuse of antibiotics

2C.D4

Antibiotics were discovered in the 1920s and were first used in the Second World War. They have prevented millions of deaths. With the rise of 'superbugs', some antibiotics are now kept in reserve for the most serious diseases. There is a desperate need, however, to develop new types.

Lifestyle choices

Getting a tan

Jodie goes regularly to a tanning salon and spends long periods on a sunbed. One day she notices a dark freckle on her arm. She is worried and visits her doctor. The doctor doesn't think the freckle is skin cancer, but she warns her that people with pale skin like hers shouldn't use sunbeds and should avoid sunbathing.

2C.P9

Radiation as a cause of cancer

Ultraviolet radiation (see Unit 1) from the Sun or from sunbeds can damage skin cells. This ages our skin and can lead to a type of skin cancer called a **melanoma**. These occur mostly in fair-skinned people.

Any agent that increases the risk of cancer is called a **carcinogen**. Some carcinogens are physical agents, like radiation. Others are chemical carcinogens.

What happens when we develop cancer?

When a cell becomes cancerous, it starts to divide uncontrollably. Many new cancer cells are produced. The cancer cells often form a clump of cells called a tumour. Sometimes some of these cancerous cells spread to other places in the body. Here, they form new tumours. Eventually surgery cannot remove all the tumours from a person's body.

A cell becomes cancerous because of a change to its DNA. This is called a **mutation**. Carcinogens cause harmful mutations.

The effects of smoking

Jodie is also a cigarette smoker. Smoking is the most common way in which people become exposed to chemical carcinogens.

Chemicals in cigarette smoke also affect our circulatory systems. When Jodie smokes, her heart rate rises. So does her blood

Know more

In the last 30 years, rates of malignant (cancerous) melanoma in the UK have increased more rapidly than any of the other 'top 10' cancers. Since 1979, rates have increased five times in males, and more than tripled in females.

Know more

Most cases of skin cancer – around 100 000 in the UK every year – are not melanomas.

Non-melanoma skin cancer is easily treatable, and survival rates are high.

...carcinogens

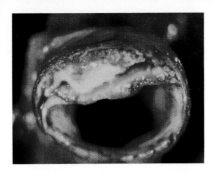

Smoking reduces the blood's ability to carry oxygen.

pressure. Raised blood pressure is a major factor contributing to **strokes**. It can also damage the lining of her arteries. This damage may lead to **atherosclerosis**, where fatty deposits form on the artery walls. Atherosclerosis in coronary arteries – the blood vessels that supply the heart with oxygen – leads to heart attacks.

Type of coronary heart disease	Number of cases and exposure to cigarette smoke		
	Never exposed	Occasional exposure	Regular exposure
non-fatal heart attack	14	63	50
fatal heart attack	3	11	11

A study carried out in America looked at 32 000 nurses, who were healthy at the start of the study. Rates of heart disease over the next ten years showed how coronary heart disease is linked to smoking

Asthma

Jodie's friend Claire has asthma, a condition that affects the airways in her lungs. Many factors, such as cigarette smoke, can trigger her asthma. When Jodie smokes, Claire leaves the room. Poor air quality in polluted environments can also affect her.

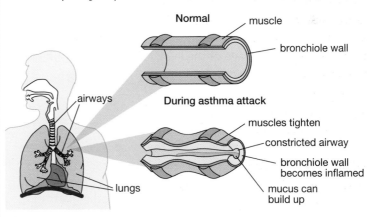

Asthma is brought on by changes to the airways, or bronchioles, in the lungs

During an asthma attack, Claire coughs and wheezes. She finds it difficult to breathe and her chest feels tight. She must take steps to keep her asthma under control. These include using an inhaler to relieve the symptoms, but also making decisions about her lifestyle.

Claire avoids certain foods and eats a lot of fresh fruit and vegetables. She exercises regularly, but is careful not to overdo this. Her flat is kept very clean (many people with asthma are sensitive to the droppings from dust mites) and well-ventilated (this helps remove gases produced by heating and cooking).

Research

Find some data to compare how the incidence of asthma in the UK has changed as pollution has decreased in recent years.

The use and misuse of drugs

Your assessment criteria:

2C.P9 Describe how lifestyle choices can affect human health

Unfit to drive

Jason is a police officer. He suspects a driver to be under the influence of drink or drugs. He stops the car and carries out a roadside breath test on the driver.

2C.P9

Alcohol

Alcohol affects how our brain functions. It is a **sedative**, or depressant. It lowers a person's awareness of what's going on. Even low amounts of alcohol increase a driver's response time. Being unable to react quickly while driving could have fatal consequences on the road.

Higher amounts of alcohol can inhibit the part of the brain that controls breathing, and even cause death. Long-term alcohol abuse can lead to damage of the liver. It is estimated that up to 1 in 3 adults drinks enough alcohol to risk liver damage.

Other misused drugs

There's currently no roadside test in the UK for so-called 'recreational' drugs, but Jason checks the person's eyes, balance, walking and co-ordination. Like alcohol, these drugs impair concentration and slow reaction times, and the driver can often misjudge speed. The drugs act on the brain and other parts of the nervous system to affect mood, perception and consciousness.

Drug	Effect
amphetamines, e.g. ecstasy, speed	**stimulants**
cannabis	changes a person's mood; produces feelings of closeness to people and experiences of increased intensity
cocaine	stimulant
LSD	alters perception and produces hallucinations
opiates, e.g. heroin, morphine, codeine	have a painkilling effect and produce a feeling of euphoria (happiness)

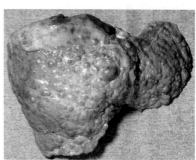

Cirrhosis of the liver involves the formation of scar tissue

Know more

Tranquillisers and barbiturates are also depressant drugs.

Know more

Some drugs affect the way our body holds on to water and how much urine we produce.

Alcohol and caffeine will increase the amount of urine produced.

Ecstasy has the opposite effect on water balance. It decreases the amount of urine produced.

...drugs and alcohol

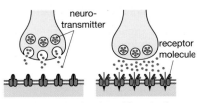

A neurotransmitter is released from the first nerve. It moves across the gap between the nerves. As it reaches the next nerve, it locks into a receptor. The second nerve is stimulated.

Nerve impulse transmission

Research

The use of drugs affects many organs in the human body. Research why and how the liver may be one of the major organs affected by long-term drug use.

Research

Recreational drugs are illegal. They are divided into three classes: A, B and C. Find out which drugs are currently in each class, and what the classes mean. From your knowledge of the drugs' effects, explain why each has been placed in the different classes.

Discuss

Some countries, such as the Netherlands, have more liberal laws on drug use than the UK. Some people believe that the laws in this country should be relaxed. They say that more easily available, cheaper drugs would mean less crime. Discuss this issue from a scientific and a social viewpoint.

The effect of drugs on the nervous system

2C.P9

The messages that nerves carry around the body are called nerve impulses. A nerve impulse is carried from one nerve to another by a chemical called a **neurotransmitter**. Drugs affect different types of neurotransmitter in the brain, or the receptor molecules they lock on to. This is how many produce their effects.

Drugs also affect other systems in the body, often producing unwanted effects. The body has control systems that keep its internal environment constant. Many drugs affect this control.

Many drugs are addictive

Many drugs can have an impact on long-term behaviour. People can quickly become dependent on some drugs. The person develops a need for the drug. This need might be psychological, when the person finds it difficult to get through the day without the drug. Or it may be **physiological**, when the person's body can no longer function without the drug.

Treatment and **rehabilitation** – getting the person back to full health and a normal life without the drug – are important.

Wider issues arising from drug misuse

People who are heavy drug users are more at risk of developing mental health problems. These include psychoses (where the ability to distinguish between what is real or imagined is affected), anxiety, depression and dementia. Behavioural changes as a result of drug use can lead to crime. Or the user may turn to crime to obtain money to fuel the drug habit. The misuse of drugs presents a challenge to the stability of the user's family.

The use of recreational drugs has led to an increase in the transmission of disease. It can also result in unwanted pregnancies. Mental and behavioural problems and accidents can lead to the death of the user.

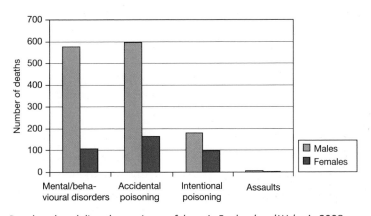

Deaths related directly to misuse of drugs in England and Wales in 2008

🔍 ...drug addiction

Inherited conditions

Your assessment criteria:

2C.M6 Explain the use of pedigree analysis

2C.D4 Evaluate the use of antibiotics, pedigree analysis and vaccination programmes in the treatment and prevention of childhood illnesses

Cystic fibrosis

Jack has a disease called cystic fibrosis. He needs vigorous physiotherapy every few days to keep his lungs working. Fifty years ago, children with cystic fibrosis would have been unlikely to live beyond the age of five. Today, half will live beyond the age of 35. And scientists are working all the time to improve this.

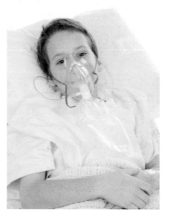

2C.M6

Inherited diseases

Cystic fibrosis is an example of a disease that's inherited, or genetic. Sufferers produce mucus that is thicker and stickier than normal. This mucus blocks Jack's airways in his respiratory system, making it difficult for him to breathe. His respiratory system can get infected easily.

Cystic fibrosis also reduces the secretion of digestive juices from the **pancreas**. This makes it more difficult to digest food.

The genetics of cystic fibrosis

Cystic fibrosis is caused if a certain gene is defective. The gene is located on chromosome 7. It codes for a protein called CFTR. This protein controls the movement of water and ions in and out of certain cells, such as those of the **epithelium** lining the lungs.

One of each of our pairs of chromosomes came from our mother, and one from our father. If a person has one normal allele (see Unit 1), the person can still produce CFTR. The person does not have cystic fibrosis but is a **carrier**. They can pass the defective gene on to their children. A person who has two defective alleles has cystic fibrosis.

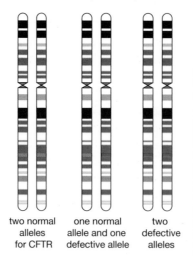

two normal alleles for CFTR

one normal allele and one defective allele

two defective alleles

It takes two defective alleles for a person to suffer from cystic fibrosis

Research

A disease called sickle cell anaemia affects the red blood cells. Find out more about the disease, its effects on the body, and why it's common in African populations.

...single gene disorders

Predicting the inheritance of cystic fibrosis

2C.D4

Over two million people in the UK carry the cystic fibrosis gene. That's about 1 in every 25 of the population.

With our knowledge of genetics, we can sometimes predict the possibility of someone being born with cystic fibrosis. We construct a **pedigree** to show patterns in the inheritance of a disease in a family.

Think about

How do we know that A, E and F are carriers of cystic fibrosis?

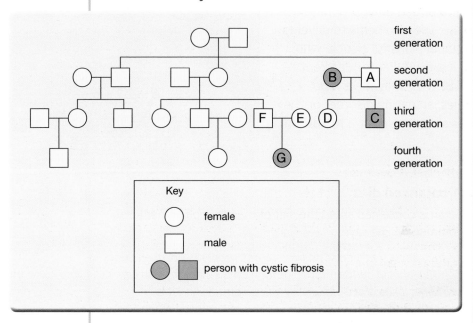

A family pedigree showing the inheritance of cystic fibrosis

Research

Evaluate the use of pedigrees in controlling genetic conditions. Remember to include negative as well as positive points. Try to include and process some data.

Genetic counsellors interpret the results of pedigrees along with genetic tests using cheek cells or blood cells, to see if potential parents are carriers.

They can then make a decision as to whether they have children or not. If both parents are carriers, there's a 1 in 4 chance of any child born having cystic fibrosis.

Research

Scientists are attempting to use gene therapy to treat cystic fibrosis. They are hoping that one day they may be able to cure the disease by introducing a normal version of the cystic fibrosis gene to the person's epithelial cells. Find out about gene therapy, and how successful it's been so far.

...pedigree analysis

Diet and exercise

Your assessment criteria:

1C.9   List some benefits of exercise on health.

2C.P9   Describe how lifestyle choices can affect human health

Healthy diets

Sarah is a community dietician. She gives advice to people on how to stay healthy through a proper diet and an appropriate lifestyle. She also helps to develop nutritional plans for people who need a special diet for different reasons. They may have food allergies, an eating disorder or they may want to train for a marathon.

1C.9
2C.P9

A balanced diet

Sarah is concerned about the diet of many people in her local community. She says:

'Many people don't find the time to eat properly. I explain that our diet should contain types of food called carbohydrates, proteins, lipids (fats), vitamins and minerals. And it's important that these must be in the correct proportions to provide a balanced diet.'

The food we eat provides the raw materials for growth, and for the normal functioning and repair of cells and body tissues. It also provides the energy we need to stay alive and be active.

Food nutrient	Role of nutrient in the body	Sources of the nutrient
carbohydrates	provide energy	bread, pasta, potatoes, rice
proteins	for growth and development, and repair	animal proteins: meat, fish, eggs, cheese non-animal proteins: nuts, beans, cereals, mycoprotein
lipids (fats)	for growth and development, e.g. of nervous tissue, and for energy storage	animal fats, vegetable oils, butter and margarine

Part of Sarah's information leaflet on a balanced diet

...diet and health

Carbohydrates, proteins and lipids (fats) are required in relatively large amounts in a balanced diet. Vitamins and minerals are required in much lower amounts, but are needed for healthy growth and development. Some are necessary for enzymes to function and for us to obtain energy from our food.

Sarah continues:

'I encourage people to increase the amount of fish oil in their diet for good health, and to use plant oils rather than solid animal fats to reduce the risk of heart disease. I also suggest that they eat more wholegrain sources of carbohydrate, which release glucose slowly into the blood.'

Balancing energy requirements

We all need a certain amount of energy just to live. This is called our **basal metabolic rate**, or **BMR**. Depending on age and gender, our BMR is 45 to 70% of our total energy expenditure. So the amount of energy we need to take in from our food depends on our age and gender. Also, the more active a lifestyle a person has, the more energy they need.

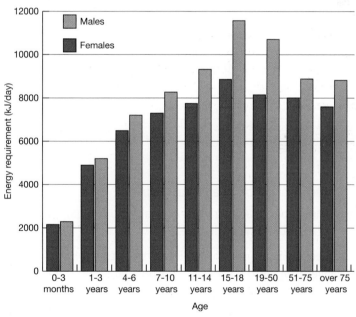

The estimated average energy requirements of people of different ages

Activity	Energy requirement, kJ/h
sitting	420
typing rapidly	590
dressing	630
walking, 3 mph	840
jogging, 6 mph	2400

The energy required to do various activities

It's important to balance the energy in the foods we eat with the amount of energy we need for our daily activities. In the UK today, many people eat food containing far more energy than they actually need. Our bodies convert excess carbohydrate to fat. This gets stored under our skin and around body organs. This fat can make us overweight or obese.

🔎...BMR calculator

1C.9
2C.P9

The importance of exercise

It is easy to eat more than we need if we don't take very much exercise. Exercise isn't only important for our energy balance. It's also important for our overall health. It keeps our heart and other muscles in our body healthy. People who exercise regularly reduce the risk of many illnesses. These include heart disease, type 2 diabetes and diseases of the circulatory system. And chemicals released during exercise also affect our mood and give us a sense of well-being.

Body mass index

Sarah continues about her work.

'People don't often realise how their need for energy depends on their body size. I can show people how to calculate their body mass index (BMI), to find out if they are the ideal weight for their height, or over- or underweight.'

$$BMI = \frac{weight, kg}{(height, m)^2}$$

'I have to explain that the information from a BMI can sometimes be misleading. It's inappropriate for pregnant women, for instance. And a BMI might suggest that a very fit person, with a high proportion of muscle, is obese!'

Consequences of the wrong diet

Too much food, or a diet rich in animal fats, can lead to serious conditions such as heart disease.

- If a person is overweight, their heart has to work harder to deliver oxygen to body cells. This puts strain on the heart.

- Excess fat in the diet can lead to fatty deposits that build up in the arteries (blood vessels). The arteries are made narrower and can become more rigid. This increases blood pressure. High blood pressure can lead to a stroke if a blood vessel bursts in the brain.

- If fatty deposits build up in the coronary arteries, which supply blood to the heart, then a blood clot could form. This can cause a heart attack.

- Diabetes (type 2) and cancer are also more likely if a person is overweight.

Think about

Sarah advises women who are pregnant and breastfeeding about their extra energy requirements. The recommended extra intake of energy during the last three months of pregnancy is 80 kJ per day. Someone who's breastfeeding needs an extra 2100 kJ per day. Why is this extra energy required?

A BMI calculator shows you quickly if you are overweight, within a normal range, or underweight

🔍 ...BMI calculator

Lifestyle factors

The dietician Sarah appreciates, from talking with people in her community, why they don't always have healthy lifestyles. Some of their comments are shown here.

It's quicker to cook a 'ready meal' than prepare more healthy food.

Fresh fruit and vegetables are more expensive than fast food.

I'm so busy that I can't find the time to exercise.

I can't get my children to eat vegetables.

Deficiencies in our diet

In some parts of the world, ecological and social factors mean that diets have insufficient protein. Diseases called kwashiorkor and marasmus occur. Sarah says that deficiency diseases resulting from a poor diet may still occur in the UK. She says,

'We produce vitamin D in our skin when the Sun shines. I've always checked on old people in the winter, to make sure that they don't become deficient in this vitamin.'

The latest research suggests that up a quarter of people in the UK could be deficient in vitamin D. A disease called rickets was common many years ago, and now it's reappearing. We now believe that vitamin D deficiency is connected with some deaths of young children.

Anorexia nervosa

Sarah also works with people who have different kinds of eating disorders. Some have a condition called **anorexia nervosa**.

Because of the society we live in, many people feel under pressure to be thin. But some have a mistaken perception of their body size. They may imagine themselves to be overweight when actually they're not. They reduce their food intake to very low levels.

With insufficient protein in their diet, muscles are broken down to provide energy and the body wastes away. A lack of glucose reduces mental function. Anorexia that's untreated is usually fatal.

Sarah says:

'I help patients to gradually establish healthy eating habits to restore their body weight. It is also important to try to tackle the psychological reasons that lead people into this condition.'

...deficiency disease

Assessment Checklist

To achieve a Pass grade, my portfolio of evidence must show that I can:

Assessment Criteria	Description	✓
2A.P1	Describe the role of genes and the environment in variation	
2A.P2	Describe how characteristics are used to classify organisms	
2A.P3	Describe the different ways in which organisms show interdependence	
2B.P4	Describe the impact that different human activities have on ecosystems	
2B.P5	Describe how living and non-living indicators can be used to measure levels of pollutants	
2B.P6	Describe the different methods used to help reduce the impact of human activities on ecosystems	
2C.P7	Describe how pathogens affect human health	
2C.P8	Describe two different treatment regimes: one used to prevent a disease and one used to treat a disease	
2C.P9	Describe how lifestyle choices can affect human health	

If you do not meet all the Level 2 Pass criteria for this Unit then your work will be assessed against these Level 1 criteria. If your work meets all these criteria you will achieve a Level 1 Pass for this Unit. If you do not achieve all these Level 1 criteria you will get a U (Unclassified) for this Unit.

Assessment Criteria	Description	✓
1A.1	Distinguish between variation due to genes and variation due to environmental factors	
1A.2	Construct simple keys to classify organisms	
1A.3	Construct food chains and food webs	
1B.4	Identify human activities that affect an ecosystem	
1B.5	Identify living and non-living indicators and the type of pollution they measure	
1B.6	Describe how recycling and re-using materials can reduce the impact that human activities have on an ecosystem	
1C.7	List the different biological, social and inherited factors that affect human health	
1C.8	Identify measures that can be taken to prevent and treat infectious disease	
1C.9	List some benefits of exercise on health	

To achieve a Merit grade, my portfolio of evidence must also show that I can:

Assessment Criteria	Description	✓
2A.M1	Explain the role of genes and the environment in evolution	
2A.M2	Discuss the factors that affect the relationship between different organisms	
2B.M3	Analyse the effects of pollutants on ecosystems	
2B.M4	Discuss the advantages and disadvantages of methods used to reduce the impact of human activity on ecosystems	
2C.M5	Explain how bacteria can become resistant to antibiotics	
2C.M6	Explain the use of pedigree analysis	
2C.M7	Discuss the advantages and disadvantages of vaccination programmes	

To achieve a Distinction grade, my portfolio of evidence must also show that I can:

Assessment Criteria	Description	✓
2A.D1	Evaluate the impact of genes and the environment on the survival or extinction of organisms	
2B.D2	Explain the long-term effects of pollutants on living organisms and ecosystems	
2B.D3	Evaluate the success of methods to reduce the impact of human activity on an ecosystem, for a given scenario	
2C.D4	Evaluate the use of antibiotics, pedigree analysis and vaccination programmes in the treatment and prevention of childhood illnesses	

Unit 5 **Applications of Chemical Substances**

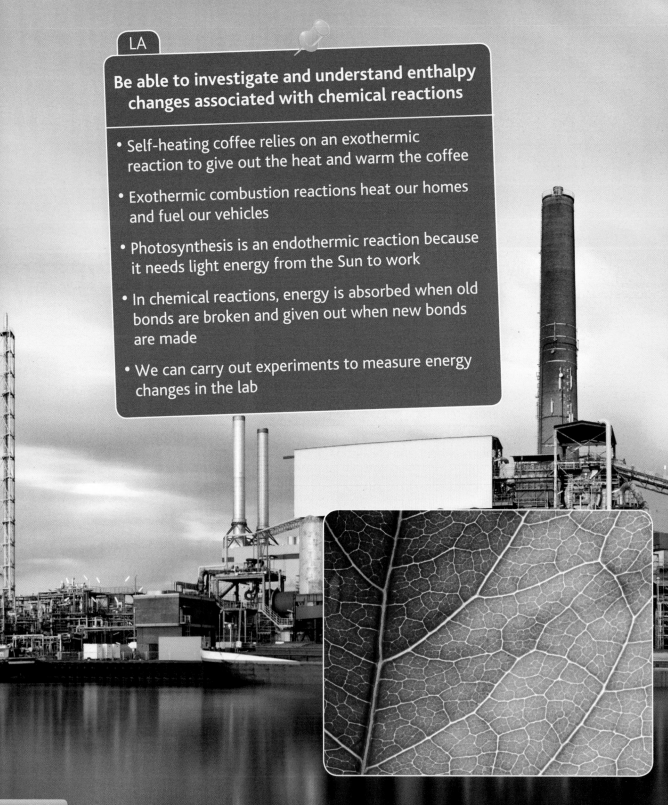

LA

Be able to investigate and understand enthalpy changes associated with chemical reactions

- Self-heating coffee relies on an exothermic reaction to give out the heat and warm the coffee

- Exothermic combustion reactions heat our homes and fuel our vehicles

- Photosynthesis is an endothermic reaction because it needs light energy from the Sun to work

- In chemical reactions, energy is absorbed when old bonds are broken and given out when new bonds are made

- We can carry out experiments to measure energy changes in the lab

LA

Be able to explore the uses of nanochemicals and new materials

- Nanoparticles are measured in billionths of a metre

- Nanochemistry could help us make a computer the size of a sugar lump

- The Kevlar lining in a Bladerunner hoodie makes it bullet- and knife-proof

- Lenses in glasses that darken in sunlight are smart materials

LA

Be able to investigate organic compounds used in society

- The petrochemical industry makes many everyday essential materials like detergents, medicines and dyes

- LPG fuel is a mix of the organic compounds propane and butane

- Designer plastics can be made to order

- PVC can be rigid like drainpipes or soft like clingfilm; it all depends on what's added

- We know that our ancestors have been brewing beer for at least 12 000 years

Exothermic and endothermic reactions

Your assessment criteria:

2A.P1 Investigate temperature changes associated with exothermic and endothermic reactions using primary data

2A.M1 Explain why an overall reaction is exothermic or endothermic

Self-heating food

The army needs to provide hot convenience food for soldiers away from base. Ideally the meals should need no cooking pans. The solution is self-heating food. Part of the food packaging contains chemicals. The meal is sealed in a separate section. When the chemicals react together, heat is given out. This warms the food.

2A.P1

Hot and cold reactions

When water is added to calcium oxide in a beaker, the beaker gets very hot. Heat is given out. The reaction is:

$$CaO(s) + H_2O(l) \rightarrow Ca(OH)_2(s)$$

Some self-heating food packs use this reaction to warm the food.

This is an **exothermic reaction**. In an exothermic reaction, heat is transferred from the **system** (the reacting chemicals) to the **surroundings** (the beaker, the bench, the air). The temperature of the surroundings rises. The reaction gives out heat energy.

We can show this on an **energy profile diagram**.

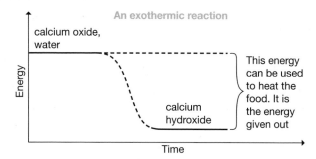

An exothermic reaction

calcium oxide, water

Energy

calcium hydroxide

This energy can be used to heat the food. It is the energy given out

Time

Energy profile diagram: calcium oxide reacting with water

Cold packs are used by athletes to treat sprains. One section of the pack contains water. The other section contains a salt such as ammonium nitrate. When they mix, the ammonium nitrate dissolves. This needs energy, so heat is taken in.

This is an **endothermic reaction**. In an endothermic reaction, heat is transferred from the surroundings to the system. The temperature of the surroundings (including the pack) falls. The pack becomes cold. The reaction takes in heat energy.

Making use of an exothermic reaction: self-heating food

Making use of an endothermic reaction: a cold pack

...smart packaging

We can show an endothermic reaction on an energy profile diagram.

2A.P1

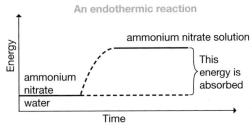

Energy profile diagram: ammonium nitrate dissolving in water

Know more

The heat given out or absorbed during a reaction is called the **enthalpy** change of a reaction.

Making and breaking bonds

2A.M1

In a chemical reaction, old bonds are broken and new ones are made. When calcium oxide reacts with water, these bonds are broken:

- the calcium–oxygen bonds in calcium oxide
- the oxygen–hydrogen bonds in water.

New bonds are made in forming calcium hydroxide.

Breaking old bonds needs energy. It is endothermic.

Making new bonds gives out energy. It is exothermic.

It is a balancing act between the energy needed to break bonds and the energy released in making new ones. This decides whether the reaction is exothermic or endothermic.

Think about

An acid neutralises an alkali. The reaction is exothermic. The heat given out is called the heat of neutralisation. Which needs more energy: breaking the old bonds or making the new ones?

Showing the energy changes

Bond breaking and bond making can be shown on the energy profile diagram of the reaction.

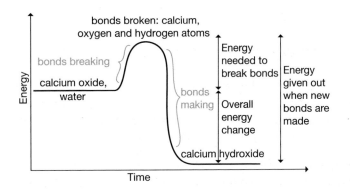

Energy profile diagram: bond breaking and bond making for the reaction between calcium oxide and water

Think about

What information about the exothermic reaction is needed in order to design self-heating meals?

🔍 ...calcium oxide

Measuring energy changes

Your assessment criteria:

1A.1 Measure the temperature changes associated with chemical reactions

2A.P1 Investigate temperature changes associated with exothermic and endothermic reactions using primary data

2A.D1 Calculate the energy changes that take place during exothermic and endothermic reactions

Keeping your energy up

Many sports drinks contain glucose. The glucose is a source of energy. Glucose contains carbon, hydrogen and oxygen. In your body cells, the glucose slowly reacts with oxygen. This is respiration. The reaction is exothermic. Energy is given out. This keeps you warm and gives you energy to move.

1A.1
2A.P1

Energy measurements

Food scientists carry out investigations to measure how much energy is given out when different foods burn. This energy change is the energy available from the food when we digest it. We can measure energy changes in the lab by measuring temperature changes.

Energy change on dissolving

Measure the temperature of a known volume of pure water (such as $25\,cm^3$).

Add a known mass (such as $3\,g$) of soluble solid, such as ammonium chloride or sodium carbonate. Stir until it is dissolved.

Measure the highest or lowest temperature reached.

Temperature change = final temperature − initial temperature

polystyrene cup with lid

$25\,cm^3$ of deionised water plus $3\,g$ of solute

Energy change on neutralisation

Measure $25\,cm^3$ each of dilute hydrochloric acid and dilute sodium hydroxide into separate measuring cylinders.

Pour the acid into a poly(styrene) cup and measure its temperature.

Add the alkali, stir and measure the biggest temperature change.

You can calculate the temperature change as for dissolving.

Combustion reactions

Combustion reactions are always exothermic. We use the energy given out to keep us warm, cook our food and power our cars. Alcohol is increasingly being used to replace petrol as vehicle fuel.

> **Know more**
>
> *Some soluble solids give out heat energy when they dissolve, others take heat energy in.*

> **Think about**
>
> *Why does using a poly(styrene) cup give more accurate results than using a glass beaker?*

🔍 ...respiration

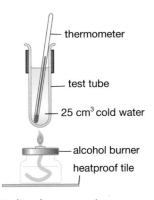

Finding the energy given out when alcohol burns

Know more

*The **specific heat capacity** of a substance is the heat energy required to raise the temperature of 1 g of the substance by 1 K, or 1 °C. This is 4.2 J for water.*

Think about

Why do we use the unit J/K/g for specific heat capacity values?

We can measure the energy given out when alcohol burns. See the diagram.

Measure the mass of the alcohol burner and alcohol.

Ignite the alcohol and allow it to heat 25 cm³ water in the test tube.

Measure the temperature rise of the water.

Measure the final mass of the alcohol burner.

This apparatus can be used to measure the heat energy given out by different fuels and by foods such as crisps, crackers and corn puffs.

1A.1
2A.P1

How much energy was given out when the alcohol burnt?

2A.D1

We use the formula:

heat energy absorbed by water = mass of water (g) × specific heat capacity (J/K/g) × temperature rise (K)

The specific heat capacity of water is 4.2 J/K/g.

If the mass of water is 25 g and the temperature rise is 30 °C, the heat absorbed by the water = 25 × 4.2 × 30 = 3150 J

If the initial mass of the alcohol burner is 62.5 g and the final mass 62.0 g, we know that 0.5 g alcohol has been burnt.

So the heat absorbed by the water when 1 g alcohol burns

$$= \frac{3150}{0.5} = 6300 \text{ J}$$

Positive and negative temperature changes

Scientists use plus and minus signs to show whether heat energy is gained or lost by the substances reacting.

* In an *exothermic* reaction, the substances lose energy: the heat energy is absorbed by the water (and other surroundings) and the temperature of the water rises. But the temperature change of the reaction is given a negative sign because the reacting substances have *lost* energy.

* In an *endothermic* reaction, the substances absorb heat from the water (and other surroundings) so that the temperature of the water decreases. The temperature change of the reaction is given a positive sign because the reacting substances have *gained* energy.

$\mathcal{P}$...combustion

Organic compounds

Crude oil

Fawley refinery lies on the edge of Southampton Water and is the largest oil refinery in the UK. It processes 22 million tonnes of crude oil a year. We use the products to heat our homes, fuel our cars, make new roads and a multitude of chemical goods from cosmetics to car tyres.

Think about

Crude oil arrives at Fawley refinery by ship. What infrastructure is needed at Fawley, apart from the fractionating columns? Think about transporting the products too.

1B.2 2B.P2

What is crude oil?

Crude oil is thick, black and a bit smelly. It is a mixture of chemicals called **hydrocarbons**. Hydrocarbons contain carbon and hydrogen atoms only. Crude oil straight from the ground is not very useful, but if the mixture is sorted into its separate hydrocarbons, the products become very useful.

Getting sorted

The hydrocarbon mixture is sorted in **fractionating columns** at **oil refineries**. Crude oil is firstly heated until it vaporises. The crude oil vapour rises up the fractionating column and starts

Your assessment criteria:

1B.2 Identify the uses of the main fractions from the distillation of crude oil

2B.P2 Describe the fractional distillation of crude oil to produce a range of useful products

2B.M2 Explain how fractional distillation separates compounds due to different boiling ranges

2B.D2 Analyse the relationship between the boiling range and the length of carbon chain of fractions

Know more

Oil formed millions of years ago. It resulted in millions of tonnes of carbon being locked up in rocks. Here, it could not cause global warming. Now we take the oil out of the ground and use it as a fuel and to make other materials. The carbon usually ends up as carbon dioxide in the air. This causes global warming.

A fractionating column at an oil refinery

...fractional distillation

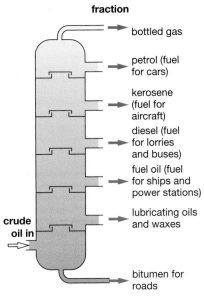

A fractional distillation (fractionating) column

to cool. The different hydrocarbons in crude oil reach different heights in the fractionating column before they condense back to liquids. Trays in the fractionating column collect the different hydrocarbons as they liquefy. The gases reach the top of the tower before being collected.

The products collected are called **fractions**. Each fraction contains several similar hydrocarbons. The process is called **fractional distillation**.

1B.2
2B.P2

How fractional distillation works

2B.M2

The different hydrocarbons in crude oil contain different numbers of carbon and hydrogen atoms bonded together. Each fraction collected during distillation contains hydrocarbons with a small range of numbers of carbon atoms. The table shows the number of carbon atoms in the hydrocarbons of each fraction and their boiling points.

Fraction	Number of carbon atoms in the hydrocarbon	Boiling range (°C)
bottled gas	1–4	–160 to 20
petrol	5–11	20 to 60
kerosene	10–16	120 to 240
diesel	15–25	220 to 250
fuel oil	20–27	250 to 300
lubricating oil	27–70	300 to 350
bitumen	over 70	over 350

As the number of carbon atoms increases, the boiling point also increases. Because the crude oil vapour cools as it travels up the fractionating column, different fractions condense at different heights. The crude oil is sorted.

Know more

*Some fractions – for example petrol and diesel – are used as they are. Other fractions are used in the **petrochemical industry**. They become the reactants for many different chemical reactions. There may be many steps. The eventual products are the materials we rely on like detergents, medicines, dyes, cosmetics, food additives – the list is endless.*

Boiling range and carbon atoms

2B.D2

The hydrocarbon molecules in crude oil have chains of carbon atoms. They are held together with strong covalent bonds. But the hydrocarbon molecules are also weakly attracted to each other. These attractions are called **intermolecular forces** and are very much less strong than a covalent bond. Before the hydrocarbon can boil, energy is needed to overcome the intermolecular forces. Longer hydrocarbon molecules with more carbon atoms have more intermolecular forces along their molecules and so higher boiling points.

Think about

Why do the hydrocarbons in fuel oil have higher boiling points than the hydrocarbons in petrol?

Organic chemistry

Organic produce

Organic food is grown without artificial fertilisers. Organic farmers use organic methods such as spreading farmyard manure as fertiliser. Organic clothes are made from fibres like cotton which is grown organically. 'Organic' has a different meaning in chemistry. Organic compounds are all those that contain carbon. Organic chemistry is the study of these compounds.

2B.P3

Carbon molecules

Carbon atoms have four electrons in their outer shell. They can make four covalent bonds, as they do in diamond. But carbon atoms can also join up with each other in long chains. These can be short or thousands of carbon atoms long. The chains may join up with other atoms to make very big molecules. Some of these molecules are the basis of life. They are **organic compounds**.

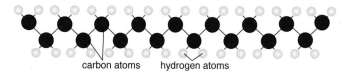

carbon atoms   hydrogen atoms

Types of formulae

Propane is one of the gases in bottled gas. It has the formula C_3H_8.

We use three different types of formula to describe propane:

- **molecular formula** – this is type of formula we are used to and is C_3H_8

- **structural formula** – this gives us more information about how the carbon atoms are bonded together, by breaking the molecule into chunks and listing the formula of each chunk. The structural formula of propane is $CH_3CH_2CH_3$.

A model of a propane molecule

$\mathcal{P}$ ...organic compounds

2B.P3

- **displayed formula** – this shows every atom and every bond in the molecule. We use a straight line to show a single covalent bond. The displayed formula for propane is:

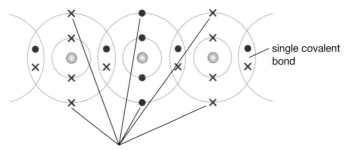

└single covalent bonds

2B.M3

Organic molecule bonding

The photo on the opposite page shows the three-dimensional image of a propane molecule. When each carbon atom makes four single covalent bonds, the bonds are arranged in a pyramid-type or **tetrahedral** structure.

single covalent bond

electrons available to form other covalent bonds

Two electrons are shared in a single covalent bond between two carbon atoms

Double bonds can also form between carbon atoms. These are shown by double lines, as in the displayed formula of propene:

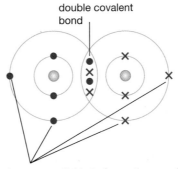

double covalent bond

electrons available to form other covalent bonds

Four electrons are shared in a double covalent bond between two carbon atoms

└double covalent bond

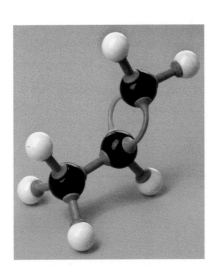

A model of a propene molecule

> **Think about**
>
> *What is the molecular formula for propene? Write the structural formula for propene.*

Alkanes and alkenes

High-performance cars

Racing cars and some sports cars have high-performance engines. They need a fuel to match. Petrol fuels contain a blend of hydrocarbons called alkanes. Different blends have different 'octane ratings'. For example, 95-octane premium unleaded has an octane rating of 95. It is suitable for most family cars. High-performance cars need higher octane ratings. Using the right fuel means the fuel will burn in a controlled way.

Your assessment criteria:

1B.3 Name alkanes and alkenes from structural and displayed formulae

2B.P3 Draw accurately the structural and displayed formulae of organic molecules

2B.P5 Describe the uses of organic compounds in our society

2B.M3 Describe the bonding and structure of organic molecules

1B.3
2B.P3

Alkanes

The hydrocarbons in crude oil are **alkanes**. Alkanes are a family of organic compounds. The smallest alkane molecule has one carbon atom bonded to four hydrogen atoms. It is methane. CH_4 is its molecular (and structural) formula. The displayed formula shows all the atoms and bonds.

The table shows other members of the alkane family.

High-performance cars need high-octane fuel

Alkane	Molecular formula	Structural formula	Displayed formula
methane	CH_4	CH_4	H | H—C—H | H
ethane	C_2H_6	CH_3CH_3	H H | | H—C—C—H | | H H
propane	C_3H_8	$CH_3CH_2CH_3$	H H H | | | H—C—C—C—H | | | H H H
butane	C_4H_{10}	$CH_3CH_2CH_2CH_3$	H H H H | | | | H—C—C—C—C—H | | | | H H H H
pentane	C_5H_{12}	$CH_3CH_2CH_2CH_2CH_3$	H H H H H | | | | | H—C—C—C—C—C—H | | | | | H H H H H
octane	C_8H_{18}	$CH_3CH_2CH_2CH_2CH_2CH_2CH_2CH_3$	H H H H H H H H | | | | | | | | H—C—C—C—C—C—C—C—C—H | | | | | | | | H H H H H H H H

...methane

Know more

Organic compound names follow patterns. Meth- means one; eth- means two; prop- means three; but- means four; pent- means five; oct- means eight. It's the number of carbon atoms. The ending -ane or -ene tells you whether it's an alkane or an alkene.

Know more

Butene is C_4H_8, pentene is C_5H_{10}. All alkenes have one double covalent bond between two of the carbon atoms. The rest are single covalent bonds.

Bottled gas used for gas barbecues is butane

Both petrol and LPG fuel are sold here

Think about

How can you work out the formula of an alkane? Crude oil has alkanes with up to 70 carbon atoms. What is the formula of an alkane with 20 carbon atoms?

Alkenes

Alkenes are another family of hydrocarbons. The first alkene has two carbon atoms joined with a double covalent bond, and four hydrogen atoms. It is ethene. Its molecular formula is C_2H_4. Its displayed formula is shown.

Ethene

The next alkene is propene. Propene also has a double covalent bond between two carbon atoms. Its molecular formula is C_3H_6. Its displayed formula is shown.

Propene

Using alkanes and alkenes

Alkanes are not very reactive. But they do make good fuels. Methane is the main gas in natural gas. Octane is one of the alkanes in petrol. We use propane and butane in bottled gas including Calor gas ('Camping Gaz') and in **LPG fuel**. Some cars use LPG fuel instead of petrol.

The alkene ethene is used in the petrochemical industry to make plastics such as poly(ethene) and other synthetic materials.

The government is backing LPG

Over 1400 filling stations around the UK sell LPG fuel. There are several reasons why people have LPG cars:

*   running costs are cut by up to 50%
*   there is 20% less carbon in the exhaust gases
*   the engine is quieter
*   we have plenty of LPG – we even export it
*   the road tax is lower
*   LPG has less government duty than petrol or diesel, so it is cheaper.

Structures

Displayed formulae are two-dimensional. They do not show the real shape of a molecule. Models like 'molymods' (shown below) show molecules in three dimensions.

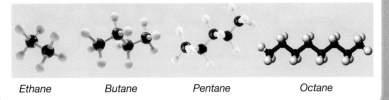

Ethane   Butane   Pentane   Octane

Useful organic molecules

Your assessment criteria:
1B.5 Identify uses of ethene, ethanol and ethanoic acid
2B.P5 Describe the uses of organic compounds in our society

Designer molecules

The chemicals from crude oil are useful starting points for making many different substances. It's a bit like building with Lego bricks. We choose the right molecules from the crude oil fractions, and then add to them or change them or link them together to give a substance with the properties we need. It's designer chemistry.

1B.5
2B.P5

Making plastics

Plastics have very long molecules. They are made by joining small molecules end to end. The small molecules are called **monomers**. The long plastic molecules are called **polymers**. Different monomers make different plastics.

Plastic bags are made from poly(ethene). Poly(ethene), also called polythene, is made from ethene. Ethene is the monomer. Ethene is a product of the petrochemical industry. High pressure and a catalyst are used to make the ethene molecules join up into the polymer molecules. This is called **polymerisation**.

Ethene is:

$$H_2C=CH_2$$

Poly(ethene) is:

$$\left[\begin{array}{cc} H & H \\ | & | \\ -C-C- \\ | & | \\ H & H \end{array} \right]_n$$

The *n* means the formula is repeated many times.

The double bond in ethene breaks open and joins with another ethene molecule. Poly(ethene) molecules can be 10 000 carbon atoms long. Poly(ethene) is an **addition polymer**.

Model of a poly(ethene) molecule

Know more

Ethene is also used to make the alcohol called ethanol. Water will react with ethene under the right reaction conditions. The equation is:

$$C_2H_4(g) + H_2O(g) \rightleftharpoons C_2H_5OH(g)$$

The reaction happens at 300 °C and 60 atmospheres with a catalyst.

Know more

Poly(ethene) was discovered by accident in 1933 when an experiment went wrong. Several explosions later, scientists realised they had made poly(ethene).

...uses of poly(ethene)

Know more

F is the group 7 (halogen) element fluorine. See Unit 2.

A slippery plastic

Teflon™ is a plastic made from the monomer tetrafluoroethene.

Tetrafluoroethene is:

$$\begin{array}{c} F \\ F \end{array}\!\!>\!C\!=\!C\!<\!\!\begin{array}{c} F \\ F \end{array}$$

When it polymerises, the polymer poly(tetrafluoroethene), or PTFE for short, trade name 'Teflon', is made.

Teflon is:

$$\left[\begin{array}{cc} \overset{F}{\underset{F}{|}} & \overset{F}{\underset{F}{|}} \\ -C & -C- \\ \end{array}\right]_n$$

The *n* means the formula is repeated many times.

The carbon–fluorine bonds in Teflon are very strong bonds. It makes Teflon very unreactive and slippery. In fact, Teflon has the lowest friction of any material we know. It is used to coat space suits because it protects astronauts from scrapes, it will not react with the environment and it is heat resistant. Teflon is also the non-stick coating on saucepans and frying pans.

Discuss

Teflon is also used to insulate electric cables in spacecraft. What property must it have to make it suitable for this?

Research

Teflon has many other uses. Research these.

Think about

Why is CH_2Cl_2 called dichloromethane?

And a paint stripper

Methane is CH_4 and one of the gases produced from crude oil. Chemists can swap the hydrogen atoms in methane for chlorine atoms. If two hydrogens are exchanged, the product is:

$$H-\overset{\overset{\textstyle H}{|}}{\underset{\underset{\textstyle Cl}{|}}{C}}-Cl$$

Discuss

Dichloromethane is toxic and thought to be carcinogenic. That means it causes cancer. What safety information should be printed on paint stripper containers?

Its molecular formula is CH_2Cl_2 and it is called dichloromethane. Dichloromethane does not dissolve in water, but it will dissolve many other things, including paint and varnish. It is the active chemical found in paint strippers.

...uses of Teflon

PVC and PVCu

A fashion statement

The fashion industry uses PVC fabric as a cheaper alternative to leather. It is made into clothes, bags, belts and shoes. PVC is a plastic. It can be bonded to cotton material or used on its own.

2B.P5

Making PVC

PVC stands for **p**oly**v**inyl**c**hloride. It is the old name for poly(chloroethene). The monomer used to make PVC is chloroethene.

Chloroethene is an organic compound made from crude oil. When it polymerises, the double bond breaks open and the monomers join up in a long chain.

chloroethene

PVC

The PVC made by polymerisation is hard and rigid. Technicians use **nanochemistry** to make the polymer flexible. Small molecules called **plasticisers** are added. These act as molecular ball bearings. They fit between the polymer chains and allow the long polymer chains to slide over each other. The PVC is now flexible and can be used as a leather substitute.

Cling film is also made from PVC. Plasticisers make the PVC flexible

We have many uses for PVC. Plastic window frames, guttering and drainpipes are just a few. The PVC used to make window frames needs to be rigid. It does not need plasticisers. This PVC is known as **PVCu** or unplasticised PVC.

Know more

Cl is the group 7 (halogen) element chlorine.

Know more

*PVCu is rigid because without plasticisers the long polymer chains attract each other. This **intermolecular force** holds the chains in place.*

Know more

uPVC, PVCu and PVC-U are the same thing. It was originally uPVC in the UK. The 'u' was moved to the end of the name to fit in with the rest of Europe.

...intermolecular forces

85% of all window frames are now made from PVCu

Think about

What other materials can be used to make window frames? Which is best?

Know more

The PVC industry is currently developing less harmful plasticisers.

Discuss

Car manufacturers often use PVC for car upholstery. What are the good and bad points about using PVC?

Research

Why are some plastic food wraps now made from poly(ethene) instead of PVC?

Why PVC and PVCu?

2B.D4

Builders choose PVCu windows, guttering and drainpipes because:

- it does not rot
- it resists weathering – it is not affected by rain, sun or frost
- it is tough
- it keeps its shape
- it can be reshaped at high temperatures.

We can use PVC to make cling film because:

- it is transparent
- it clings to many different surfaces
- it stretches
- it does not let food smells pass through.

But, some governments and environmental groups such as Greenpeace have concerns about PVC and PVCu.

- The raw materials used to make PVC come from crude oil. Crude oil is a finite resource.

- Making PVC produces harmful chemicals called **dioxins**. Dioxins dissolve in body fat and are difficult to excrete. They can harm several body organs and systems.

- The plasticisers in PVC can leak out and pose health risks. They are soluble in fats and oils, found in foods like cheese. Once inside our bodies, they can disrupt our endocrine system (the body system that produces hormones).

- PVC has been difficult to recycle in the past because of its high chlorine content. Since 2000, EU initiatives have improved the technology needed to recycle it, and increasingly less is sent to landfill.

- Burning PVC makes more dioxins.

PVC food wrap is often used for fresh produce

...Greenpeace

Ethanol

Your assessment criteria:

1B.5 Identify uses of ethene, ethanol and ethanoic acid

2B.P3 Draw accurately the structural and displayed formulae of organic molecules

2B.P5 Describe the uses of organic compounds in society

Brewing beer

We have been brewing beer in Europe for 5000 years. Today, it is a skilled job. The percentage of alcohol is carefully monitored. The alcohol in beer is ethanol. It is made by fermenting sugar from barley. Hops may be added to give a bitter flavour.

Fermentation tanks at a brewery

Know more

Beer contains between 3% and 5% ethanol, depending on the type. Wine contains between 9% and 14% ethanol. Spirits like vodka contain up to 40% ethanol.

1B.5
2B.P3

The alcohol family

Alcohols are a family of organic compounds. **Ethanol** is just one example.

Alcohols contain carbon, hydrogen and oxygen. A molecule of ethanol has two carbon atoms, six hydrogen atoms and one oxygen atom. Its molecular formula is C_2H_5OH.
The displayed formula is:

Ethanol

The structural formula of ethanol is CH_3CH_2OH.

All alcohols contain an oxygen atom bonded to a hydrogen atom. It is called the **OH group**.

Know more

*The letters 'eth' tell us there are two carbon atoms.
'ol' is the ending used for alcohols.*

Know more

*There are many alcohols. Methanol is CH_3OH.
Propan-1-ol is C_3H_7OH.*

...fermentation

Making ethanol

The first step in brewing is changing the starch in barley to sugar. Yeast is then used to ferment the sugar. Yeast is a single-celled living organism. It uses the sugar as food. It produces ethanol and carbon dioxide. This is called fermentation. The carbon dioxide gas bubbles off and the ethanol stays in the mixture.

Fermentation in brewing

Ethanol in cosmetics

Ethanol is a colourless liquid that boils at 78 °C. It has many uses in cosmetics.

- It is used in acne treatments because it is antibacterial.
- It is used to dissolve other ingredients.
- It is used in skin toners and aftershave. It evaporates quickly so the skin feels cool.

An important property of alcohols

Alcohols burn in oxygen. They are flammable. The reaction is:

$$C_2H_5OH + 3O_2 \rightarrow 2CO_2 + 3H_2O$$

This is an exothermic reaction: heat is given out. Alcohols make good fuels.

Know more

Ethanol has many other uses in industry. Like alkanes and alkenes, it is used as a starting point in making many other chemicals. It is also used as a solvent. This means that like water it is used to dissolve other chemicals.

Discuss

Ordinary petrol-fuelled cars in the UK can run on 5% blends of ethanol. Targets are in place for all motor fuel in the UK to contain 5% biofuel by 2014. We make bioethanol from sugar beet in the UK. Should the government encourage greater use of bioethanol?

Uses of ethanol

Replacing petrol

Ethanol can be used to replace petrol in vehicles. It reduces our dependence on crude oil. The US and Brazil grow lots of corn and sugar cane. They ferment some of it to make the **biofuel** ethanol, often called **bioethanol**. The ethanol is mixed with petrol.

Running cars from plants

Bioethanol is a **renewable** source of energy. It is made from plants and we can grow more plants.

Sugar cane is used to make biofuel

2B.P5

Carbon dioxide is used when plants photosynthesise. It is released when the ethanol fuel is burnt. It balances out. Making bioethanol is a sustainable industry.

carbon dioxide, water, sunlight → (photosynthesis) → sugar in plants → (fermentation) → ethanol → (combustion in cars) → carbon dioxide, water, energy

There is a drawback. Huge areas of land are needed to grow plants for bioethanol. We also need this land to grow food.

...bioethanol

Ethanoic acid

Your assessment criteria:

1B.5 Identify uses of ethene, ethanol and ethanoic acid.

2B.P3 Draw accurately the structural and displayed formulae of organic molecules

2B.P5 Describe the uses of organic compounds in society

2B.M5 Explain the problems associated with the use of organic molecules

The sweet shop

A confectioner makes sweets of many different flavours. Fruity flavours come from chemicals called esters. Esters occur naturally in fruits and flowers. Synthetic esters can be made in a laboratory. Scientists can make esters that smell and taste like bananas or strawberries, or any other fruit flavour.

1B.5 2B.P3

Organic acids

The **esters** that give us fruity flavours are all made from an alcohol and an **organic acid**. The organic acid called ethanoic acid is used to make pear and banana flavours.

Ethanoic acid:

- is a **carboxylic acid** (this is the chemical family)
- has the molecular formula CH_3COOH
- has the displayed formula:

$$H-\overset{\displaystyle H}{\underset{\displaystyle H}{C}}-C\overset{\displaystyle O}{\underset{\displaystyle O-H}{}}$$

Ethanoic acid

All carboxylic acids include the COOH group:

$$-C\overset{\displaystyle O}{\underset{\displaystyle O-H}{}}$$

This is the **carboxylic acid group**.

2B.P5

Uses of ethanoic acid

Making esters

The general equation for making an ester is:

alcohol + carboxylic acid ⟶ ester + water

A few drops of sulfuric acid are needed as a catalyst.

Know more

Ethanoic acid is corrosive.

Think about

What is the structural formula for ethanoic acid?

Know more

Methanoic acid is HCOOH. Ant stings are itchy because they inject you with methanoic acid.

🔍...artificial flavours

Food scientists make different esters by using different alcohols and acids. They all result in different flavours. The table shows the reactants needed to produce two particular esters.

Alcohol	Acid	Ester	Smell
ethanol	ethanoic acid	ethyl ethanoate	pear
butanol	ethanoic acid	butyl ethanoate	blueberry/banana

Esters are also used in perfumes. They give the fruity or flowery smells. The ester must evaporate easily, that is be **volatile**. Then enough particles reach your nose for you to detect the smell. Expensive perfumes may have natural esters such as in rose oil or sandalwood. Synthetic esters are used in cheaper perfumes, including those used in bath products, room sprays, perfumed fabric fresheners and polishes.

Vinegar

We have been using a dilute solution of ethanoic acid for centuries. It is vinegar. Vinegar is made when certain bacteria mix with wine, beer or cider. The bacteria make the ethanol react with oxygen and this makes ethanoic acid. It happens naturally when wine or beer goes off.

We add vinegar to our food. We use it in cooking. We use it to preserve food like pickles. The old name for ethanoic acid is acetic acid. You will still find this name used on the ingredients lists of some foods.

Onions pickled in vinegar

Production of ester-based perfumes is big business

Think about

Ethanoic acid behaves like other acids. How would you expect it to react with:

* *universal indicator solution*
* *an alkali*
* *a metal*
* *a carbonate?*

The good and the bad

If the food label says **flavouring**, you may be eating esters made in a laboratory. If the food label says **natural flavouring**, the flavouring was made by nature. It's the same chemical, just made in different ways. Artificial flavourings do not need E-numbers. Many doctors are worried that artificial flavourings cause hyperactivity and allergies in children.

Nutritional food label

Discuss

Artificial flavours do not have to be listed separately on ingredients lists. Sweets and soft drinks can contain many flavours. Should they be listed? Should artificial flavourings have E-numbers?

...vinegar

Identifying organic molecules

Drug testing

The International Olympic Committee aims for all athletes to be drug free. They have a long list of banned substances. Urine samples from Olympic competitors are routinely checked for these performance-enhancing drugs. Scientists carry out a series of reliable tests that will identify the drugs.

Your assessment criteria:

1B.4 Identify an alkene and an alkane using primary observations

2B.P4 Identify an alkene and a carboxylic acid using primary observations

2B.M4 Explain how a series of experiments can be used to identify organic compounds based on their solubility and reactions

2B.D3 Explain the results of experiments to identify organic compounds in terms of their reaction type, structural and displayed formulae, and bonding

1B.4
2B.P4

Laboratory tests

Performance-enhancing drugs are organic compounds. The Olympic scientists use electronic equipment to test urine samples. We can carry out simpler test-tube reactions to identify some organic compounds.

Identifying an alkene

Ethene gas is an alkene. If ethene is bubbled through orange bromine water, the solution turns colourless. This is the test for an alkene. All alkenes decolorise bromine water, but alkanes do not.

Identifying an alcohol

Ethanol is an alcohol. Acidified potassium dichromate(VI) solution is orange. When it is added to ethanol and shaken, the colour changes to green. This confirms the presence of an alcohol such as ethanol.

Identifying a carboxylic acid

Ethanoic acid is a carboxylic acid. All acids have some common properties, including reacting with carbonates to produce carbon dioxide gas. If dilute ethanoic acid is added to sodium carbonate or its solution, carbon dioxide gas is given off, which turns lime water milky.

There is effervescence (fizzing) when dilute ethanoic acid is added to sodium carbonate

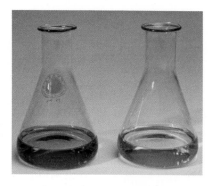

The flask on the left contains bromine water. Ethene gas has been bubbled through the flask on the right

The test tube on the left is potassium dichromate(VI) solution. The test tube on the right shows the positive test for ethanol

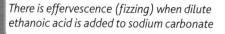
...drug testing

Think about

What makes a good chemical test?

Is it an alkane, alkene, ethanol or ethanoic acid?

2B.M4

Scientists work through a series of tests to identify unknown compounds, including testing their solubility in water. You can follow the diagram to find the identity of an unknown colourless liquid.

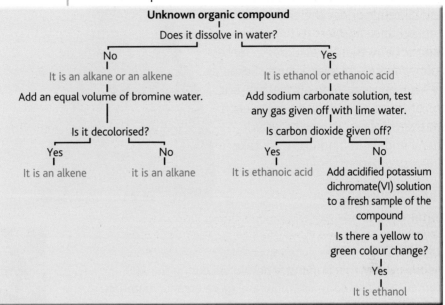

Unknown organic compound

Does it dissolve in water?

No — It is an alkane or an alkene — Add an equal volume of bromine water. — Is it decolorised?
- **Yes** — It is an alkene
- **No** — it is an alkane

Yes — It is ethanol or ethanoic acid — Add sodium carbonate solution, test any gas given off with lime water. — Is carbon dioxide given off?
- **Yes** — It is ethanoic acid
- **No** — Add acidified potassium dichromate(VI) solution to a fresh sample of the compound — Is there a yellow to green colour change? — **Yes** — It is ethanol

Think about

Why is there no colour change when methane is bubbled through bromine water?

2B.D3

All the compounds in a family of organic chemicals have the same **functional group**. All alkenes have a double bond, alcohols have an OH group and carboxylic acids have a COOH group. The functional groups are the reactive part of a compound, so all the compounds in a family have similar chemical reactions.

Alkenes (e.g. ethene)	Ethanol	Ethanoic acid
The double bond breaks and makes new bonds with the bromine atoms in bromine water.	Acidified potassium dichromate(VI) is an oxidising agent. When added to ethanol, it **oxidises** it to ethanoic acid. $CH_3CH_2OH + 2[O] \rightarrow CH_3COOH + H_2O$	This hydrogen atom makes the compound an acid because it can form a hydrogen ion.
This is dibromoethane. It is colourless.	*This is the oxygen from the oxidising agent.*	The reaction with sodium carbonate is: $2CH_3COOH + Na_2CO_3 \rightarrow 2CH_3COONa + H_2O + CO_2$
This type of reaction is called an **addition reaction**.	The potassium dichromate(VI) is changed and the new compound is green. This is an **oxidation reaction**.	This is a **neutralisation reaction**.

Organic problems

Your assessment criteria:

2B.M5 Explain the problems associated with the use of organic molecules

2B.D4 Evaluate the benefits and drawbacks of using organic materials

The disappearing plastic bag

At some supermarkets, cashiers hide their plastic bags under the checkout. They encourage shoppers to bring their own bags or buy their 'green' bags. Some shops now charge for plastic bags. Some towns have banned them altogether. But billions of them are still given away each year in the UK. They can be recycled, but many end up in landfills. They take 1000 years to decompose.

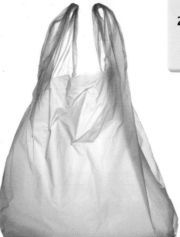

2B.M5

Plastic problems

As the petrochemical industry developed during the 20th century, we started to use more and more organic materials. But using organic molecules has brought problems, too.

*   ***Risk of fire.*** Alkanes, alkenes, alcohols and many other organic compounds are **flammable**. That means they easily burn. Since many alkanes, alkenes and alcohols are liquids at room temperature, the burning liquid can flow and spread the flames. This is a big fire hazard and flammable organic compounds must be stored and used safely.

*   ***Products of combustion.*** If there is enough oxygen present, the products will include carbon dioxide and water.

    For example, $C_5H_{12}(l) + 8O_2(g) \rightarrow 5CO_2(g) + 6H_2O(l)$

    Carbon dioxide is a greenhouse gas.

    If there is not enough oxygen present, carbon monoxide may be a product.

    For example, $2C_5H_{12}(l) + 11O_2(g) \rightarrow 10CO(g) + 12H_2O(l)$

    Carbon monoxide is very toxic and causes unconsciousness followed by death.

    Combustion also produces other toxins, such as dioxins (see page 167) and heavy metals. Many of the fatalities from domestic fires are due to inhaling fumes from burning plastics.

A flammable organic liquid is burning and spreading the fire

Know more

*If sufficient oxygen is present to produce carbon dioxide and water, it is called **complete combustion**. If insufficient oxygen is present and carbon monoxide forms, it is called **incomplete combustion**.*

🔍 ...PVC plastic

2B.M5

2B.D4

Know more

A composite material contains two or more materials moulded together.

- **Disposal.** Recycling plastics is expensive because they are difficult to sort. Many still end up in landfill sites where they are estimated to take up to 1000 years to decompose. Most plastics are **non-biodegradable** which means they are not easily broken down by water, air or microbes. Discarded plastic becomes an eyesore and a threat to wildlife.

  Some plastic waste is disposed of by incineration (large-scale burning in special containers). The problem of burning most plastics is that the combustion products are toxic.

  The good news is that some waste plastic is now being used to make a wood–plastic composite board which can be used as a building material.

The tall smoke stack on an incinerator used to burn plastic waste takes any toxic waste high into the atmosphere

Think about

Do the benefits of poly(ethene) outweigh its disadvantages when we use it to make supermarket plastic bags? What are the alternatives?

Think about

Cornish farmers cover their early potato crops with poly(ethene) sheets. The extra warmth produces new potatoes earlier in the season and farmers make more money from their crop. The poly(ethene) sheets cannot be reused and have to be disposed of. Is this a good use of poly(ethene)?

Amazing poly(ethene) or not?

Poly(ethene) is a cheap, light and strong plastic. Its strong chemical bonds make it chemically resistant and it does not decompose easily. It can be moulded, dyed any colour and is a good thermal and electrical insulator. That's why we use it to make many items from poly(ethene) bags to polytunnels for crops.

Poly(ethene) is one of the few plastics that does not have toxic combustion products. Since it contains carbon and hydrogen only, the products on burning are carbon dioxide and water only. Waste poly(ethene) can be processed into blocks and used as fuel. The energy produced when they burn can be used to produce electricity in power stations and in other industries. However, the carbon dioxide given off is a greenhouse gas.

Poly(ethene) is made from crude oil, a finite resource that will run out one day. Discarded poly(ethene), like most other plastics, does not decompose in the environment.

Think about

Discarded small plastic pellets, formed during plastic manufacture, are often mistaken for food by marine life. What effect do you think this has?

Most of this rubbish washed up along the Thames estuary is plastic; some of it is poly(ethene)

Nanochemistry

Green rocket fuel

One big problem with space travel is getting off the ground. Space technicians are developing a new rocket fuel. It is a mixture of 'nanoscale' aluminium powder and ice. It doesn't work with ordinary aluminium powder. The particles are too big. Nanoscale aluminium has very small particles. They react explosively with water. The products are less polluting than ordinary rocket fuel.

1C.6
2C.P6

How small?

We use kilometres, metres, centimetres and millimetres to measure everyday sizes. **Nanometres** are used to measure very small things. One nanometre (1 nm) is one billionth of a metre. The smallest bacteria we know are 200 nm long. A gold atom is 0.28 nm across.

Sizewise, a nanometre to a metre is like a marble to the Earth.

Size	How many metres?
kilometre (km)	1000
metre (m)	1
centimetre (cm)	0.01
millimetre (mm)	0.001
nanometre (nm)	0.000 000 001

Chemistry usually works on a large scale. But nanochemistry is about making individual atoms and molecules work for us. It is chemistry on the **nanoscale**. Nanochemistry is different to ordinary chemistry. This is because single atoms and molecules have different properties to bulk substances.

Know more

We could measure very small things in metres. But the numbers get difficult to handle. A gold atom is 0.000 000 000 28 m across.

Know more

Nanochemistry couldn't be studied until we had a microscope powerful enough to see single atoms.

...carbon nanotubes

The buckyball 'buckminsterfullerene'

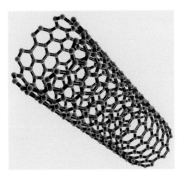

A carbon nanotube

Useful nanostructures

1C.6
2C.P6

Shape is important in nanochemistry. We used to think carbon could be either diamond or graphite. Then **fullerenes** were discovered. These are different structures of carbon atoms. Two fullerenes used in nanochemistry are **buckyballs** and **nanotubes**.

Fullerene	Shape
buckyball	hollow, spherical (ball-like)
carbon nanotube	hollow, cylindrical (tube-like)

The first buckyball discovered was buckminsterfullerene, C_{60}. It has 60 carbon atoms covalently bonded in a football pattern. It is 0.7 nm across. Other buckyballs have been discovered.

Carbon nanotubes have many formulae. Their diameters are measured in nanometres, but they can be up to several millimetres long. Carbon nanotubes are very strong. They are good conductors of electricity and heat.

Producing nanotubes

2C.P6

The best nanotubes are made by **arc-discharge**. Two graphite (carbon) electrodes are placed close together in an atmosphere of helium gas in a special container. A current of 50 amps passes, there is a spark and the anode vaporises. Black carbon powder covers the apparatus, but the carbon on the cathode contains nanotubes.

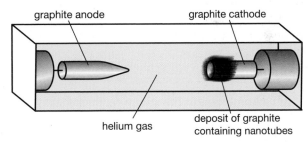

graphite anode   graphite cathode

helium gas   deposit of graphite containing nanotubes

The way ahead

Discovering buckyballs and carbon nanotubes was very exciting, but scientists wanted to find uses for them. Some suggested uses were:

- Drugs could be put inside nanotubes. This would enable a cancer drug to be delivered straight to a tumour.

- Carbon nanowires, just a few nanometres wide, could enable the production of nanoscale electronic circuits.

- Buckyballs or nanotubes could act as molecular ball bearings.

This is nanochemistry.

Research

Nanotubes have many other possible uses. Find out about some of these.

Think about

Explain the meanings of these words:
nanochemistry   nanoscale
nanostructure   nanometre
nanotubes

Using nanochemistry

Your assessment criteria:

2C.M6 Explain the benefits of using nanochemicals, smart and specialised materials

2C.D5 Evaluate the benefits and drawbacks of using nanochemicals, smart and specialised materials

Smelly socks

A mixture of sweat and bacteria can make your socks smell. Anti-odour socks are treated with nanosilver. The tiny silver particles penetrate the fibres and stop bacteria forming. Your feet may sweat, but your socks will stay fresh. Nanosilver is also being used in shirts and sportswear to keep them odour free.

2C.M6

Everyday nanoparticles

Many cosmetics and other everyday items now contain **nanoparticles** (nanoscale particles).

Sun creams

Ultraviolet (UV) light burns your skin. Most sun creams contain titanium(IV) oxide and zinc oxide. These reflect the harmful UV light. They also make a thick, white, greasy layer on your skin. But in some sun creams, the titanium(IV) oxide and zinc oxide are ground to nanoparticles. The 'cream' now appears transparent, but still works.

Mascara

There are many different carbon buckyballs. Their colours range from yellow/orange to brown and black. It all depends on the number of carbon atoms in the structure. Buckyballs make good mascara colours. No extra dye is needed. They easily roll on the eye lashes and are very soft to touch.

Buckyball mascara needs no dye

Know more

Nanoparticles of copper are being used in some self-tanning lotions. They penetrate the skin and your tan lasts longer.

...anti-odour socks

Textiles

Nanoparticles can be used to treat fabrics, to make them:

- antibacterial
- stain resistant
- wrinkle resistant
- flame retardant
- waterproof
- resistant to UV light.

In fact, almost any property you need can be created, even colour. Carbon nanotubes can be spun into fibres. Different thicknesses of nanotubes have different colours. The fibres do not need to be dyed. You just choose the right thickness of nanotubes.

Sports equipment

Nanochemistry has improved sports equipment. Golf clubs can have nanoscale metal coatings to make them stronger. Golf balls can also have nanoscale coatings to make them go straighter. Tennis rackets with nanoparticles of silicon(IV) oxide have more power. Carbon nanotubes make badminton rackets, ice hockey sticks and baseball bats lightweight and very hardwearing.

Processors

Computers store information on silicon microchips. Computer designers are using nanochemistry to design smaller and more powerful processors. They can grow **nanowires** directly on silicon crystals and use them to link components in extremely small circuits. The nanowires allow several layers of silicon to be built up, possibly resulting in a 3D microchip.

The performance of sports equipment can be improved with nanochemistry

Research

A battery with silicon nanowires would last ten times longer in your mobile before it needed recharging. Find out more about nanobatteries.

Discuss

Ordinary silver has been tested and is safe to use. Nanosilver has different properties. What tests should all nanomaterials have? What regulations do we need?

The concerns

Safety checks on nanomaterials are not yet regulated. Nanoparticles are small enough to penetrate your skin, and they can move round your body. Health workers are concerned. They do not know what the effects are.

Nanosilver is slowly washed out of clothes. It kills twice as many bacteria as bleach. The water authorities are concerned it could stop bacterial breakdown in sewage treatment.

Bacteria break down sewage into harmless products. Nanoparticles could affect this action

...sun creams and nanochemistry

Smart materials

Smart sunglasses

Photochromic lenses in glasses and sunglasses darken as the Sun gets brighter. When the Sun dims or you go indoors, the lenses become clear. Photochromic lenses are smart materials.

2C.P6

What are smart materials?

Smart materials change with a stimulus. The stimulus must be a change in the environment, like light, temperature, stress or pressure. In **photochromic** lenses, the stimulus is UV light. The change is the amount of visible light that is let through. The change is **reversible**. The lenses can go darker, then lighter again as the light changes.

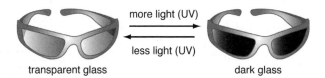

more light (UV) →
← less light (UV)

transparent glass   dark glass

There are other types of smart materials.

In **thermochromic** materials, the stimulus is heat. The change is their colour. The colour change happens at a definite temperature. The change is reversible. Thermochromic substances can be added to dyes, paint, paper and inks.

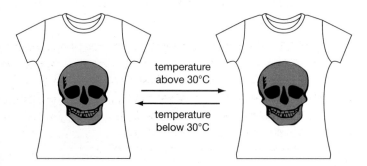

temperature above 30°C →
← temperature below 30°C

Thermochromic dyes in T-shirts change colour at about 30 °C. When you first put the T-shirt on, its temperature is below this. The T-shirt warms up with your body heat and its colour changes when it gets over 30 °C

Know more

Thermochromic dyes in the plastic of babies' bottles can show when the milk is cool enough for the baby to drink.

Thermochromic dyes in toothbrushes can be designed to change colour after two minutes in the hand. Your teeth should be clean by then.

🔍 ...transition sunglasses

Piezoelectric materials produce a voltage when they are under stress. This means that squeezing a piezoelectric material and changing its shape makes electricity. The change is reversible: a small voltage across a piezoelectric material changes its shape.

Piezoelectric materials are used in microphones on electric acoustic guitars. They are found under the bridge. They pick up the vibrations from the strings and produce a voltage. The voltage is detected and you hear the music through an amplifier.

2C.P6

Producing photochromic lenses

2C.M6

Lenses in sunglasses are plastic. To make them photochromic, they are dipped in either silver chloride solution or silver bromide solution. The lenses absorb some of the silver compounds. When these silver compounds are exposed to UV light, they change shape. This causes them to absorb some of the visible and UV light falling on them.

UV light is normally only found outside, in sunshine. So photochromic lenses darken outside and protect the wearer from the sun's glare.

Think about

Car windscreens do not let UV light pass though. How useful are photochromic glasses for driving?

Can you suggest other uses for photochromic substances?

Think about

What environmental considerations do manufacturers of smart materials need to take?

Benefits and drawbacks

2C.D5

Many new smart materials are emerging from laboratories. They are providing opportunities to develop new technology such as artificial muscles, and sensors in bridges to detect weaknesses. Their properties are far superior to their 'dumb' equivalents. The main drawback is cost. Manufacturing processes are more complicated and this raises the market price. The manufacturing cost of photochromic lenses is 20 times that of normal plastic lenses.

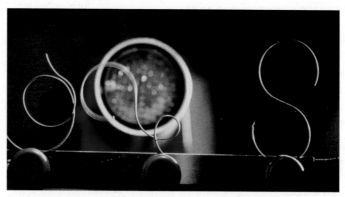

The shape memory nickel/titanium alloy is reverting to an S shape as it is heated. Memory alloys are used in medical devices, including dental braces

Discuss

If you could use nanochemistry to design a new smart material, what properties would it have?

🔍 ... artificial muscles

Specialised materials

A futuristic film set

A futuristic film must use state-of-the-art materials in its props. Costumes must be made from the newest materials with special properties.

Your assessment criteria:

2C.P6 Describe a use of nanochemicals, smart and specialised materials

2C.M6 Explain the benefits of using nanochemicals, smart and specialised materials

2C.D5 Evaluate the benefits and drawbacks of nanochemicals, smart and specialised materials

2C.P6

State-of-the-art materials

Wool, cotton and silk are natural fibres. We make use of their natural properties when we make materials from them.

We can design synthetic polymers with almost any special properties we want.

Gore-Tex™

Raincoats can be made from nylon. Nylon is lightweight, tough and keeps the rain out. But it also keeps your sweat in. Water vapour from sweat makes you cold and wet inside the raincoat.

Gore-Tex™ material keeps you dry inside and out. It lets your sweat pass through and keeps the rain out. It has all the properties of nylon, but is breathable as well.

Thinsulate™

Thinsulate™ provides warmth without bulk. Its name is made from the words **thin** and **insulate**. Its polymer fibres are thinner than other insulating materials such as wool. They tangle and trap air. Air is a poor conductor of heat, so you do not lose body heat. The gaps between the fibres also let water vapour from sweat out. You keep dry and warm.

> ### Know more
>
> Lycra™ is 80% polyurethane. It is lightweight, stretchy and used to make sportswear.

Head-hugging and stylish, but also very warm

...Gore-Tex ...Thinsulate

2C.P6

Kevlar™

Kevlar™ is a very strong polymer. It is five times stronger than steel. It owes its strength to its chemical structure and how it is woven. The polymer is made and spun into ropes or fibres. Each fibre is made of millions of layers, each one molecule thick. The fibres can then be woven into material. It is used in bullet-proof clothing. The fibre layers can absorb the energy from a bullet or a stab from a knife.

Kevlar™ has many other uses: to strengthen tyres, to make cables for suspension bridges, sailboard sails, canoes and protective clothing.

Know more

New materials used in swimsuits mimic shark skin. Polyurethane sections are water repellent and reduce drag.

2C.M6

How does Gore-Tex™ work?

Gore-Tex™ material has at least three layers. The middle layer is Teflon™. It has small pores – over 1 billion per square centimetre. These are big enough to let water vapour molecules through. Your sweat escapes. Water drops from rain are too big to pass the other way. You keep dry.

Think about

What other uses for Gore-Tex™ can you think of?

Research

Why is titanium dioxide a specialised material?

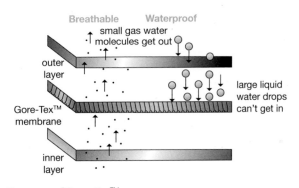

Structure of Gore-Tex™

2C.D5

Benefits and drawbacks

Gore-Tex™ is used to make clothing for industry, the military, fire and safety personnel and the police. When Gore-Tex™ is treated with carbon nanoparticles it can be used to make fire fighters' jackets. The nanoparticles make it antistatic. This means it cannot spark a fire in dangerous conditions. So fire fighters can wear it in buildings where gas may be escaping. The drawback of this protective clothing is cost. Extra manufacturing processes and treatments make Gore-Tex™ clothing more expensive than normal working jackets.

Discuss

What are the advantages and drawbacks of using Gore-Tex™ outdoor gear such as walking boots and jackets?

🔍 ... Gore-Tex membrane

Assessment Checklist

To achieve a Pass grade, my portfolio of evidence must show that I can:

Assessment Criteria	Description	✓
2A.P1	Investigate temperature changes associated with exothermic and endothermic reactions using primary data	
2B.P2	Describe the fractional distillation of crude oil to produce a range of useful products	
2B.P3	Draw accurately the structural and displayed formulae of organic molecules	
2B.P4	Identify an alkene and a carboxylic acid using primary observations	
2B.P5	Describe the uses of organic compounds in our society	
2C.P6	Describe a use of nanochemicals, smart and specialised materials	

If you do not meet all the Level 2 Pass criteria for this Unit then your work will be assessed against these Level 1 criteria. If your work meets all these criteria you will achieve a Level 1 Pass for this Unit. If you do not achieve all these Level 1 criteria you will get a U (Unclassified) for this Unit.

Assessment Criteria	Description	✓
1A.1	Measure the temperature changes associated with chemical reactions	
1B.2	Identify the uses of the main fractions from the distillation of crude oil	
1B.3	Name alkanes and alkenes from structural and displayed formulae	
1B.4	Identify an alkene and an alkane using primary observations	
1B.5	Identify uses of ethene, ethanol and ethanoic acid	
1C.6	Define nanochemicals	

To achieve a Merit grade, my portfolio of evidence must also show that I can:

Assessment Criteria	Description	✓
2A.M1	Explain why an overall reaction is exothermic or endothermic	
2B.M2	Explain how fractional distillation separates compounds due to different boiling ranges	
2B.M3	Describe the structure and bonding of organic molecules	
2B.M4	Explain how a series of experiments can be used to identify organic compounds based on their solubility and reactions	
2B.M5	Explain the problems associated with the use of organic molecules	
2C.M6	Explain the benefits of using nanochemicals, smart and specialised materials	

To achieve a Distinction grade, my portfolio of evidence must also show that I can:

Assessment Criteria	Description	✓
2A.D1	Calculate the energy changes that take place during exothermic and endothermic reactions	
2B.D2	Analyse the relationship between the boiling range and the length of carbon chain of fractions	
2B.D3	Explain the results of experiments to identify organic compounds in terms of their reaction type, structural and displayed formulae, and bonding	
2B.D4	Evaluate the benefits and drawbacks of using organic materials	
2C.D5	Evaluate the benefits and drawbacks of using nanochemicals, smart and specialised materials	

Unit 6 Applications of Physical Science

Be able to investigate motion

- If all goes to plan, by 2013 *Bloodhound SSC* will be the fastest car in the world, travelling faster than 1000 mph along a desert track in South Africa. *Thrust SSC* is the current record holder – it travelled faster than the speed of sound (330 m/s) in 1997

- The space shuttle flew at 17 500 miles per hour to remain in orbit at about 200 miles above the Earth's surface

- If a car crashes at 45 miles per hour (70 km/h), 1 in 10 drivers die; if the car crashes at 55 miles per hour (90 km/h), 8 in 10 drivers die

Be able to investigate forces

- Satellites orbit the Earth above the atmosphere so there are no drag forces; they do not need to burn fuel to stay moving in their orbit

- Formula 1 cars decelerate 60 times quicker than trains, and stop in one-sixtieth of the distance if they travel at the same speed at the start

Be able to investigate light and sound waves

- The mosquito noise is an irritating high-pitched sound that can only be heard by young people; some use it as a silent ring tone on their mobiles; some shopkeepers play it to deter young people from gathering near their shops

- Lasers produce very intense beams of light; their uses include tattoo removal, CD players, barcode scanning, pointers, medical operations, and very precise industrial cutting

- The use of lasers must be controlled as they can burn human tissue

Be able to investigate electricity

- The first human life saved using a heart defibrillator was in 1947; modern portable defibrillators can check whether the patient needs an electric shock, as well as deciding what type of shock is needed and giving instructions to the user

- Many electrical sensors are used in intensive care wards; they can check a patient's oxygen levels, internal fluid pressure and heart activity, as well as carrying out tasks like breathing for the patient and keeping them at a constant temperature

Measuring motion

Your assessment criteria:

1A.2 Measure distance for simple experiments

2A.P2 Calculate speed and velocity for simple experiments

1A.1 Produce accurate graphs to represent uniform motion using primary data

2A.P1 Produce accurate graphs to represent uniform and non-uniform motion using primary data

2A.M1 Interpret graphs to identify objects that are stationary, moving at a constant speed and moving with increasing or decreasing speed

2A.D1 Calculate the gradient for distance–time graphs and the gradient and area of speed–time graphs

Speeding

If a car is travelling fast, the driver has less time to react if a person steps into the road or a car pulls out. Speed cameras detect motorists who are travelling over the speed limit. People caught speeding are fined and may receive penalty points on their license.

1A.2
2A.P2

Measuring motion

Distance travelled is usually measured in metres (m) using a ruler or measuring tape.

Time is usually measured in seconds (s) using a stopclock.

The **speed** of an object measures how fast it travels, in metres per second (m/s), or sometimes in kilometres per hour (km/h). Trains can travel at about 190 km per hour; people walk at about 6 km per hour.

Speed is calculated using:
speed = distance ÷ time

A car's speedometer shows the speed of the car at a particular point in time; the speed changes during a journey

Traffic speed cameras take two photographs, half a second apart. The photographs show lines on the road and the car's change in position in that half second.

We can also measure average speed over a whole journey:
average speed = total distance travelled ÷ total time taken

If a train takes 3 hours to travel 300 km between two cities, its **average speed** is 100 km/h. Although it has a top speed of nearly 200 km/h, the train spends some of the journey time stopped at stations.

Displacement is the distance moved in a certain direction. If the train travels north for the whole journey, its displacement is 300 km north. If it zig-zags between the two cities so that the total distance covered is 450 km, the final displacement is still 300 km north.

Velocity measures how fast something travels in a certain direction. Velocity is calculated using:
velocity = displacement ÷ time
The train's average velocity is 100 km/h north.

Know more

In the UK, road signs show distances in miles and speed limits in miles per hour (mph). 30 miles per hour is about the same as 50 km per hour (50 km/h).

Know more

To calculate the distance travelled or displacement, use:
distance = speed × time
displacement = velocity × time

🔍...distance–time graph

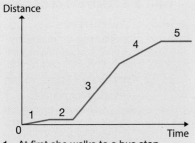

1   At first she walks to a bus stop.
2   Then she waits for a bus.
3   The bus travels quickly at first.
4   The bus slows down.
5   The bus stops.

A distance–time graph

Motion graphs

A **distance–time graph** is a plot of the distance travelled against the time taken for a journey. The slope (gradient) of the graph tells us how fast the moving object travels at any point.

- A shallow slope shows slow speed.
- A steep slope shows fast speed.
- A flat line shows the object is not moving.
- If the object moves backwards, the line slopes downwards.

The distance–time graph on the left shows a girl's journey to school. Each section of the graph has a different slope because she travels at a different speed at different times.

Acceleration measures how quickly the velocity (speed) of an object changes:

acceleration = change in velocity ÷ time taken

If the speed is in metres per second, m/s, the acceleration is in m/s per second, which is written m/s^2.

A **velocity–time graph** plots the velocity of a moving object at all times during a journey. Its slope shows acceleration.

- A shallow slope shows slow changes in speed (low acceleration).
- A steep slope shows fast changes in speed (high acceleration).
- A flat line shows a steady speed – no acceleration.
- If the object slows down, the line slopes downwards.

1A.1
2A.P1
2A.M1

Think about

What would a velocity–time graph look like for your journey to school?

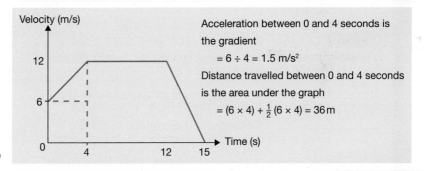

Acceleration between 0 and 4 seconds is the gradient

= 6 ÷ 4 = 1.5 m/s²

Distance travelled between 0 and 4 seconds is the area under the graph

$= (6 \times 4) + \frac{1}{2}(6 \times 4) = 36\,m$

A velocity–time graph

Think about

In factories, it is necessary to monitor the speed of the production line. How could this be done?

Calculations using motion graphs

2A.D1

- Speed is shown by the gradient of a distance–time graph. The gradient is calculated using:
  change in distance ÷ change in time

- Acceleration is shown by the gradient of a velocity–time graph. The gradient is calculated using:
  change in speed ÷ change in time

- The distance travelled is shown by the area under a velocity–time graph. It can be easier to divide the area into several smaller areas to calculate this.

🔍 ...velocity–time graph

Energy transformations

Energy and sport

You're at a large sporting event. The spectators jump to their feet as the players run and shout, and the sound system blasts out a loud announcement. Lots of different types of energy are involved.

Your assessment criteria:

1A.3 Draw energy transformation diagrams for simple experiments

2A.P3 Describe the conservation of energy for simple experiments, including energy transformation diagrams

2A.D2 Explain how changes in energy will affect transportation and stopping distances

1A.3
2A.P3

Energy transformation and conservation

When anything happens, energy is transferred from an energy store to its surroundings. A car engine transfers chemical energy from fuel to kinetic energy in the engine. This can be shown on an energy transformation diagram:

chemical energy ➜ kinetic energy

In all energy transfers, no energy is lost or created. This is the **law of energy conservation**. All forms of energy involved in the transfer must be shown. The car engine also produces unwanted heat and sound energy (to the surroundings) so the complete diagram looks like this:

chemical energy ➜ kinetic energy + heat energy + sound energy

Some transfers happen in more than one stage. The battery in a radio changes chemical energy to electrical energy and unwanted heat energy. The radio changes electrical energy into sound energy and unwanted heat energy. At each stage, all the energy is accounted for.

In the battery: chemical energy ➜ electrical energy + heat energy

In the radio: electrical energy ➜ sound energy + heat energy

Know more

*Energy is measured in **joules** (J). You use about one joule of energy picking up a football.*

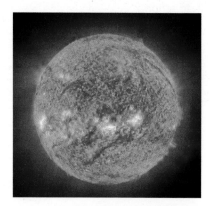

Nuclear reactions in the Sun provide all our energy on Earth

Know more

Several types of energy can be involved. An exploding firework gives out heat, light and sound, as well as particles with kinetic and potential energy.

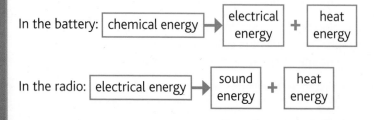

🔍...types of energy

Sankey diagrams show the types of energy involved *and* their relative amounts. The width of each part of the arrow indicates the amount of energy involved.

This Sankey diagram is for a car engine. The energy input is from fuel which stores chemical energy. The useful energy output makes the car move, and wasted forms of energy include heat and sound energy which spread to the surroundings.

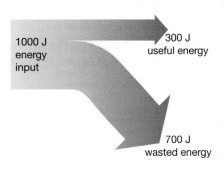

1000 J energy input

300 J useful energy

700 J wasted energy

We can draw a Sankey diagram for the car at any speed. At lower speeds, less energy is wasted so the useful energy arrow is thicker and the wasted energy arrow is thinner.

1A.3
2A.P3

The train's nose is smooth and pointed to reduce drag forces

Transportation and energy changes

2A.D2

When a car slows down, its kinetic energy is transferred to the surroundings as heat energy. The brake pads and discs, and the road and tyres heat up. Faster cars have a longer **stopping distance** because more energy must be transferred in braking.

All vehicles use more fuel when they travel faster. **Drag** forces increase as speed increases, and energy is used more quickly to overcome these. This energy is wasted as heat energy to the surroundings. A streamlined shape reduces the drag forces, so fuel consumption is lower. High-speed trains and sports cars reach high speeds because they are streamlined (which reduces drag forces) and because they have powerful engines (to overcome drag forces at high speeds).

Discuss

Which forms of transport shown here waste the least energy?

...energy transformation

Kinetic and potential energy

Roller-coaster ride

Many people love the thrill of a roller-coaster. The ride is exciting because you accelerate when you shoot down the track. Gravitational potential energy at the top of the track changes to kinetic energy.

Energy changes make this a thrilling ride

Your assessment criteria:

2A.P3 Describe the conservation of energy for simple experiments, including energy transformation diagrams

2A.M2 Calculate kinetic energy and changes in gravitational potential energy

2A.D2 Explain how changes in energy will affect transportation and stopping distances

2A.P3

Kinetic energy and potential energy

Moving objects have **kinetic energy**. Objects have more kinetic energy if they move faster, or are heavier.

Objects that have been lifted up gain energy and store it as **gravitational potential energy**. When an object falls, it changes the stored potential energy into kinetic energy. As it falls further it changes more stored energy into kinetic energy and moves faster.

On the roller-coaster ride, energy is conserved – the gravitational potential energy changes to kinetic energy at the bottom of each trough, and back to gravitational potential energy at each peak.

A child on a swing moves fastest at the lowest point. Then the swing and child have most kinetic energy and least gravitational potential energy. When the swing reaches the highest point, it stops moving very briefly before falling again. At this point, all the energy is gravitational potential energy. As the child swings, the energy keeps changing between kinetic energy and potential energy.

Sometimes we talk about '**elastic potential energy**'. This is energy gained and stored when an elastic object, such as a balloon, a spring or an elastic band, is stretched. This stored energy can be used to make things move.

Gravitational potential energy changes to kinetic energy and back again

Know more

*After a while the swing stops because of energy transfer as heat, caused by **friction** where moving parts rub, and by **drag** (the continual pushing against the air).*

🔍...kinetic energy

Think about

What energy transfers take place for a person on a fairground ride, in terms of kinetic and potential energy?

Climbing steps increases your gravitational potential energy

Calculating kinetic and potential energy

2A.M2

A moving object has kinetic energy which depends on the mass of the object and its speed. Kinetic energy (KE) is measured in joules and is calculated using:

KE = ½ mass × speed²

with mass in kg and speed in m/s.

The kinetic energy of Jack (mass 60 kg) walking at a speed of 2 m/s is ½ × 60 × 2² = 120 joules.

Objects gain gravitational potential energy if they are lifted up. Gravitational potential energy (PE), again in joules, is calculated using:

PE = mass × acceleration due to gravity × change in height

with mass in kg and height in m.

On Earth, acceleration due to gravity is about $10\,m/s^2$.

If Jack climbs up steps so that he is 6 m higher, the gravitational potential energy he gains is 60 × 10 × 6 = 3600 joules. The energy needed for this comes from the chemical energy in the food he has eaten.

Making energy changes efficient

2A.D2

When energy changes take place there is always some energy transfer as heat, or 'wasted energy'. We can't prevent wasted energy, but we can reduce it. Moving parts cause friction, wasting energy in the form of heat energy. Efficient energy transfers reduce this effect by smoothing or lubricating moving parts. Manufacturers try to design machines to make them as efficient as possible.

Scientists study images like this one of the space shuttle glowing during re-entry to change its design and improve efficiency

Research

Find out some design features that help improve the efficiency of energy changes from kinetic energy to gravitational potential energy in leisure equipment, such as trampolines and slides.

...potential energy

193

Forces and work

Your assessment criteria:

1B.4 Identify the forces on objects

2B.P4 Describe the effects of balanced and unbalanced forces on objects

1B.5 Describe work done in terms of forces moving through a distance

2B.P5 Calculate the work done by forces acting on objects for simple experiments

2B.D3 Explain the various forces involved, and their approximate sizes, in a variety of applications

Bungee jumping

Jumping from a tall crane or bridge held by an elastic rope is fun for some people. As you fall, potential energy changes to kinetic energy. The thrill of the jump comes because you accelerate. The elastic rope stretches as you fall, absorbing some energy so you bounce back up.

1B.4
2B.P4

Squashing and stretching

Some objects are elastic – when we stretch or squash them they change shape. When the force is removed, they change back to their original shape. Other objects, like plasticine, are not elastic – once their shape is changed it stays changed.

When you sit on a car seat, you squash the springs inside the seat. We say your weight is a **compressive force** because it compresses, or squashes, the springs. When you stretch an elastic band, we say it is in tension. The force stretching the elastic band is a **tensile force.**

Sometimes a force is compressive and tensile. If you load a beam, the middle of the beam bends downwards. The underside of the beam is stretched and in tension. The top of the beam is being compressed.

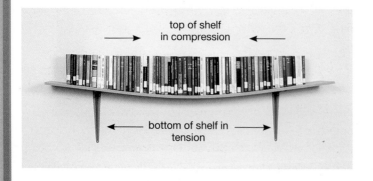

top of shelf in compression

bottom of shelf in tension

Know more

Arch bridges are designed so the weight of traffic squashes each stone onto its neighbour. Stone is very strong when it is compressed.

Know more

Suspension bridges use stretched steel cables to hold the bridge up. Steel is strongest when it is in tension.

...effects of forces

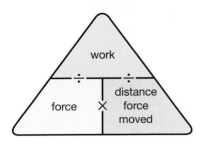

Use this triangle for calculations to do with work. Cover up what you need to find out and the rest of the triangle shows you how to calculate it

Work done by a force

1B.5
2B.P5

If a force moves something, it transfers energy. More energy is transferred if a larger force is used, or it moves further. The energy transferred is called **work done**.

- A person does more work lifting a 5 kg mass than a 1 kg mass.

- The person does more work lifting a weight by 2 m rather than by 1 m.

Work done is measured in joules (J). It is calculated using:

work   =   force   × distance moved
(joules, J) (newtons, N)   (metres, m)

Friction and drag forces increase with speed. A car's engine does more work at fast speeds because the engine has to produce a larger force.

When a car brakes, its energy is transferred to the brakes and surroundings. The work done stopping the car is (braking force × braking distance). A smaller braking force increases the braking distance. A faster speed means more energy must be transferred so the braking distance increases.

If a force doesn't move, no work is done. A weightlifter does work lifting the weights, but does no work holding them in the air. No energy is transferred to the weights when they do not move.

This bridge collapsed in 2007, partly due to design flaws

Research

Find out more about building regulations. Why are they necessary and how do they help people to be confident that buildings are safe?

Good design

2B.D3

When springs are extended too far, they deform and do not go back to their original size. If this happened to the springs in weighing scales, the scales would not give a true reading.

If an object that is too heavy crosses a beam or a bridge, the forces may damage it and make it weaker. Engineers need to build in protection.

Every time a new structure or piece of equipment is designed, the forces that will be exerted on it must be thought about, so that it can be used easily without being damaged. This applies to things in the home like door hinges and chairs, as well as larger items like theme park rides and planes.

🔍 ...work done

Effects of forces

Your assessment criteria:

1B.4 Identify the forces on objects

2B.P4 Describe the effects of balanced and unbalanced forces on objects

2B.P6 Describe how friction and normal reaction forces are produced in response to an applied force

2B.M3 Calculate the force on objects, in relation to their mass and acceleration for an application

2B.D3 Explain the various forces involved, and their approximate sizes, in a variety of applications

Tug of war

In a tug of war, two teams pull in opposite directions on a rope. If the teams are well matched, both teams pull as hard as each other and the forces are balanced. No team moves much, however hard they pull. In the end, one team gets tired and the other team can pull harder than them, winning the contest.

Matched teams mean the forces are balanced

1B.4
2B.P4
2B.P6

Balanced forces

Forces happen when one object affects another object. They happen when something pushes, pulls or twists an object. Forces include weight, magnetic forces, friction and tension in string. Usually more than one force acts on an object. We can combine the effects of these forces to give a **resultant force**. Forces are measured in **newtons** (**N**).

Imagine two friends pushing a heavy object along the floor. Each friend pushes with a force of 40 N.

- Forces acting in the same direction add together. If the friends push in the same direction, they may be able to move the object. Their resultant force is 80 N.

- Forces acting in opposite directions subtract and cancel each other out. If the friends push in opposite directions, the object won't move. The resultant force is zero.

Forces acting on an object that are equal in size but acting in opposite directions are **balanced forces**.

Balanced forces mean that:

- an object that isn't moving stays still

- a moving object keeps moving in a straight line at a steady speed.

Know more

*When an object feels a force, it pushes back with an equal force in the opposite direction. If you push on a wall, the wall pushes back on your hand. This is a **reaction force**.*

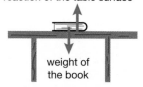

reaction of the table surface

weight of the book

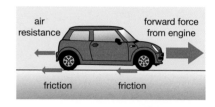

air resistance / forward force from engine

friction / friction

The car travels at a steady speed, because the force from the engine forwards is equal to friction and air resistance backwards

🔍 ...resultant force

Know more

The weight of an object affects the friction force between it and a surface. For example, it is easier to push a light book across the table than a heavy book.

Unbalanced forces

2B.P4

Unbalanced forces on an object mean there is a resultant force. This can change the way the object moves.

- An object **accelerates** (speeds up) if the resultant force is in the direction that it's moving.

- An object **decelerates** (slows down) if the resultant force is in the opposite direction to its movement.

- An object changes direction if the resultant force is in a different direction.

A ball thrown upwards slows down because its weight acts downwards – the opposite direction to its movement. Once it starts to fall back down, the ball accelerates because the weight acts in the same direction as its motion.

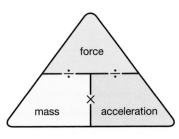

Use this triangle for calculations. Cover up what you need to find out, and the rest of the triangle shows you how to calculate it

Force and acceleration

2B.M3

The amount of acceleration depends on the mass of the object and the size of the force. A large mass needs a larger force to accelerate it than a smaller mass. The same mass accelerates more if a larger force pushes on it. We calculate the acceleration using:

force = mass × acceleration

Force is in N, mass in kg and acceleration in m/s². For example, a runner, mass 60 kg, accelerates by 2 m/s². The force needed is 60 × 2 = 120 N.

Think about

How can a driver control the forces acting on a car so that it reaches different steady speeds?

Changing forces

2B.D3

It can be hard to identify all the forces on an object. But if an object isn't moving, all the forces on it must be balanced.

Some forces change.

- Drag is a force that slows down moving objects. It is larger when the object travels faster. When the drag matches the driving force, the object reaches a top speed, or **terminal velocity**.

- Reaction forces only exist when another force is applied. If you stand on the floor, a reaction force acts upwards in the opposite direction to your weight, so you don't fall through the floor. When you step away, the reaction force disappears.

Research

Find out how drag forces can be controlled in different sports.

...acceleration

Forces on cars

Your assessment criteria:

1B.6 Identify friction forces and situations where they occur

2B.P6 Describe how friction and normal reaction forces are produced in response to an applied force

2B.M4 Explain how friction and normal reaction forces are produced in response to an applied force

Car crashes

When a car crashes, the driver and passengers can feel enormous forces. Crashes at quite slow speeds can still kill and injure people. Modern cars include many safety features to reduce the forces felt by passengers and to make accidents less likely.

Test crashes are done to rate the safety of different cars

1B.6
2B.P6

Braking

Friction is a force that slows down moving objects. It enables cars to brake. When the brake pedal is pressed, friction between the car's brake pads and the wheel make the wheel turn less quickly, and stop.

The contact between the tyres and the road is very important. When tyres grip the road well, friction between the tyres and the road can stop the car when the wheels stop turning. Otherwise, the wheels stop turning but the car slides across the road. In countries where very cold weather is normal, drivers fit snow chains or winter tyres that grip well in ice or snow.

Black skid marks are from rubber tyres sliding across the road as the vehicle skids. Skids are worse at high speeds

Know more

In icy weather, a mixture of grit and salt is spread on roads. The grit makes the road less slippery and the salt helps the ice to melt.

Think about

List several occasions when it is likely that a driver will skid.

 ...friction

Braking safely

Friction forces happen when objects are moving over each other. Rough edges on the surfaces catch, making it harder for the objects to move relative to one another. Friction can be useful – road surfaces are rough so car tyres can grip and use friction to be steered safely.

Friction is never bigger than the force causing motion. These forces act in opposite directions.

Friction is smaller than the driving force when an object accelerates. When a car accelerates, friction and drag (air resistance) forces are smaller than the force from the engine.

A braking system called **ABS** helps a driver to keep control of a car if it skids. When the driver brakes, sensors in the brakes check that the wheels are still turning. If they are not, the system repeatedly stops and starts the brakes. This helps the tyres to grip the road, allowing the driver to steer.

Keeping passengers safe

When a car crashes, it stops suddenly. But the people inside keep moving until something stops them. A sudden stop involves a very large deceleration, so the passengers feel a very large force and can be injured. Cars are designed so that these forces are reduced.

- Seatbelts keep people in their seats so they are not thrown through a windscreen or into hard objects in the car.

- Seatbelts are very slightly elastic. When the car stops, the seatbelt stretches slightly as the person is thrown forwards. The person takes a fraction of a second longer to stop, which is enough to reduce the force they feel.

- **Air bags** are normally hidden inside the steering wheel or dashboard. If a car crashes, these pop open creating a cushion filled with gas. The person is thrown forward but falls onto the cushion, which reduces the forces they feel.

- The front and back of a car are designed to crumple a lot if there is a crash. This means the car takes a split second longer to stop and so the forces are reduced. The car's **crumple zones** will be badly damaged but the centre part of the car is less damaged.

After a crash, seatbelts cannot be re-used

Research

What other safety features are designed in modern cars? Which features do you think are best at reducing injuries and deaths?

Parachutes and rockets

Your assessment criteria:

1B.6 Identify friction forces and situations where they occur

2B.P6 Describe how friction and normal reaction forces are produced in response to an applied force

2B.M4 Explain how friction and normal reaction forces are produced in response to an applied force

2B.D3 Explain the various forces involved, and their approximate sizes, in a variety of applications

Why the *Beagle* didn't land safely

Beagle 2 was a small space probe that was sent to Mars in 2003 to find out more about the planet. The probe was dropped onto the surface of Mars but failed to land safely. Parachutes did not slow it down as much as scientists expected and so it crash-landed and was damaged.

1B.6
2B.P6

Slowing down

Drag slows down moving objects. It depends on:

- the object's speed – there is more drag at fast speeds

- the object's surface area – there is more drag if the surface area is large

- the stuff the object moves through – there is more drag if this is thicker, for example, a liquid.

Gravity

Gravity is a force that attracts two objects together. The size of gravity depends on the mass of the objects and their distance apart. The Earth has such a large mass that it attracts small, nearby objects (like us) to its surface. Our weight is caused by the force of gravity.

The Earth's gravity affects the motion of other objects that are further away, like the Moon, but its effect is weaker at a distance.

Other planets and moons all have their own gravity. The Moon's gravity is less than Earth's, because the Moon's mass is less than Earth's.

Landing a probe safely on Mars is a challenge for scientists

Know more

The drag on a parachute on Mars is less than on the Earth because the atmosphere of Mars is less dense than the Earth's.

2B.M4

Parachutes

When any object falls, it feels two main forces: its weight acting downwards and drag acting upwards.

1 When an object starts falling, there is a downwards force so it accelerates. Weight is much bigger than drag.

2 As the speed increases, so does the upward drag. The weight acting down stays the same. The resultant force gets smaller so there is less acceleration.

3 Eventually, there is no resultant force: drag and weight are equal. The object keeps falling, at a steady speed or terminal velocity.

🔍 ...gravity ... terminal velocity

2B.M4

Research

Find out about the world record for the highest sky dive. How was the speed of the dive controlled?

A parachute slows down a falling object. If it opens while an object is falling:

1 Drag increases because the parachute's surface area is bigger.

2 The upward drag force becomes larger than the weight. The resultant force is upwards so the object slows down (decelerates).

3 As the speed decreases, the drag get less so the resultant force gets smaller until drag and weight are equal. The object keeps falling but at a slower steady speed (terminal velocity).

In each case the skydiver falls at his terminal velocity, but this is slower when the parachute is open

Huge amounts of fuel are needed so the rocket can break away from the Earth's gravity

Research

What effect does the Moon's gravity have on things on Earth?

2B.D3

Rockets

Beagle 2 was sent off on its mission using a rocket. Rockets leave the Earth so fast that gravity is not strong enough to pull them back. As the rocket moves further away from Earth, the pull of gravity is less so the force needed to move away is less. As the rocket moved closer to Mars, Mars's gravity started to attract it more than the Earth's gravity.

Landing safely

One theory of why *Beagle 2* fell heavily is that the atmosphere on Mars was not as thick as scientists believed. The parachutes weren't big enough, or didn't open in time, to provide enough drag to slow *Beagle* down enough to avoid damage.

🔍 ...rocket forces

Lenses

Lighting a fire with a lens

Can you light a fire without matches? Some explorers use a magnifying glass, or even the glass from the bottom of a bottle. If the Sun's heat and light is focused through the glass onto dry scraps of paper or wood, they can catch fire. Litter that includes glass can be a fire hazard among dry materials.

2C.P7

Refraction and lenses

Light travels incredibly fast in air, but slows down in **transparent** materials like glass. If light enters a glass block along an imaginary **normal** (this means at right angles to the boundary), it keeps going in a straight line. If it enters at another angle, it changes direction. This is called **refraction**.

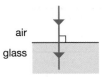

Light entering the glass at an angle of 90°.

The light ray slows down when it enters the more dense glass. It enters the glass along the normal. Its direction does not change.

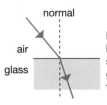

Light enters the glass block at an angle, it slows down in the glass and refracts towards the normal.

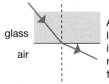

As the light ray leaves the glass block, it speeds up and refracts away from the normal.

Refraction is used by diamond cutters in the jewellery trade to make a diamond appear more impressive

Know more

In empty space, light travels faster than anything else in the Universe – 300 thousand km per second! Even so, it takes light 8 minutes to reach the Earth from the Sun.

...refraction

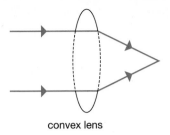

convex lens

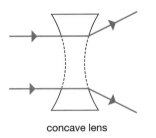

concave lens

Lenses are pieces of glass or transparent plastic, shaped to control the way light travels through them by using refraction.

- A **convex lens** is thicker in the middle than at the edges. It focuses a beam of light to the lens's **focal point**. It is a *converging* lens.

- A **concave lens** is thinner in the middle than at the edges. It spreads light out. It is a *diverging* lens.

Lenses with very curved surfaces are more powerful than flatter lenses. Their focal length is shorter. The image forms closer to the lens.

Ray diagrams

Light always travels in straight lines called rays. **Ray diagrams** show how light travels from the **object** we are viewing, through the lens to form an **image** that we see. The type of image depends on the position of the object. It may be:

- upside down or upright

- **magnified** (larger) or **diminished** (smaller) than the object

- a **real image** (on the other side of the lens to the object) or a **virtual image** (on the same side of the lens as the object).

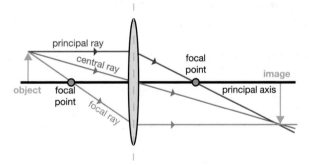

A ray diagram for a convex lens. The image here is upside down, larger than the object, and real

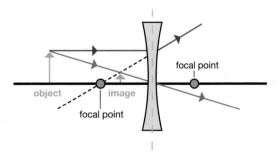

A ray diagram for a concave lens. The image is always upright, smaller than the object, and virtual

Research

Find out the difference between a real image and a virtual image.

Using lenses

Your assessment criteria:

2C.P7 Describe, using diagrams, reflection and refraction of light for simple applications

2C.M5 Describe how lenses and mirrors can affect rays of light

2C.D4 Explain how reflection and refraction of light can be used in applications

Seeing clearly

Being able to see clearly can be a matter of life or death. The eyes of animals, birds and fish all contain lenses, but their shapes are different. Some animals, like hawks, are hunters and need to focus clearly on their prey. Other animals, like rabbits and mice, are likely to be eaten. So they need good all-round vision to spot hunters in time. Some animals, like owls, need to see in the dark.

2C.P7

The structure of the human eye

The eye uses a convex lens to focus images onto the back of the eye.

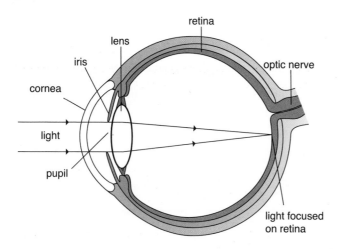

The cornea is a transparent covering. It protects the front of the eye as well as working with the fluid in the eyeball to focus light.

The lens allows you to focus on near and distant objects by changing its shape. It makes small adjustments so the image on the retina is clear. The lens is thicker when you focus close up. It is thinner when you focus on distant objects.

The pupil is the dark spot in the centre of your eyes – it lets light into the eye.

The iris surrounds the pupil, controlling its size. This controls how much light goes into the eye. In bright light, the pupil is small.

The **retina** is the covering of light-sensitive cells at the back of the eyeball. These cells detect the image, sending signals along the optic nerve to the brain.

Rabbits have eyes on the sides of their heads to help them see all around while grazing

Know more

Your eyes see everything upside down. Your brain makes the changes so you see the world upright.

🔍 ...structure of the eye

The concave lenses of the spectacles help the eyes to focus on distant objects

Correcting eye problems

2C.M5

Many people do not see clearly because their eyes do not focus light onto their retina.

- Distant objects are blurred if you are **short-sighted**. The image is formed in front of the retina, possibly because the eyeball is slightly too long. To correct short sight, a concave lens is used to spread the rays slightly before they enter the eye.

- Nearby objects are blurred if you are **long-sighted**. The image is formed behind the retina, possibly because the eyeball is slightly too short. To correct long sight, a convex lens is used to bend the rays together slightly before they enter the eye.

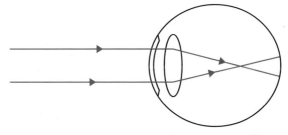

Short-sighted people focus the image of a distant object in front of the retina; a concave spectacle or contact lens corrects this

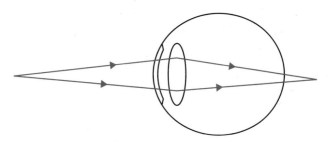

Long-sighted people focus the image of a near object behind the retina; a convex spectacle or contact lens corrects this

Laser surgery

2C.D4

Short and long sight can be corrected with surgery. A laser is used to reshape the cornea by burning away cells just under, or at, the surface. The shape of the cornea is made more curved (so it focuses more) to correct long sight. The shape is made less curved to correct short sight.

Laser eye surgery has not been in use for long in the UK. This means that its long-term effects are not known. As with all surgery, sometimes things go wrong and patients may have permanent eye damage.

Research

Find out more about laser surgery. Is it suitable for all eye problems? Do most doctors think its benefits outweigh its risks?

Reflection

Look behind you!

It's important that drivers know what vehicles behind them are doing. A driver can look behind quickly and safely using mirrors on the windscreen and at the sides of the car. The image is formed from light that has been reflected from the mirror.

1C.7
2C.P7

Reflection of light

Light reflects (bounces) off almost all surfaces. Light-coloured surfaces reflect more light than dark-coloured ones. We see things because the reflected light enters our eyes. When light is reflected off a flat mirror, we see an image that is:

- the same size as the object

- the same distance from the mirror as the object

- behind the mirror

- a **virtual image** (which means it can be seen, but it can't be projected onto a screen)

- laterally inverted (left becomes right).

When a single ray of light is reflected from a mirror, it obeys the **law of reflection**:

The angle of reflection is the same as the angle of incidence.

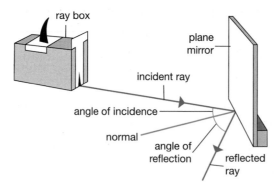

Normal: an imaginary line at right angles to the mirror
Angle of reflection: the angle between the normal and the reflected ray
Angle of incidence: the angle between the normal and the incident ray
Incident ray: the incoming ray
Reflected ray: the ray reflected off the mirror

This shows one way to test the law of reflection

Your assessment criteria:

1C.7 Describe, using diagrams, reflection of light in plane mirrors for simple applications

2C.P7 Describe, using diagrams, reflection and refraction of light for simple applications

2C.M5 Describe how lenses and mirrors can affect rays of light

2C.D4 Explain how reflection and refraction of light can be used in applications

The word 'AMBULANCE' on the front of the vehicle is written backwards, with each letter turned around too. In the rear-view mirror of a car in front, the word is seen normally, and the driver knows to get out of the way

Know more

Wing mirrors on vehicles are convex (they bulge out in the centre). This allows drivers to see more of the car's surroundings. The image is smaller.

...law of reflection

Reflection from convex and concave surfaces. What happens if you look in the bowl of a spoon and bring the spoon up close to your eye?

How curved mirrors affect light
2C.M5

Mirrors can be curved.

The centre of a **concave mirror** curves inwards. Concave mirrors magnify the image of a close object, so they are used in shaving mirrors. They concentrate light into a beam, so are used in reflector bulbs.

The centre of a **convex mirror** curves outward. Convex mirrors show a wide view of the surroundings and are used in security mirrors and car wing mirrors.

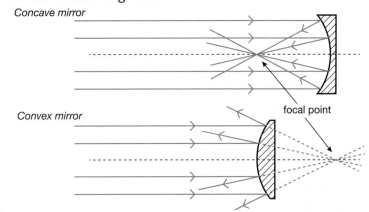

Concave mirror

focal point

Convex mirror

Telescopes
2C.D4

Telescopes are used to make distant objects appear closer. These objects are usually very dim, so a system of lenses and mirrors is needed to collect the light and concentrate it to give an image bright enough to see.

Refracting (astronomical) telescopes use two convex lenses. The objective lens collects and focuses light from distant objects. The eyepiece lens magnifies the image.

Reflecting (Newtonian) telescopes use a primary concave mirror instead of an objective lens to collect and focus light. They also have a second flat mirror to reflect light to the eyepiece lens. There is less distortion of the image with reflecting telescopes, compared with refracting telescopes.

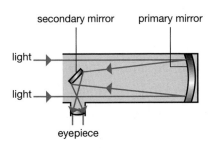

Reflecting telescope

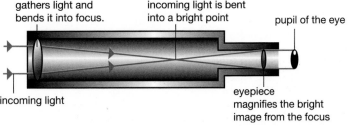

Refracting telescope

Internal reflection

Your assessment criteria:

2C.P7 Describe, using diagrams, reflection and refraction of light for simple applications

2C.D4 Explain how reflection and refraction of light can be used in applications

Optical fibre Christmas trees

One of the latest fashions in Christmas decorations is the optical fibre tree. The main trunk lights up and light shines out of the ends of the fronds. They look simple, so it's hard to realise how optical fibres have changed our lives, especially in communications and medicine.

2C.P7

Total internal reflection

The inside surface of transparent objects behaves like a mirror when light hits the surface at certain angles. This is called **total internal reflection**.

All transparent materials have a **critical angle**. Light refracts in the usual way if the angle of incidence is smaller than the critical angle. Otherwise it reflects off the inside surface.

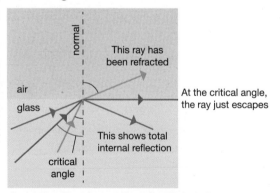

The angle of incidence affects how light behaves inside a glass block

A **prism** is triangular wedge of glass or transparent plastic. Light reflects off the inside walls of the prism. It may travel back the way it came (as in safety reflectors fixed in the road, called cat's eyes) or travel at right angles (as in periscopes).

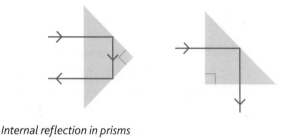

Internal reflection in prisms

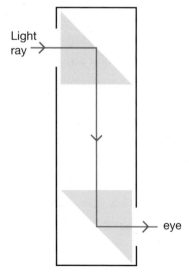

A periscope uses two prisms

...total internal reflection ... optical fibres

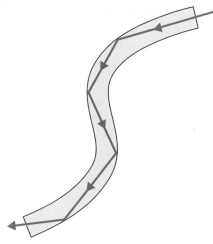

In an optical fibre, total internal reflection takes place many times

Optical fibres

Optical fibres are thin fibres made of glass or plastic which may be as thin as a single hair. Light entering one end of the fibre repeatedly reflects at angles larger than the critical angle. It comes out at the far end because it cannot escape from the sides of the fibre.

Using optical fibres in surgery

Optical fibres enable us to 'see round corners'. They are very useful to doctors for seeing inside the human body. An **endoscope** has thin flexible bundles of optical fibres to shine light into a patient's body. Another bundle of optical fibres sends reflections back so the doctor can view an image of what is happening inside the body. This can be used to diagnose problems, or even to carry out operations using **keyhole surgery**. Very intense light from a laser can be sent through optical fibres to make cuts or to seal off blood vessels.

2C.P7

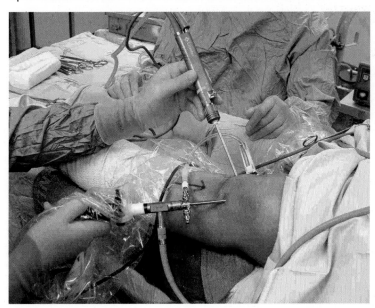

Keyhole surgery allows patients to recover more quickly than after traditional operations

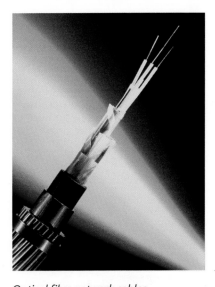

Optical fibre network cables

Know more

An optical fibre system 28 000 km long, mostly under the sea, connects North America, the UK and Japan.

Using optical fibres in communications

Optical fibres are also used for rapid communication in telephone networks, cable TV and Internet connections. Light signals can travel for many kilometres through the fibres. Many signals can be carried at the same time along one optical fibre. Cables are thinner and lighter than ever before, but can carry more information and with less distortion than copper cables.

2C.D4

🔎 ...endoscope

Sound and ultrasound

Your assessment criteria:

1C.8 Describe how sound is reflected for simple applications

2C.P8 Describe the importance of a medium for the transmission of sound waves through a variety of substances for simple applications

2C.M6 Describe the propagation of sound waves, including compression and rarefaction

2C.D5 Explain how sound waves can be applied in everyday uses

Voice recognition

People with serious eyesight problems, or disabilities with their hands, can use computers with the help of voice-recognition software. They speak into a microphone, and the words are changed into electrical signals and saved as a text file.

1C.8
2C.P8

Sound waves

Sound is produced when something vibrates. The vibrations transfer sound energy from one place to another.

- Larger vibrations make the sound louder.

- Faster vibrations make the sound higher pitched. One vibration per second has a frequency of 1 hertz. Humans hear low-pitched sounds, from about 20 hertz, up to very high-pitched sounds of about 20 000 hertz.

An echo is reflected sound. Sound reflects off boundaries between different materials.

When something vibrates, it makes nearby particles vibrate. These will bunch up or spread apart, creating regular pressure changes. This causes sound waves to travel away from the vibrating object. Energy is transmitted.

Sound waves must travel through a medium such as a solid, liquid or gas. Sound travels fastest in solids because the particles are closely packed. It does not travel at all in a vacuum (empty space).

Spoken words represented as an electrical signal

2C.M6

Sound waves transfer energy by creating a series of pressure differences in the air, which our ears, microphones and other sound sensors can detect.

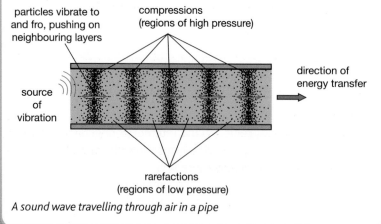

A sound wave travelling through air in a pipe

Know more

The loudest sounds on Earth come from the eruption of volcanoes. The loudest man-made sounds are from the launch pads of space rockets. However, in space these rockets are completely silent because sound cannot travel through empty space.

...voice-recognition software

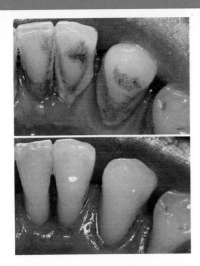

Ultrasound can clean plaque from teeth

Applications of ultrasound

Above 20 000 hertz, sounds are called **ultrasound**. Ultrasound is sound that is too high-pitched for humans to hear. Ultrasound waves:

- can be reflected off many materials
- are partly reflected by tissues in the body
- can be directed very precisely
- can break down some substances.

Ultrasound can be directed as a narrow beam from a transmitter. It sends pulses of ultrasound which are reflected when the beam reaches a boundary between different materials. A receiver measures how long it takes for the reflected ultrasound to return. A pulse travelling further takes longer to reach the receiver.

- In hospitals, ultrasound is used to scan organs like the heart, liver and brain. The pulses reflect in different ways off the different tissues, so a picture of structures inside the body is built up.

- Ultrasound scans in pregnancy can safely look at the baby as it develops inside the mother.

- Ultrasound reflects off cracks in metal, so aeroplane parts, engines and other solid items can be checked.

- In the ocean, ultrasound reflects off the seabed or objects lying beneath the transmitter. The time taken for signals to reach the receiver is measured and used to calculate the depth of the seabed or object. The technique can identify fish or whales, and locate the position of sunken ships. This is called **sonar**.

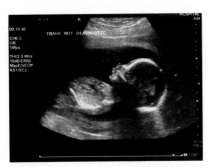

Ultrasound scan of a 20-week-old unborn baby

If a beam of ultrasound is directed at some things, it can force them to break apart. It can break down kidney stones, so patients don't need an operation. It can break up plaque which has built up on teeth. It can even dislodge dirt from delicate objects like jewellery.

Benefits and disadvantages of ultrasound

Ultrasound has been used for many years to examine patients internally without operating. No serious side-effects are known. As ultrasound is becoming more widely used, its safety record is becoming more reliable. However, scans need to be interpreted properly, otherwise doctors may not have the correct information before treating a patient.

Research

How do some animals use ultrasound?

Electric circuits

Your assessment criteria:

1D.9 Describe, using diagrams, how to build series and parallel circuits

2D.P9 Measure currents and voltages in series and parallel electric circuits

2D.M7 Calculate resistances from measured currents and voltages

2D.D6 Analyse an everyday life situation in which the resistance of a conducting wire is not constant

Restarting the heart

The first few minutes after a heart attack are critical. A heart attack stops the heart beating correctly and the beating must be restarted fast. A defibrillator can be used to give the heart an electric shock to restart it. Defibrillators have been installed in places like shopping centres, sports centres, railway stations and airports. This can save lives.

1D.9
2D.P9

Measurements in series and parallel circuits

Current is measured in amps (A) using an **ammeter**. It is connected in series and is part of the loop of conductors.

Voltage is measured in volts (V) using a **voltmeter**. It is connected in parallel with a component, and can be added to the circuit as an extra loop.

A **series circuit** is a single loop of conductors.

- The current is the same in all places in a series circuit. The ammeter has the same reading wherever it is in the circuit.

- The voltage is shared between the components. The readings on the voltmeters show that $V = V_1 + V_2$.

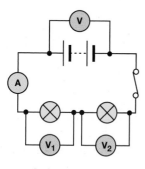

Series circuit

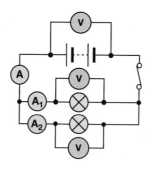

Parallel circuit

A **parallel circuit** has more than one loop, forming separate paths for the charges. Each loop links to the battery.

- The current is shared between the loops of a parallel circuit. The ammeter reading $A = A_1 + A_2$.

- The voltage is the same in each loop. The voltmeter reading is the same across the battery and for each loop.

Know more

Humans can produce about 0.01 to 0.1 volts inside their bodies, but electric eels can produce about 600 volts.

...series circuit ... parallel circuit

Measuring resistance

Resistance (see Unit 3) can be measured directly using an **ohmmeter** or by using readings from an ammeter and voltmeter. Several readings of current and voltage may be plotted on a graph. The resistance at any voltage is calculated using values from the graph since:

$$\text{resistance (ohms, } \Omega) = \frac{\text{voltage (volts, V)}}{\text{current (amps, A)}}$$

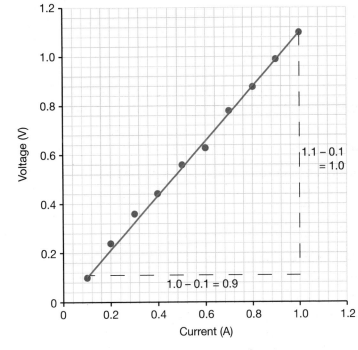

Using this graph, the resistance = 1.0 ÷ 0.9 = 1.1 ohms

Changing resistance

The resistance of some materials stays constant as the voltage changes. These materials obey Ohm's law, as long as the temperature stays constant. Doubling the voltage doubles the current.

Many materials do not obey Ohm's law. A filament in a light bulb heats up and glows as the voltage increases:

- at low voltages and small currents, the resistance is constant

- at higher voltages and currents, the wire heats up

- hotter wires have a higher resistance and the current does not increase as quickly as the voltage does; doubling the voltage does not double the current.

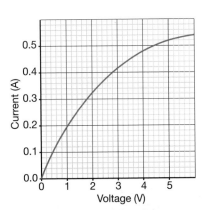

At 1 V, the current is 0.2 A and the resistance is 5 Ω. At 3 V, the current is only about 0.4 A and the resistance has increased to 7.5 Ω

🔍 ...Ohm's law

Electric sensors

The intelligent house

Intelligent houses may automatically shut curtains when it is dark, turn on lights and the TV when people come in, even turn around to follow the Sun or let chosen friends in when you are out. These things are already possible using sensors.

1D.10
2D.P10

Sensors and indicators

A **sensor** is a device that detects a change in the environment, such as the temperature. In an electric circuit it can cause a change in current, which can make something happen.

Temperature sensors

A circuit using a **thermistor** detects if the temperature is too high or too low. The electrical resistance of a thermistor falls as the temperature increases. This means the current in the circuit gets bigger. So a thermistor is used in sensor circuits which turn things on automatically, such as greenhouse heaters or fire alarms.

Farmers lose money if crops are damaged by frost. A sensor circuit can be designed so that heaters come on when the temperature drops too low

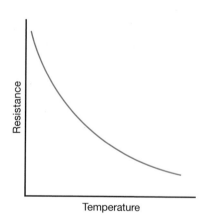

As the temperature increases, the resistance of the thermistor falls and the current increases

🔍 ...thermistor

Light sensors

1D.10
2D.P10

The resistance of a **light-dependent resistor (LDR)** falls as the amount of light falling on it increases. This means the current in the circuit gets bigger. A sensor circuit using an LDR can detect when light levels change. It can be used to turn things on automatically, such as lights when it gets dark.

These lights are controlled by a sensor; they come on when daylight fades

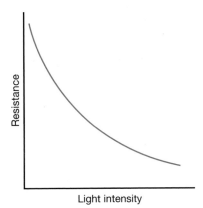

As the light gets brighter, the resistance of the LDR falls and the current increases

2D.M8

Using your results

Experiments using LDRs may compare the resistance and light intensity. Enough results are needed to plot a smooth curve over the range of light intensity. If results using different LDRs are included on one graph, the most suitable LDR can be chosen. The most suitable LDR has the biggest change in resistance over the range of light intensities that it is used in.

Similar experiments using thermistors at different temperatures can be used to find the most suitable thermistors for an application. The most suitable thermistor has a large change in resistance over the temperature range that it will be used in.

2D.D7

Choosing the best component

Thermistors and LDRs control circuits automatically. The circuit may be improved if it turns on or off over a narrow range of brightness or temperature, or it may be improved if the component works over a very wide range of temperatures and light intensities.

An LDR used in streetlights that turn on automatically does not need to be as sensitive as an LDR in a camera light meter. Thermistors used in hospital incubators must be sensitive over a smaller temperature range than thermistors used in engines or spacecraft, which face extreme changes in temperature.

> **Think about**
>
> *How many sensors do you use in your home? List them and what they do.*

> **Research**
>
> *Many circuits use a resistor and an LDR arranged to switch a circuit on when the light levels are low. This arrangement is called a potential divider. Find out more about how a potential divider works.*

🔍 ...LDR ...potential divider

Assessment Checklist

To achieve a Pass grade, my portfolio of evidence must show that I can:

Assessment Criteria	Description	✓
2A.P1	Produce accurate graphs to represent uniform and non-uniform motion using primary data	
2A.P2	Calculate speed and velocity for simple experiments	
2A.P3	Describe the conservation of energy for simple experiments, including energy transformation diagrams	
2B.P4	Describe the effects of balanced and unbalanced forces on objects	
2B.P5	Calculate the work done by forces acting on objects for simple experiments	
2B.P6	Describe how friction and normal reaction forces are produced in response to an applied force	
2C.P7	Describe, using diagrams, reflection and refraction of light for simple applications	
2C.P8	Describe the importance of a medium for the transmission of sound waves through a variety of substances for simple applications	
2D.P9	Measure currents and voltages in series and parallel electric circuits	
2D.P10	Investigate an application of thermistors or LDRs using primary data	

If you do not meet all the Level 2 Pass criteria for this Unit then your work will be assessed against these Level 1 criteria. If your work meets all these criteria you will achieve a Level 1 Pass for this Unit. If you do not achieve all these Level 1 criteria you will get a U (Unclassified) for this Unit.

Assessment Criteria	Description	✓
1A.1	Produce accurate graphs to represent uniform motion using primary data	
1A.2	Measure distance for simple experiments	
1A.3	Draw energy transformation diagrams for simple experiments	
1B.4	Identify the forces on objects	
1B.5	Describe work done in terms of forces moving through a distance	
1B.6	Identify friction forces and situations where they occur	
1C.7	Describe, using diagrams, reflection of light in plane mirrors for simple applications	
1C.8	Describe how sound is reflected for simple applications	
1D.9	Describe, using diagrams, how to build series and parallel circuits	
1D.10	Describe the use of a thermistor or LDR for an application	

To achieve a Merit grade, my portfolio of evidence must also show that I can:

Assessment Criteria	Description	✓
2A.M1	Interpret graphs to identify objects that are stationary, moving at a constant speed and moving with increasing or decreasing speed	
2A.M2	Calculate kinetic energy and changes in gravitational potential energy	
2B.M3	Calculate the force on objects, in relation to their mass and acceleration for an application	
2B.M4	Explain how friction and normal reaction forces are produced in response to an applied force	
2C.M5	Describe how lenses and mirrors can affect rays of light	
2C.M6	Describe the propagation of sound waves, including compression and rarefaction	
2D.M7	Calculate resistances from measured currents and voltages	
2D.M8	Mathematically or graphically process the results of the investigation into thermistors or LDRs to draw conclusions	

To achieve a Distinction grade, my portfolio of evidence must also show that I can:

Assessment Criteria	Description	✓
2A.D1	Calculate the gradient for distance–time graphs and the gradient and area of speed–time graphs	
2A.D2	Explain how changes in energy will affect transportation and stopping distances	
2B.D3	Explain the various forces involved, and their approximate sizes, in a variety of applications	
2C.D4	Explain how reflection and refraction of light can be used in applications	
2C.D5	Explain how sound waves can be applied in everyday uses	
2D.D6	Analyse an everyday life situation in which the resistance of a conducting wire is not constant	
2D.D7	Evaluate the investigation into thermistors or LDRs, suggesting improvements to a real-life application	

LA

Be able to investigate factors that contribute to healthy living

- Scientists have found a clear link between lifestyle, health and disease; people who lead unhealthy lifestyles are more likely to suffer from certain diseases

- We are said to be sitting on an 'obesity time bomb' because the number of children suffering from obesity is increasing. The number of year 6 pupils who are obese has risen to 19%, and those who are considered to be overweight is 14.4% (NHS Information Centre).This could have serious consequences for the health care of the nation in the future

- Some people's diets can make them sick; people with coeliac disease have intolerance to wheat and it can cause diarrhoea, stomach cramps and mouth ulcers

LA

Be able to investigate how some treatments are used when illness occurs

- The overuse of antibiotics for infections may be responsible for new bacteria that are resistant to antibiotics, such as MRSA

- You cannot receive just any type of blood if you need a blood transplant; you need blood that is complementary or a match to your own type

- Currently gene therapy is being developed for diseases like HIV and cancer, and could provide an effective treatment in the future

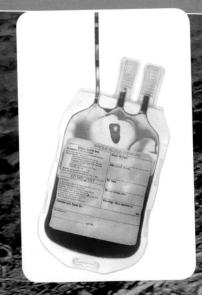

Know how preventative measures can be used to support healthy living

- Not only does your stomach acid digest food, it also plays an important part of your first line of defence

- Vaccinations are actually small doses of the pathogen you need defence against; they are inactive so they cannot give you the disease – a flu vaccine will not give you flu

- Doctors can now check for a number of different diseases before they start to cause problems; this helps treatment and increases survival rate

Healthy living

Are you healthy?

Do you enjoy an evening on the sofa, watching TV, eating junk food and doing very little exercise? This may sound tempting and is common for some people. This type of lifestyle is proving to be a real concern. There are fears we are heading for an 'obesity epidemic'. This will result in more people becoming ill.

Your assessment criteria:

1A.1 Explain the importance of a balanced diet and exercise

2A.P1 Describe the possible effects of diet and exercise on the functioning of the human body

2A.M1 Explain how the diet and exercise plan will affect the functioning of the human body

2A.D1 Evaluate the diet and exercise plan, and justify the menus and activities chosen

1A.1
2A.P1

Factors that affect health

'Health' can be thought of as the general state of your body and mind. If someone is healthy then their mind and body are functioning well and they can live a full and active life. If someone is in a poor state of health, their body or mind or both are not working well.

Health is affected by a number of factors:

- **lifestyle** – the way we choose to live our lives

- **diet** – what we eat

- **exercise** – how active we are

- **physical illness** – things that can go wrong with our bodies, either caught (infectious) or developed (non-infectious)

- **mental illness** – things that can go wrong with our minds.

These factors are interrelated. For example, a lifestyle can be one that involves little exercise and therefore this can affect health. A poor diet can lead to a non-infectious physical illness such as heart disease. A lifestyle choice such as smoking can lead to a non-infectious disease such as lung cancer. Our health is in a constant state of change and the choices we make can directly affect it.

Know more

Half of the world's population live on a diet of mainly rice.

Rice is a healthy food but rice alone cannot supply all the nutrients we need

🔍...health and fitness

Discuss

Are healthier people happier? What do you think?

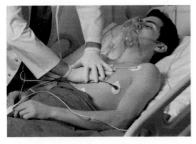

Even if you're not overweight, an inappropriate diet and lack of exercise can put pressure on your heart

Think about

Exercise doesn't have to mean going to the gym. Suggest how someone who is fairly inactive might increase the amount of exercise they take. How might a small increase in exercise affect the functioning of their body?

Think about

What would you do to assess someone's general state of health?

The benefits of a healthy lifestyle

2A.M1

A healthy lifestyle can have both **physiological effects** and **psychological effects**.

- If we control our diet and take exercise, our bodies become fitter. This can reduce the risk of some physiological conditions (physical illnesses) such as diabetes and heart disease.

- A healthy lifestyle in turn can affect our minds. We look better, we start to feel better about ourselves and this improves our moods. There is some evidence to suggest that this can help control psychological problems (mental illnesses) like depression.

Evaluating health

2A.D1

We may feel healthy, but can only decide how fit we really are by looking at our eating and exercise habits. It is easy not to notice how much we eat and drink, or what we are eating and drinking, and what the effects might be.

Some people need to structure their eating and exercise habits. For some this requires advice from dieticians, medical practitioners or fitness coaches. These experts help in evaluating current lifestyles, designing appropriate plans and reviewing a person's progress towards their goals.

A fitness programme can help a person reach their health goals

🔍 ...healthy lifestyle

Food and diet

Middle-age spread

It is a joke among middle-aged people that they only eat the same or less than they did when they were young and yet they still put on weight! This is often called 'middle-age spread'. One theory is that the energy and nutrient requirements for the two age groups are different. Teenagers are growing and are very active, which means their energy requirements are high. Middle-aged people need less energy from their diets – being careful about what they eat will still not allow them to eat as if they were a teenager!

Your assessment criteria:

1A.1 Explain the importance of a balanced diet and exercise

1A.2 Identify a balanced diet for teenagers

2A.P1 Describe the possible effects of diet and exercise on the functioning of the human body

2A.M1 Explain how the diet and exercise plan will affect the functioning of the human body

2A.D1 Evaluate the diet and exercise plan, and justify the menus and activities chosen

1A.1
2A.P1

We all need food

We all need food as our source of **nutrition**. It provides us with energy to carry out everyday activities, and essential **nutrients** for maintaining and repairing our bodies. If our meals over a period of time do not provide the right mix of nutrients in the right quantities, we can gain too much weight, lose too much weight or damage our health in other ways.

The nutrients we need are shown in the table.

Nutrients	Why we need it
carbohydrates (sugar and starch)	These are our major energy source. The amount you need depends on the type of carbohydrate, who you are and how you live your life.
lipids (fats and oils)	These are energy sources and also have other functions in the body, such as making cell membranes.
protein	This is needed for growth and repair of the body. The amount you need depends on the type of protein, who you are and how you live your life.
vitamins and minerals	These are essential substances needed in very small amounts for the maintenance and effective working of the body.

Carbohydrates and fats are energy providers. Food with a lot of sugar or a lot of fat has a high energy content, or **calorific value**. If we eat more than we need, the body stores the excess in the form of body fat and we put on weight.

If we eat too much or too little food of the wrong types this can affect how our bodies function and can lead to health problems.

Know more

We need many different vitamins, for example vitamin C and vitamin B12, and several minerals such as magnesium and iron. Each one has a 'recommended daily amount'.

Know more

The calorific value of food measured in kilocalories, kcal (often just called 'calories'), or kilojoules, kJ. We all need different amounts of energy from our food – see Unit 4.

🔍 ...calorific values

1A.2
2A.P1

Becoming a teenager

As children hit adolescence they grow fast! For girls, this happens around 10–11 years of age. For boys it happens at around 12–13 years. This growth places extra demands on the body for both energy and nutrients. Therefore, a balanced diet for a teenager will be slightly different than that for a middle-aged person.

Extra energy needs to be obtained from foods that also provide nutrients for growth, not just energy. Therefore high-fat and high-carbohydrate foods, such as takeaways and fast foods, need to be balanced with foods rich in nutrients, such as wholegrain breads and cereals, fruits, legumes, nuts, vegetables, fish and lean meats.

Extra calcium is needed for growing bones. Dairy products such as milk can help boost calcium intake.

2A.M1

Are you on a diet?

The word 'diet' can mean different things to different people – it means what you eat! A **balanced diet** provides all the nutrients needed, in the right proportions.

Sometimes people adopt eating plans to either lose or gain weight – so their dietary requirements will change. If a person is regularly consuming too many calories (energy units) per day, then a diet plan would aim to reduce the number of those calories. If the diet plan is followed, the body responds by using some of its energy and the person might lose weight. Combining this reduction in calorie intake with an exercise plan may improve the person's health.

Some people's diet changes dramatically when they are on holiday because they allow themselves 'treats' which are high in calories. This may have the consequence of weight gain, and also affects blood sugar levels and mood.

2A.D1

Evaluating diet

When we evaluate what we eat, we need to look at the type of food we are eating. Packaged food in the UK contains nutritional information on the pack. This tells us the calorific value and the quantities of each of the major nutrients in 100 g of the food.

We can use these data to calculate the calories we take in:

$$\text{number of calories} = \frac{1}{100} \times \frac{\text{calorific value}}{\text{per 100 g}} \times \frac{\text{amount of}}{\text{food in grams}}$$

For example, if we eat 100 g of cake which has a calorific value of 379 kcal per 100 g, we would be consuming 379 kcals.

Would a person on a healthy eating plan be able to justify that piece of cake?

Think about

How might the dietary needs of a 60-year-old man compare to those of a 13-year-old boy? How might lifestyle and personal circumstances affect these dietary needs?

Think about

How would you explain the need for a low-calorie diet to an overweight person?

Unbalanced diets

Super-skinny

Models are often employed because they are slim and look elegant in clothes. We assume they must be healthy because they are so slim, but model Luisel Ramos proved this assumption wrong. Luisel died at the age of 21 from a heart attack. She weighed only 44 kg. It is alleged her heart failure was a direct result of an eating disorder. Luisel was rumoured to have eaten only lettuce leaves and Diet Coke for a week before she died.

Your assessment criteria:

1A.1 Explain the importance of a balanced diet and exercise

1A.2 Identify a balanced diet for teenagers

2A.P1 Describe the possible effects of diet and exercise on the functioning of the human body

2A.M1 Explain how the diet and exercise plan will affect the functioning of the human body

2A.D1 Evaluate the diet and exercise plan, and justify the menus and activities chosen

1A.1
1A.2
2A.P1

Getting the balance right

When a person eats too much it can be called **overnutrition**. This can lead to weight gain and in extreme cases can lead to **obesity**. There are a number of health conditions, such as heart disease, that are associated with being overweight or obese.

If a person eats too little they will suffer from **undernutrition**. They are not consuming enough calories and nutrients. The body responds by first breaking down its own fat and using it for energy. Weight loss occurs. After fat stores have been used up, the body may break down its other tissues, such as muscle and tissues in internal organs. This can lead to a number of different nutrient deficiencies and serious health problems, possibly death.

Eating disorders

In the UK and other wealthy nations, the choice of what we eat is under our own control. For some people this control goes wrong and they can develop **eating disorders**.

Know more

Eating disorders are around ten times more common in girls and women than in boys and men.

🔍 ...undernutrition

1A.1
1A.2
2A.P1

The eating disorders **anorexia nervosa** and **bulimia** are both serious psychological conditions, leading to severe physical problems, and in extreme cases death.

The anorexia nervosa sufferer has a greatly reduced appetite and obsessive control of what they eat, or even a complete avoidance of food.

The bulimia sufferer alternates between eating excessive amounts of food (bingeing) and making themselves sick, or using laxatives (purging), in order to maintain a chosen weight.

Food allergies

In some people certain types of food cause an **allergic reaction**. This may be mild or extreme. Sometimes, if appropriate treatment is not obtained, it can be fatal. The most well known food allergies are to peanuts and eggs.

2A.M1

Dealing with undernutrition

Undernutrition can occur for a number of reasons. In today's society it can still occur because of poverty, or when natural disasters such as flood or drought ruin food supplies. In parts of society with plenty of food available, undernutrition can occur because of psychological eating disorders.

Whatever the cause, undernutrition is debilitating and can lead to death. It is therefore important to treat it appropriately. Treatment can mean providing more food or food rich in different types of nutrient. In the case of a psychological disorder, long-term treatment is required to change a person's attitude to food and the way they view themselves.

A high-protein shake is sometimes recommended for people who need to put on body mass

2A.D1

Crash diets

Explaining to someone that their diet needs to change can be difficult, particularly if they do not see the need for change. For this reason, diet plans need to be justified and trained nutritionists are often used. They have an in-depth knowledge of the nutritional value of foods and can advise clients. For example, they can explain why one kind of pizza might have 300 kcal per 100 g and a different type of the same size might have 500 kcal per 100 g. If you were trying to lose weight, which would you eat?

Know more

About 1% of all 16–18 year-olds suffer from anorexia nervosa.

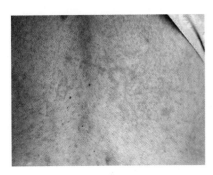

This rash has been caused by an allergic reaction to seafood

Discuss

What power does the mind have over a successful diet plan? What could be the potential consequences of putting an overweight person on a calorie-restricted diet?

A crash diet is unlikely to be the right kind of diet plan for an obese person

Fit and healthy

Looking good, feeling good?

A very muscular body is something that some men aspire to. More visible muscles are often seen as attractive and 'fit'. But this is not always the case. Appearances can be deceptive. A person who looks good might not be fully fit and healthy.

1A.1
2A.P1
2A.P2

Exercise for fitness

If a person looks good but their lifestyle means that they take little or no regular exercise, then they may still be unfit.

Fitness is the ability to do what your body is required to do. It can include agility, stamina, balance, speed and flexibility. Fitness is different for different people.

The amount of exercise needed to maintain fitness depends on the fitness level of the person and the goals set. For example, if you were an Olympic marathon runner, jogging one mile in nine minutes would count as only a **mild intensity** activity. For many people, though, it would be a **high intensity** activity. For most people, experts recommend about 30 minutes of **moderate exercise** every day to keep fit.

The fitness level you can achieve depends on your current physical state. Some people have restricted **mobility** (ability to move). These may be very obese people, those recovering from surgery or those with chronic conditions that affect mobility, such as degenerative joint and muscle diseases (like arthritis). These people would need to work on exercises that gradually increase their range of mobility and flexibility. Small gains in fitness could have a significant impact on their lifestyle.

Exercise plans can be developed to suit different people's needs

Your assessment criteria:

1A.1 Explain the importance of a balanced diet and exercise

2A.P1 Describe the possible effects of diet and exercise on the functioning of the human body

2A.P2 Develop a diet and exercise plan based on level and type of exercise and appropriate nutritional balance, to promote healthy living for an individual

2A.M1 Explain how the diet and exercise plan will affect the functioning of the human body

2A.D1 Evaluate the diet and exercise plan, and justify the menus and activities chosen

Know more

*Being **agile** means you can move in sudden bursts in different directions, like running in zig-zags down a football pitch. Being **flexible** means you have a wide range of movement around your joints and may be able to 'do the splits'.*

If you can't do this, does it mean you're not fit?

Know more

It is estimated that only 37% of men and 24% of women take enough exercise.

...exercise and health

Personal computers can take people through fitness programmes

The right type of exercise

Different activities in a health and fitness plan have different effects on the functioning of the body. Some examples are shown in the table.

Activity	Effect on the body
aerobic exercise (such as running, cycling)	Improves speed and agility, increases lung capacity and **cardiovascular fitness** (how fit your heart and circulatory system is), reduces stress and can lead to weight loss.
yoga	Improves balance and flexibility, can tone up parts of the body and reduce stress.
weights	Builds up and tones muscles, can change body shape and appearance.
jogging	Increases lung capacity and cardiovascular fitness, reduces stress and can lead to weight loss.
swimming	Improves speed, stamina, cardiovascular fitness and tones the body. Can lead to weight loss and reduces stress.

Think about

Are you fit? List the activities that you do which contribute to your fitness.

Discuss

What might be a realistic goal for someone who is extremely unfit?

Evaluating fitness

Different **physiological measurements** can be made to establish how fit someone is:

- **resting pulse rate** – the normal pulse rate when not exercising
- **recovery time** – how long it takes for the pulse and breathing rate to return to normal after exercise
- **body mass index (BMI)** – shown by this ratio:

$$\frac{\text{weight}}{(\text{height})^2}$$

- percentage of body fat
- waist circumference
- waist/hip ratio.

There is a range of devices on the market for making these measurements.

An evaluation of fitness should not just rely on one method – it is better to use a combination of methods.

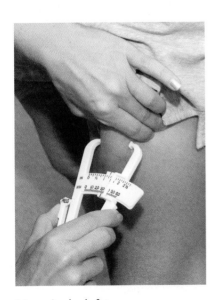

Measuring body fat

Planning for health and fitness

Getting excited about health

Too much rich food, too little exercise, and all of a sudden we feel unhealthy. The good news is that it is never too late to do something about it. By following a healthy living plan and establishing good habits you can return to health. Healthy habits and exercise can be fun – even cycling with your family once a week can have a positive effect on your health.

Your assessment criteria:

1A.1 Explain the importance of a balanced diet and exercise

2A.P1 Describe the possible effects of diet and exercise on the functioning of the human body

2A.P2 Develop a diet and exercise plan based on level and type of exercise and appropriate nutritional balance, to promote healthy living for an individual

2A.M1 Explain how the diet and exercise plan will affect the functioning of the human body

2A.D1 Evaluate the diet and exercise plan, and justify the menus and activities chosen

1A.1
2A.P1

The components of a health plan

To design a health and fitness plan we need to first evaluate how healthy a person is. We can do this in a number of ways. One type of evaluation is a **physiological investigation**. This consists of taking a number of measurements for the person, such as pulse rate (see page 229).

We also need to make a **lifestyle evaluation**. This is a series of questions relating to the way the person lives their life. It could include questions on:

- diet and eating habits
- sleeping habits
- exercise habits
- job and other activities
- smoking and alcohol intake
- attitude towards food and exercise.

Once the data have been collected they are analysed, and the areas that need to be improved are decided on.

🔍 ...health and fitness plans

FITNESS PLAN

Name ————————————
Age ————————————
Height ————————————
Injuries/health conditions ————

Aims ————————————
————————————————

Date				
Body weight				
BMI				
Body fat%				
Rest pulse				
Ex.1 pulse				
Ex.2 pulse				

A fitness plan needs to take into account key measurements

2A.P2

Short-term goals may be set, with a suitable time frame.

'I would like to lose 3 kg in 2 months.'

For some people it is appropriate to set **long-term goals**.

'I need to improve my fitness to run a half-marathon within a year.'

A specific health and fitness programme can be developed that is tailor-made for the individual. It should address all the issues raised in the evaluation.

2A.M1

The benefits of a health and fitness plan

A diet and exercise plan can have beneficial effects on the health and fitness of a person. However, what is appropriate for one person may not be for another. It depends on the initial level of fitness and on the goals.

Keeping to a healthy diet can help maintain a suitable weight, with body fat and **cholesterol level** within a healthy range (high blood cholesterol increases the risk of cardiovascular disease).

Keeping to a fitness plan can benefit the heart and circulatory system, can help maintain a suitable weight and percentage of body fat, and for some people it can increase movement and flexibility and improve mental health.

Good diet and exercise regimes can help in reducing the risk of heart disease.

Fish oils are very beneficial to our health

Know more

A total cholesterol level of less than 4.0 mmol/L is considered to be healthy.

Research

What alternatives to fish oil could you find for vegetarians or people who do not like fish, which would provide the same nutritional benefits?

Think about

How would you assess the impact of a diet and exercise plan on the habits and health of a person? How could a plan be amended if a particular exercise was not working for the person?

2A.D1

Making the plan fit for purpose

A diet and fitness plan is only as good as the results it delivers. To evaluate a plan you need to look at the goals of the plan and establish whether they have been reached. For example, the person's goal might be to lose weight in order to reduce their BMI. The person's BMI – weight divided by (height)^2 – would be calculated before, during and after the programme to see if the goal has been met.

🔎 ...healthy living

Health campaigns

Smoking costs money!

One report in 2009 suggested that the effects on health of smoking costs the NHS £5 billion a year. This huge amount of money needs to be reduced, but how can this be done?

1A.3
2A.P3

Anti-smoking

Smoking has long been acknowledged as bad for your health and as having a huge impact on the functioning of the human body. Therefore, the Government and pressure groups have tried several different measures to encourage people to stop:

- increasing tax on tobacco, making smoking expensive
- adverts showing the detrimental effects of smoking
- education campaigns in schools
- banning smoking in public places
- banning displays of tobacco products in supermarkets and other large shops
- free advice and medical measures to help people to give up.

When anything has such a huge negative impact on health – smoking, excess alcohol or unhealthy eating – measures need to be taken to reduce its impact and improve the health of the nation.

Likewise when something is thought to have a positive effect on health it is encouraged, as in the recommendation to eat five portions of fruit and vegetables a day.

Your assessment criteria:

1A.3 Identify measures taken to improve the health of the population

2A.P3 Describe the ways in which health improvement measures are intended to improve the health of the population

2A.M2 Analyse rates of disease in the population in relation to lifestyle choices

2A.D2 Evaluate measures taken to improve the health of the population

Know more

It is estimated there are up to 4000 toxic chemicals in cigarette smoke.

Think about

The annual No Smoking Day has helped up to 1.5 million people give up since it was started in 1984.

...health risks of smoking ...No Smoking Day

Research

What is emphysema? What is the quality of life for people who have it?

The benefits of giving up

2A.P3

Smoking directly causes over 100 000 deaths in the UK each year and contributes to many more. Of these deaths, about 42 800 are from smoking-related cancers, 30 600 from cardiovascular disease and 29 100 from emphysema and other chronic lung diseases (www.netdoctor.co.uk). The solution is simple: if all these people were to stop smoking, the health of the population would improve and this in turn would save the Government more than £5 billion a year.

It's all in the numbers

2A.M2

The NHS Information Centre produced data in 2010 that estimated the following in England:

Cause of death	% attributed to smoking
all deaths	18
all cancer	29
all respiratory disease	36
all circulatory disease	14
all diseases of the digestive system	5

Know more

In 2011 the NHS reported that since 2004 there had been a 60% rise in liver disease in young people due to alcohol.

If we analysed these data and took no other factors into account, they clearly show us that more deaths relating to cancer and respiratory illness are attributed to (caused by) smoking as a lifestyle choice.

Discuss

Is it right to dictate to people whether they can or cannot smoke?

Do anti-smoking measures work?

2A.D2

To evaluate the effectiveness of any measure we need to look at its intended outcomes. The intended outcome of the ban on smoking in public places was to reduce the level of smoking and therefore the health-related issues caused by it.

The smoking ban was introduced in 2007. In 2008, the Health Behaviour Research Unit, University College London, carried out a study and found that more than two billion fewer cigarettes were smoked and that 400 000 people had given up in the year since the ban was introduced. The report estimated that this would prevent 40 000 deaths over the next 10 years.

Do you think this is the complete picture or is further investigation and evaluation needed? What other factors would need to be taken into account to show if the ban has been a success?

...government health campaigns

Preventing illness and disease

Ill all the time?

Imagine if we caught every virus around. We'd be ill all the time. We couldn't go to school, go to work, go out to socialise – we may not even be able to go out at all. Our lives depend on us being healthy and so we have a well-tuned system for preventing illness.

Your assessment criteria:

1B.4 Identify the role of the immune system in defending the body

2B.P4 Describe how the immune system defends the body in relation to specific and non-specific immune responses

2B.M3 Compare the different defence mechanisms the immune system uses to protect the human body

1B.4
2B.P4

The first line of defence

Illnesses can have either a **physical cause**, such as injury, or a **biological cause**, such as a pathogen infecting the body.

A broken arm is a physical cause

The human body is designed to work efficiently. It has sophisticated systems to help prevent pathogens causing illness. These involve different 'lines of defence':

- **physical barriers** help to stop pathogens entering the body
- **chemical barriers** deal with invaders if they do get in.

Pathogens can get into the body through the skin, the eyes, the ears, and through external respiratory organs (mouth and nose), digestive organs (mouth and anus), urinary organs (urethra) and reproductive organs (vagina and penis). For example, pathogens can invade through damaged skin, we can **ingest** them with our food or we can **inhale** them through the nose.

Know more

A pathogen is anything that can cause disease. It is usually a bacteria or a virus. These are types of microorganism, or microbe. See Unit 4.

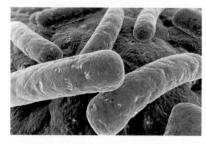

A sore throat is caused by bacteria – a biological cause

Know more

By 'chemical barrier' we mean a substance in the body that can kill or limit the effect of a pathogen.

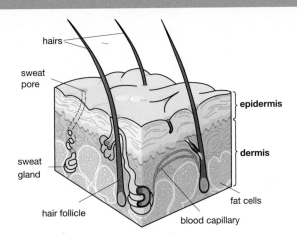

hairs

sweat pore

epidermis

dermis

sweat gland

fat cells

hair follicle

blood capillary

The skin is our most important barrier against pathogens. It is waterproof and slightly acidic

Discuss

If we have all these barriers, why do we still get ill?

Research

What would happen if we didn't have these physical and chemical barriers as a first line of defence? Find out about burn victims whose skin has been severely damaged.

Think about

How can medicine help if there is too much damage to the skin (too large a cut, graze or burn)?

Physical barriers at work

2B.M3

- When skin is broken by a cut, it rapidly blocks the break and any cut blood vessels, forming a scab. This prevents the entry of microbes and allows the skin time to heal.

- In the respiratory system we have hairs in our nose that capture large particles and **mucus**, a sticky substance that traps dirt and large pathogens. If we get infected we often make more mucus. This is a symptom of a cold. In our lungs we have **cilia** (hair-like projections that move) which help to remove mucus and pathogens from the lungs.

- In the digestive system, pathogens that have been swallowed may be killed by **stomach acid**. Special chemicals called enzymes also help to destroy pathogens. The inner lining of the gut produces mucus that can trap invading pathogens. The intestines have so-called 'good bacteria' that help prevent 'bad bacteria' taking over.

- In the **urinary system**, the flow of urine flushes bacteria out of the bladder and urethra.

Chemical barriers at work

When the physical barriers fail, we have a second line of defence known as the **immune system**. The way the immune system defends against the threat of infection often depends on the nature of the infection. The response can be **non-specific** (against general threat) or **specific** (against a particular type of infection).

For example, when you cut yourself the body responds by plugging the cut, isolating the damage from the rest of the body by **inflammation**, flooding the area with white blood cells to control pathogens and repairing the skin.

This is an example of a non-specific immune response that tries to defend against all pathogens.

The immune system

Chickenpox

Laura has chickenpox. Many children get this disease. It is caused by a virus. It is not a pleasant infection because it causes a very itchy rash that turns to blisters, as well as flu-like symptoms.

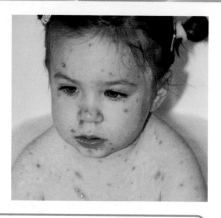

1B.4
2B.P4
1B.5
2B.P5

The second line of defence

If your body has been infected by a foreign substance or cell (**pathogen**), it responds to it and defends itself using the immune system. This fights the infection and can sometimes prevent it from reoccurring.

The immune system is made up of white blood cells which search out the infection, identify it and fight it. White blood cells are made in the bone marrow. They move around the body in the blood to where they are needed.

There are different types of white blood cell. Each has a specific way of working, depending on the threat.

Phagocytes and lymphocytes

Phagocytes are white blood cells that engulf any types of pathogen and then digest them using enzymes. Pathogens contain chemicals called antigens (usually on their outside) that are recognised as foreign to the body.

White blood cells called **lymphocytes** identify and fight against pathogens. They can stick to a pathogen, making it more likely to be destroyed. They produce **antibodies** against the antigens to help deactivate specific pathogens. They can also produce substances that counteract poisons produced by some pathogens.

Vaccination

When the pathogen is a virus and is particularly threatening (i.e. it can cause severe illness or death), a **vaccine** may be developed. **Vaccination** is when a person is given an inactive form of the pathogen that stimulates an immune response. Antibodies that work against that pathogen are produced (see Unit 4).

Your assessment criteria:

1B.4 Identify the role of the immune system in defending the body

2B.P4 Describe how the immune system defends the body in relation to specific and non-specific immune responses

1B.5 Identify how a vaccine aids in defending the body

2B.P5 Describe the changes in the human body following vaccination

2B.M3 Compare the different defence mechanisms the immune system uses to protect the human body

2B.D3 Evaluate the effectiveness of human vaccination and screening programmes

Know more

A drop of blood can contain anywhere from 7000 to 25 000 white blood cells.

Know more

*If your immune system is able to recognise a particular pathogen and fight it so that you do not get the disease, you have **immunity** against that disease.*

Research

Which conditions directly affect a person's immune system?

...immune system

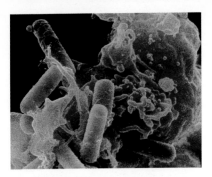

A phagocyte (orange) engulfing bacteria (blue)

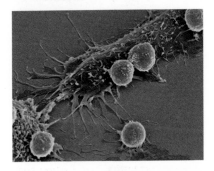

Lymphocytes (pink) attacking a cancer cell

2B.M3

Comparing defence mechansims

Look at the table below – for each of the 'threats' you can see generally how the body responds. Some of these responses are useful; others are not so useful.

Threat	Response	Specific/ non-specific	Useful or not useful
pollen	inflammation in the mucus membranes	non-specific	not useful
cut skin infected with bacteria	cut is plugged	non-specific	useful
	inflammation	non-specific	useful
	white blood cells digest and clump pathogens	non-specific	useful
	specific white blood cells called lymphocytes produce antibodies if a specific antigen is present	specific	useful
chickenpox virus	specific white blood cells called lymphocytes produce antibodies to counter infection	specific	useful

Can you think of some more 'threats' to compare?

Research

What is the difference between active and passive immunity?

Research

For what diseases are there vaccination programmes in the UK? Try to find some data about how effective they are.

2B.D3

Effectiveness of vaccination

The effectiveness of a vaccination programme is measured by how well it prevents a population from getting the disease, the likelihood of any health risks associated with being vaccinated and how many people receive it.

For example, everyone in the UK is offered the mumps, measles and rubella vaccine. Take-up of this vaccine is not as high as it could be because people have been worried about its potential side-effects.

Vaccination has one big success story. In 1979, the World Health Organisation officially recognised that smallpox, a killer disease, had been wiped off the planet.

See also Unit 4.

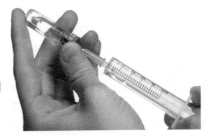

Preparing to give a vaccination

...vaccinations

Screening for disease

Your assessment criteria:

1B.6 Identify screening programmes

2B.P6 Describe the role of specific health screening programmes

2B.M4 Discuss the advantages and disadvantages of a specific health screening programme

2B.D3 Evaluate the effectiveness of human vaccination and screening programmes

Jade's fight for life

Jade Goody died from cervical cancer in 2009. If her cancer had been detected earlier she might have survived. Her well publicised fight against cervical cancer helped to raise awareness of cervical cancer screening.

**1B.6
2B.P6**

Preventative measures

Scientists have developed **screening programmes**, which help detect any abnormalities that might indicate the early stage of a disease or other condition. Screening is usually targeted at specific 'at-risk' groups. Current screening programmes include the following.

- **Breast screening** is a method of detecting breast cancer at a very early stage. The first step involves an X-ray of each breast, called a **mammogram**. This can show small changes in breast tissue which are too small to be felt either by the woman herself or by a doctor.

- **Cervical screening** is a method of detecting early abnormalities in a woman's cervix (the neck of the womb) which, if left untreated, could lead to cancer.

- **Antenatal screening** is a way of assessing whether an unborn baby (foetus) could develop or has developed an abnormality during pregnancy, for example spina bifida or Down's syndrome.

- **Newborn** or **neonatal screening** helps to identify babies who may have rare but serious conditions, including sickle cell disorders, cystic fibrosis and phenylketonuria (PKU), a disorder of the nervous system.

- **Vascular screening** usually involves a series of health checks such as height, weight, cholesterol level, blood pressure and family history, to establish the risk of cardiovascular (heart or circulatory) disease such as atherosclerosis (narrowing of the arteries).

Know more

Around 1.5 million women are screened in the UK each year for breast cancer. Screening is routine for over-50s.

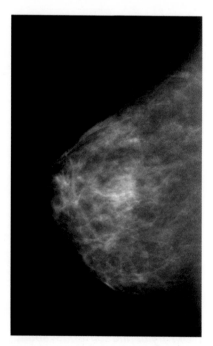

A mammogram is a screening test to detect breast cancer in its early stages

...health screening ...NHS cancer screening

1B.6
2B.P6

Know more

Prostate cancer is the most common cancer in men. In the UK, 37 000 men are diagnosed with the disease each year. Screening is possible, but is not routinely carried out.

Screening for disease is not compulsory but is recommended by health professionals.

Some types of screening, such as ante- and neonatal checks, require appointments in hospitals for specialist tests. Other screening, for example for cardiovascular disease, can be achieved by regular health checks with the GP. Some screening can be done by the individual at home, for example self-examination to check for breast or testicular lumps.

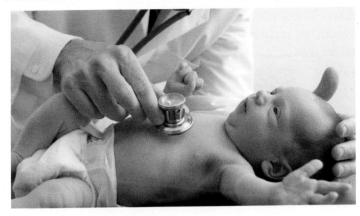

Neonatal screening can help detect some rare and serious conditions

Discuss

When funding is limited, is it better to spend money on treating conditions, or on screening for conditions?

2B.M4

How effective is screening?

Screening can be very effective in the reduction of the number of cases of certain diseases. About 1 in 20 people in the UK will develop bowel cancer during their lifetime. It is the third most common cancer in the UK, and the second leading cause of cancer deaths. Over 16 000 people die from it each year. The NHS states that regular bowel cancer screening has been shown to reduce the risk of dying from bowel cancer by 16%. Men and women aged 60 to 69 are now screened routinely.

Think about

What factors might be considered by an individual when deciding whether to be screened, or whether they want their child to be screened, for a particular disease?

2B.D3

Evaluating effectiveness

An evaluation of a screening programme relies on collecting data as evidence of its effectiveness. Effectiveness can be measured in different ways:

- the number of patients being identified and treated for the disease

- the **coverage** of the screening programme (the percentage of the target population screened)

- the reduction in serious cases of (or deaths from) the disease

- the cost-effectiveness.

Research

Find other diseases that are now screened for in the UK and their 'target population'.

Treatment options

Your assessment criteria:

2C.P8 Describe the use of anti-fungal, antiviral and analgesic treatments

2C.M5 Analyse the effectiveness of different kinds of medical treatment in health care using secondary data

2C.D4 Evaluate the use of different kinds of medical treatments, justifying your opinions

Treatment in the Middle Ages

For thousands of years, doctors relied heavily on one kind of treatment for many conditions. It didn't matter whether someone had a persistent headache or heart disease: the 'remedy' was bloodletting. Doctors would routinely cut open a blood vessel and let out blood. Fortunately our knowledge of how the human body works has increased and medicine today has a vast range of treatments available.

Physical and chemical therapies

2C.P8

Treatment options depend on whether the condition can be cured or if the aim is to control it. Some treatments control the symptoms, such as pain or discomfort, but do not cure the condition. Treatments can be thought of as either physical therapies or chemical therapies.

- A **physical therapy** is a type of treatment that does something physically to the body. An example of a physical therapy is surgery. A physical therapy is particularly useful when specific parts of the body are not functioning well.

- A **chemical therapy** is a type of treatment that uses chemicals (drugs) to treat the cause and/or the effects of an illness. For example, antibiotics are drugs that can kill bacteria that have invaded the body.

A **replacement therapy** is a physical therapy that involves replacing parts of the body that are not working well. Examples of this are transplants and blood transfusion (see page 242).

Know more

In 1920 the 'Spanish flu' epidemic caused by a flu virus claimed the lives of between 50 and 100 million people.

...transfusion ...transplants

2C.P8

The type of chemical treatment depends on the cause and the symptoms of the disease.

- **Anti-fungal** medicines kill fungi that can cause disease.

- **Antibiotics** kill specific bacteria that cause disease.

- **Antiviral** medicines slow or stop the development of specific viruses that can cause disease.

- **Analgesics** are pain killers and help control pain, they do not kill pathogens.

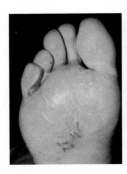

Athlete's foot is a common fungal infection that can be treated using an anti-fungal cream

Each medicine is used in a different way (i.e. cream or tablet) and prescribed or used at different doses depending on the disease and its severity.

> **Know more**
>
> *Gene and stem cell therapies are both new therapies that have exciting potential for treating some diseases.*

Effectiveness of treatments

2C.M5

The effectiveness of a medicine or treatment depends on many different factors such as when it is used, how it is used and if the diagnosis was correct in the first place. For example, if the effectiveness of antibiotics was measured from secondary data relating to curing the common cold (which is caused by a virus), then their effectiveness would be '0'.

Can you think of some other effectiveness measures?

Evaluating treatment options

2C.D4

Treatments can be evaluated from a number of different perspectives.

Medical and scientific: Is it working? What are the benefits? What is the evidence? What are the risks?

Financial: How much does it cost? Are the benefits of the treatment worth this expenditure?

Ethical: Are there any reasons why the treatment could be considered wrong? Is the treatment essential, whatever the cost?

Social: Does the treatment benefit society as a whole? Will the treatment take too much money away from other important areas?

Religious: Do religious beliefs reject the treatment?

...treating disease

Antibiotics

Arguing about antibiotics

On a visit to the doctor's surgery with a really bad cold, Julia had a disagreement with her doctor. Julia wanted an antibiotic that would cure her of her cold, but the doctor said he couldn't give her anything. He told her that antibiotics only work on bacterial infections, not on viruses.

Your assessment criteria:

1C.7 Describe how antibiotics are prescribed for use

1C.8 Identify pathogens that cannot be treated by antibiotics

2C.P7 Investigate the use and misuse of antibiotics using secondary data

2C.M5 Analyse the effectiveness of different kinds of medical treatment in health care using secondary data

2C.D4 Evaluate the use of different kinds of medical treatments, justifying your opinions

1C.7
1C.8
2C.P7

The history of antibiotics

An antibiotic is a substance that kills or slows the growth of some microbes, especially bacteria. It is made naturally by other microbes.

Antibiotic substances were discovered long ago, when the ancient Egyptians and Chinese used mould to treat infections. The breakthrough in medical treatment came when the effects of one particular organism were discovered in 1929. This was 'penicillium', discovered by Alexander Fleming. It was only in 1940 that antibiotic drugs were developed and used widely.

Types of antibiotic

There are many types of antibiotic. Each works slightly differently and acts on different types of bacteria. Some antibiotics are very good at fighting a wide range of bacteria. These are called **wide spectrum antibiotics**. Others are effective against only a few types of bacteria. These are called **narrow spectrum antibiotics**.

Some antibiotic names you may have heard of are:

penicillin   amoxicillin   tetracycline   erythromycin

Antibiotics are used to treat **bacterial infections**, including throat infections, chest infections, pneumonia, syphilis and meningitis. They work either by binding to the **cell membrane** of the bacteria and destroying it, or by stopping it **replicating**. Antibiotics cannot be used to treat infections caused by a virus.

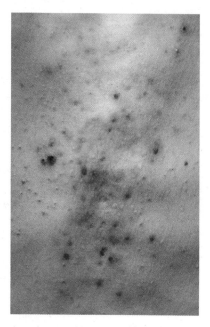

Acne is sometimes treatable with an antibiotic

Know more

Antibiotics cannot tell the difference between 'good' and 'bad' bacteria, so they can get rid of some of the bacteria you actually need.

🔍 ...antibiotics

Are antibiotics effective?

2C.M5

Antibiotics have been highly successful in treating a wide range of dangerous and potentially fatal diseases worldwide. Before penicillin was developed, bacterial infections were a major cause of death. In 1900, one third of all deaths were caused by pneumonia, tuberculosis (TB) and diarrhoea and sickness. All of these can now be effectively treated with antibiotics.

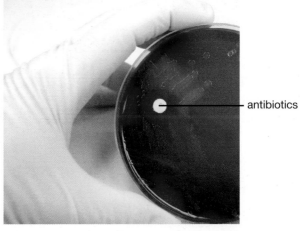

The disc in this plate contains antibiotics, which have killed the bacteria around it

But the inappropriate use and over-prescribing of antibiotics has helped to create strains of bacteria that are resistant to them. These so-called 'superbugs' are responsible for many infections that are caught in hospital. The most well known superbug is MRSA. Worryingly, a new antibiotic-resistant form of TB is now causing concern.

The development of antibiotic-resistant bacteria can be partly controlled by limiting the prescription of antibiotics. In the UK antibiotic use has declined, with the sharpest reduction in 1998. The prescribing rate for antibiotics in the UK fell in October 2004, but then increased again and continues to be higher than that in other northern European countries.

Think about

Why is it not a good idea to take only some of an antibiotic medicine?

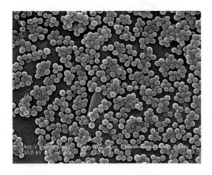

MRSA bacteria highly magnified

Discuss

Can we justify the continued use of antibiotics?

Evaluating antibiotic use

2C.D4

So how should we use antibiotics in the future? This will really depend on demand and if they remain effective. Antibiotic resistance is increasing. If doctors prescribe antibiotics less often, and if patients always complete the course of medicine prescribed, the development of resistance may slow down. It's not possible to stop resistance completely, but slowing down its spread buys us some time to develop new types of antibiotics.

...antibiotic resistance

Transfusions and transplants

A&E

Mario has been in a serious car accident, which has resulted in severe blood loss. Although doctors have managed to stop the bleeding, he has lost so much blood that his blood pressure has dropped and his organs are starting to fail. The doctors have no option but to give him a blood transfusion.

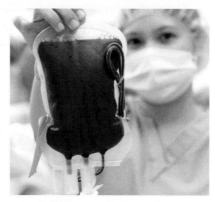

Blood transfusions save lives

1C.9
2C.P9

Blood groups and transfusions

Blood is a liquid that carries important substances around the body. Blood also helps in defending the body against infections. Depending on the type of red cell present, blood is classified into four main groups: A, B, AB and O. Depending on whether a specific protein called the Rhesus factor is present or not, blood is a further classified as + or −. Group AB is the most common blood group.

Blood cells in different groups of blood have different antigens and antibodies. This means that some bloods cannot mix.

	Blood Group		
	Group A	Group B	Group AB	Group O
Red blood cell type	A	B	AB	O
Antibodies present	Anti-B	Anti-A	None	Aniti-A and Anti-B
Antigens present	A antigen	B antigen	A and B antigens	None

🔍...blood transfusion

If someone has lost a lot of blood, it can be replaced. This process is called **transfusion**. Blood can only be replaced with blood of the same type that has been lost, or with blood without the antigens it has antibodies to. So for example, a person with Group A blood could not be transfused with Group B blood, because the antibodies in Group A blood would attack the antigens in Group B blood.

1C.9
2C.P9

Know more

Organs need to be 'donated' either from live donors or people who have died. Suitable organs are not always readily available, so people who need them are put on a waiting list. The average waiting time for a kidney transplant is 1110 days.

Think about

What could be done to reduce waiting lists?

Research

Find out where stem cells are obtained from and explain why their use can be controversial. What other conditions can they potentially treat?

Discuss

Should the Government fund stem cell research?

Discuss

Should we have our organs donated automatically on our death?

Organ donation

2C.M6

Blood transfusions are an example of a **replacement therapy**. So are organ transplants. A transplant is needed when a person's organ is no longer working. Like blood transfusions, organs need to be matched to the recipient. Careful checks need to be carried out and blood and tissue types matched before a transplant can be considered. If the match is not close enough then the donated organ would be rejected by the recipient's body. The closer the match, the lower the risk of rejection.

Even when a transplant is carried out and the match is very close, the person with the transplant needs to take drugs for life to suppress their immune system to ensure that the organ is not rejected.

Stem cell transplants

2C.D5

Stem cells are body cells that can develop into other, specialised cells that the body needs. The stem cells in bone marrow, for example, develop into our immune system. The disease leukaemia destroys the immune system. Leukaemia can be treated if stem cells are transplanted into someone with the disease.

Potential uses for stem cells include producing and transplanting tissues into damaged organs when matched donors are difficult to find and to reduce the risk of rejection.

Stem cell treatment has proven effective in some cases but it is complex and depends on multiple factors.

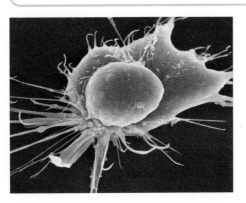

The use of this simple stem cell has medical potential but is hotly debated

🔍 ...organ transplant ...stem cells

Assessment Checklist

To achieve a Pass grade, my portfolio of evidence must show that I can:

Assessment Criteria	Description	✓
2A.P1	Describe the possible effects of diet and exercise on the functioning of the human body	
2A.P2	Develop a diet and exercise plan based on level and type of exercise and appropriate nutritional balance, to promote healthy living for an individual	
2A.P3	Describe the ways in which health improvement measures are intended to improve the health of the population	
2B.P4	Describe how the immune system defends the body in relation to specific and non-specific immune responses	
2B.P5	Describe the changes in the human body following vaccination	
2B.P6	Describe the role of specific health screening programmes	
2C.P7	Investigate the use and misuse of antibiotics using secondary data	
2C.P8	Describe the use of anti-fungal, antiviral and analgesic treatments	
2C.P9	Explain the importance of blood group matching in blood transfusions	

If you do not meet all the Level 2 Pass criteria for this Unit then your work will be assessed against these Level 1 criteria. If your work meets all these criteria you will achieve a Level 1 Pass for this Unit. If you do not achieve all these Level 1 criteria you will get a U (Unclassified) for this Unit.

Assessment Criteria	Description	✓
1A.1	Explain the importance of a balanced diet and exercise	
1A.2	Identify a balanced diet for teenagers	
1A.3	Identify measures taken to improve the health of the population	
1B.4	Identify the role of the immune system in defending the body	
1B.5	Identify how a vaccine aids in defending the body	
1B.6	Identify screening programmes	
1C.7	Describe how antibiotics are prescribed for use	
1C.8	Identify pathogens that cannot be treated by antibiotics	
1C.9	Identify the different blood groups	

To achieve a Merit grade, my portfolio of evidence must also show that I can:

Assessment Criteria	Description	✓
2A.M1	Explain how the diet and exercise plan will affect the functioning of the human body	
2A.M2	Analyse rates of disease in the population in relation to lifestyle choices	
2B.M3	Compare the different defence mechanisms the immune system uses to protect the human body	
2B.M4	Discuss the advantages and disadvantages of a specific health screening programme	
2C.M5	Analyse the effectiveness of different kinds of medical treatment in health care using secondary data	
2C.M6	Describe organ donation and approaches used to reduce rejection	

To achieve a Distinction grade, my portfolio of evidence must also show that I can:

Assessment Criteria	Description	✓
2A.D1	Evaluate the diet and exercise plan, and justify the menus and activities chosen	
2A.D2	Evaluate measures taken to improve the health of the population	
2B.D3	Evaluate the effectiveness of human vaccination and screening programmes	
2C.D4	Evaluate the use of different kinds of medical treatments, justifying your opinions	
2C.D5	Evaluate the potential benefits of stem cell therapy	

Unit 8 **Scientific Skills**

LA

Understand how to produce a good plan for an investigation

- Scientists use practical investigations to test their ideas (hypotheses), ranging from ideas about how our everyday activities might be linked with disease, to predicting the behaviour of chemicals and the properties of new materials

- Our safety depends on many of the activities carried out by scientists, including forensic science, environmental issues and whether food and drink is fit for us to eat or drink

- Scientists must use the most appropriate techniques and equipment for their investigations or their findings may not be accepted, for instance in areas such as in forensic science

LA

Be able to process, present and analyse data, and draw evidence-based conclusions

- Scientists organise their data and other information by recording it in carefully constructed tables

- Scientists display large amounts of data in a small space by using graphs and charts – for other scientists or the public

- Graphs and charts give a clear picture of relationships that couldn't be understood as clearly, if at all, in a table

- Forensic scientists – like all other scientists – must base their conclusions on experimental evidence; conclusions must not involve any preconceived ideas, bias or prejudice

Be able to evaluate evidence and investigative methods

- Data on antibiotic resistance may *support* the hypothesis that this is related to the overuse of antibiotics, but scientists would never say that a hypothesis had been *proven*

- Scientists testing a hypothesis that soil nutrients are lost by deforestation must follow up one study on nitrates with others on other nutrients; scientists always consider what extra data would support the hypothesis

- Scientists must look for ways of improving their scientific technique when collecting data – such as collecting more data and improving their techniques or measurements

An outbreak of food poisoning?

Your learning aims:

A.1   Produce a good plan for an investigation

A.2   Provide a hypothesis based on relevant scientific ideas

An investigation for environmental health

There has been an outbreak of sickness and diarrhoea in a small town. Doctors, along with the people who were ill, report the illness to the local authority.

Food poisoning is suspected. Public health scientist Sarah is co-ordinating the investigation.

A bacterium called Campylobacter is the most common cause of food poisoning

Planning the investigation

Sarah begins the investigation by interviewing the people who were ill. The interviews indicate that the people had all eaten at one of the town's restaurants and that the symptoms had begun two to three days after eating there. The diners had all eaten an item on the menu with chicken in it. Further research showed that restaurant-goers who hadn't eaten this dish had not become ill.

From this evidence and her knowledge of microorganisms, Sarah can suggest a possible explanation for the outbreak.

A hypothesis

Sarah's hypothesis is that the outbreak has been caused by food at the restaurant being contaminated by a microorganism. She says that, "because the symptoms occurred three days after the restaurant visit, this probably rules out one type of bacterium called *Staphylococcus*. All the people affected vomited, so this may rule out an organism called *Campylobacter*. I suspect that an organism called *Salmonella* may be involved, especially as the people affected all ate chicken."

But these are just suggestions. Sarah must carry out further investigative work to find support – or not – for her hypothesis.

Sarah's investigation

Sarah takes samples of the foods used to make the chicken dish. She also swabs the kitchen work surfaces and chopping boards.

Exam tip

*A possible explanation that someone suggests to explain some scientific observations is called a **hypothesis**.*

Sarah liquidises the food samples in sterile water using a homogeniser

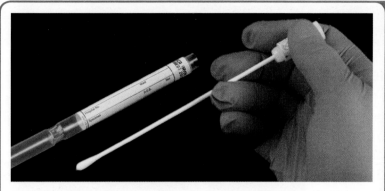

Sarah collects samples from surfaces using sterile swabs. Note that she wears gloves, for her own safety as well as to avoid contamination of the samples

From the homogenised food samples, Sarah uses a micropipette to apply small, accurately measured volumes to **agar plates**. She repeats each test.

Sarah uses several different types of agar. Each type she selects supports the growth of a different type of bacterium.

She incubates the plates at 37 °C for 24 hours and looks for any growth on them.

Sarah uses a new sterile, disposable pipette tip for each sample

Sarah's hypothesis is supported

Sarah's results support her hypothesis. No other types of bacteria that cause food poisoning grew from her samples. But she could not be absolutely certain of the identification. Or that it was definitely the bacteria in the food samples that caused the outbreak of diarrhoea and sickness.

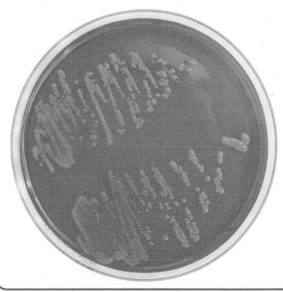

Bacteria grow only in the plate containing Brilliant Green agar. The plate is turned purple. This suggests that bacteria in the sample are Salmonella

🔍 ... writing a hypothesis

Health and safety

The Health and Safety Officer

Dai is a Health and Safety Officer in a life sciences company. His job is to produce and oversee the organisation's health and safety policy. He also ensures that these policies are complied with at all times.

Life science companies carry out research in areas of medicine and biotechnology

Identifying hazards and risks

Dai says, "Before anyone carries out any practical work, we must identify the possible hazards."

A **hazard** is something that is likely to cause harm. Substances, organisms and equipment that we think of as being harmless, may be hazardous if used in the wrong way.

We can group hazards into biological, chemical and physical.

Scientists use an international series of symbols so that investigators can identify hazards.

Caution	*Toxic*	*Flammable*	*Oxidising*
Corrosive	*Explosive*	*Harmful to environment*	

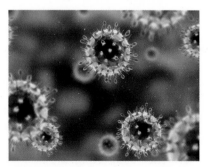

Biological hazards include body fluids, microorganisms, animals and plants, especially if mishandled

... scientific hazard symbols

Physical hazards include electrical equipment, hot objects and nuclear radiation

Hazards pose **risks** to the person carrying out the investigation. What might happen if things go wrong? A risk posed by dilute hydrochloric acid, for instance, is that if it splashes into your eyes you could lose your sight.

Minimising risk

Hazardous materials, such as chemicals or equipment in the laboratory, must be used in a way that keeps risks to an absolute minimum. One way of reducing the risk for hydrochloric acid is to wear eye protection.

Before you begin the investigation, carry out a **risk assessment**. This must include steps that need to be taken to minimise or manage the risks.

Activity				
Biological hazards	Nature of hazard, e.g. type of body fluid, living organism	Type of hazard and risk associated with hazard	Steps taken to minimise risk	Emergency procedure
Chemical hazards	Nature of hazard, e.g. chemical found, used or made	Type of hazard and risk associated with hazard	Steps taken to minimise risk	Emergency procedure
Physical hazards	Nature of hazard, e.g. sharp objects, device being used	Type of hazard and risk associated with hazard	Steps taken to minimise risk	Emergency procedure

An example of a risk assessment

You should also consider what to do at the end of the practical. Used agar plates should be left for a technician to sterilise; solutions of certain metal salts should be collected in a bottle and disposed of safely.

A full and appropriate risk assessment

To make sure that your risk assessment is full and appropriate:

- for a chemical reaction, the risk assessment should include the products as well as the reactants

- make sure the hazard and risk match, for example check the concentration of the chemical you're using; many acids are corrosive in higher concentrations, but harmful or irritant at low concentrations.

Exam tip

Make sure that you include all the hazards (using the correct terms), even if you think they will pose minimal risk.

Limescale removers

Limescale

When hard water is heated, it forms a hard, off-white solid called limescale. Limescale sticks to the heating elements of kettles and washing machines and can block water pipes. Aiguo works for a chemical company in China. He is researching safe and sustainable limescale removers ('descalers').

Limescale forms on the elements of kettles, reducing efficiency. It can flake off and end up in your tea or coffee

The reaction between limescale and acid

Limescale is mostly made of calcium carbonate. Calcium carbonate reacts with acids, such as hydrochloric acid forming soluble calcium chloride, carbon dioxide and water:

calcium carbonate (solid)	+	hydrochloric acid (solution)	→	calcium chloride (soluble)	+	carbon dioxide (gas)	+	water

Many different acids could be used as descalers. Acids such as hydrochloric acid are too corrosive to use.

Aiguo's company is researching the use of lactic acid as a limescale remover. The acid is safer than many others, and is biodegradable. Lactic acid can be produced by **fermentation**. His company has found a new way of producing it sustainably from a chemical called glycerol.

Glycerol is a waste product of biodiesel production

... experimental variable

Question

From your knowledge and understanding of chemical reactions, and observations you have made, write a hypothesis for the reaction between lactic acid and marble. Try to be quantitative: suggest what might happen to the rate of reaction if the concentration of the acid is doubled.

Exam tip

*When working with any independent variable, you have to choose an appropriate **range** over which to investigate the variable.*

Exam tip

*What you choose to measure in an investigation is called the **dependent** variable. The values measured will **depend** on the independent variable, and this is perhaps the best way of remembering its definition.*

Question

Suggest two more variables that should be controlled.

The effect of lactic acid concentration on limescale removal

Aiguo wants to investigate the best concentration of lactic acid to react with and remove the limescale. The factor he chooses to investigate is called the **independent variable**.

Aiguo chooses a range of lactic acid concentrations to test, from 0 to 10%. To help him make this decision, he carried out some preliminary investigations. He found these concentrations were suitable to react with and 'dissolve' the limescale. They also give results in a short period of time that he can measure accurately. Importantly, these concentrations of acid are not too corrosive and do not pose serious health and safety hazards.

Aiguo uses blocks of marble – another form of calcium carbonate – to carry out the test. He puts marble blocks in different concentrations of lactic acid. He then rinses and dries each block and measures the change in mass. The change in mass is called the **dependent variable**.

Controlling other variables

Aiguo needs to control other variables that may also have an influence on the test. In most investigations, it's important that you investigate just one variable at a time. So any other variables, apart from the one you're testing, must be controlled. They must not be allowed to vary.

Aiguo uses marble blocks of identical size in different concentrations of lactic acid and measures their change in mass. Each block is placed in the lactic acid for exactly 15 minutes.

The reaction between calcium carbonate and an acid

... control variable

Investigating sunscreens

Sunscreens

Emily works for a company that manufactures sunscreen creams. Sunscreens protect our skin against damaging ultraviolet (UV) radiation. Emily is testing two new sunscreens developed by the company. One of them contains nanoparticles.

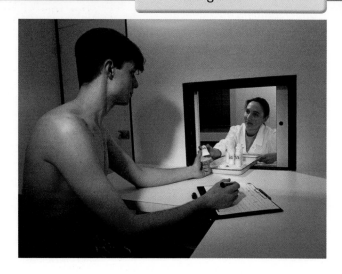

Protection against the Sun's rays

We are all exposed to UV radiation when we go out in sunshine. Some people also receive UV radiation from sunbeds or become exposed to it in their work in industry. The UV that reaches the Earth's surface is made up mostly of UVA rays, with a small component of UVB. (UVC is filtered out by the Earth's ozone layer.) Both UVA and UVB can cause skin cancer. Exposure to UVA rays can also cause the skin to age, while UVB causes sunburn. Sunscreens must protect against this radiation.

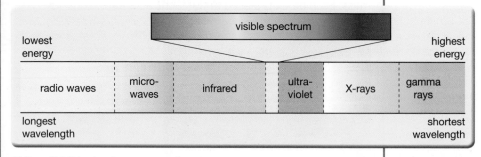

UVA and UVB in the electromagnetic spectrum

Planning her investigation

Emily says, "Sunscreens work by preventing the UV radiation from reaching our skin. Some chemicals used in our sunscreen products absorb UV radiation. Other types reflect it away from the skin."

"Any investigation into a new product must be planned very carefully. It's essential to select techniques and equipment that will enable me to collect measurements that are accurate and precise."

... accuracy and precision

"The method I use measures the UV radiation that is absorbed by a layer of the sunscreen. I coat a layer of it on a plastic sheet, then allow it to dry. I use a technique that makes sure that the sunscreen is applied evenly, at a rate of 2 mg per cm^2 of the sheet."

"I then measure the amount of radiation transmitted through the layer. The factor that I'm varying each time – the independent variable – is the wavelength of the radiation. The range of wavelengths I investigate is from 200 to 400 nm."

Experimental controls

"Experimental controls are also very important. I need to be sure that any UV absorbed is by the active ingredient in the sunscreen, and not by the plastic sheet or by the glycerol base that the sunscreen chemical is in."

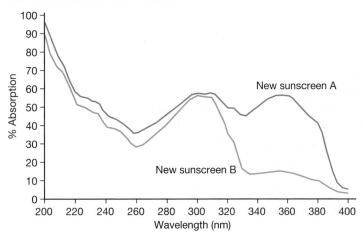

The absorbance of UV at different wavelengths by the new sunscreens

The next stage of the investigation

"I now know which sunscreen works better in absorbing radiation. So it's time to see how it will work on humans. I will choose ten healthy volunteers who are older than 18 years of age."

Emily finds the dose of UV radiation that leads to sunburn in her volunteers 16–24 hours after exposure

... independent variable range

Question

Emily keeps all other factors that might affect her investigation constant. Make a list of these.

Question

Look at the graph on the right. Which is the better sunscreen? Explain why.

Exam tip

You need to know the stages of planning an investigation:

✓ *Write a hypothesis*

✓ *Choose a factor to test (the independent variable)*

✓ *Choose a suitable range (of the independent variable) over which to investigate*

✓ *Choose what you will measure (the dependent variable)*

✓ *Select appropriate equipment/technique to carry out the investigation/measure the dependent variable*

✓ *Produce a risk assessment*

Testing the performance of limescale remover

Your learning aims:

B.1	Tabulate data in a clear, logical way
B.2, B.3	Identify and deal with anomalous results in tabulated data
B.4, B.5, B.10	Perform calculations from data, using significant figures to an appropriate level of accuracy
B.6–B.9	Draw graphs, identify anomalous results, draw lines of best fit and read off values
B.11–B.13	Describe trends and patterns in data, explain anomalous results, analyse evidence and draw a conclusion

Investigating the effectiveness of lactic acid

In their applied science class Jodie and Ben are investigating a new limescale remover containing lactic acid.

Measuring the effect of concentration

Jodie and Ben want to look at the effect of different concentrations of lactic acid limescale remover on calcium carbonate. They use calcium carbonate in the form of marble chips. The reaction is:

$$\text{calcium carbonate} + \text{lactic acid} \rightarrow \text{calcium lactate} + \text{carbon dioxide} + \text{water}$$

They have decided to measure the amount of carbon dioxide produced. Jodie thinks it would be difficult to measure how much calcium carbonate reacts as the reaction proceeds. She says, "We would have to remove the marble chips from the acid and weigh them."

Jodie makes a series of solutions of different concentrations of the limescale remover. Ben pours equal volumes of each into five conical flasks.

They add an equal mass of crushed marble chips to each and time how long it takes to collect $50\,\text{cm}^3$ of carbon dioxide. They repeat each experiment.

Question

Explain the difficulties with trying to measure the calcium carbonate that has reacted.

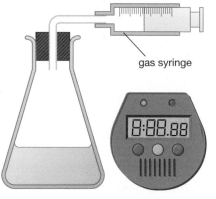

The equipment they use includes a gas syringe. It has an accuracy of 1%

... collecting data

Recording and processing results

Jodie and Ben record the results in a table.

Concentration of lactic acid (mol/dm^3)	Time taken for 50 cm^3 of carbon dioxide to be produced (seconds)						Average time taken for 50 cm^3 of carbon dioxide to be produced, seconds
	Experiment 1	Experiment 2	Experiment 3	Experiment 4	Experiment 5	Experiment 6	
0.25	483	485	499	495	488		490
0.50	243	244	235	235	233		238
0.75	170	162	166	165	171		167
1.00	87	129	122	117	119	123	122
1.25	103	105	96	97	98		100
1.50	77	81	82	80	85		81
1.75	72	68	67	73	71		70
2.00	60	55	61	65	58		60

Exam tip

Make sure the column headings in your tables describe accurately what you're measuring.

Exam tip

*Note that the averages in the table are all whole numbers. Look at the data for the 2.00 mol/dm³ lactic acid. The average is 59.8. But each of the recorded values has only two **significant figures**. So the averages can't have more.*

Exam tip

If you think an anomalous result comes from an error in the experimental work, you should omit it when calculating the average. You may want to carry out another repeat. But if you have sufficient consistent data, this may not be necessary.

They calculate the average time taken for 50 cm^3 of carbon dioxide to be produced for each concentration of lactic acid. Ben says, "Calculating the average, or mean, of a repeated set of measurements will give us the best estimate we can get of the true value."

Repeatability

The results show good **repeatability**. Each time Jodie and Ben repeated the experiment, their results were quite consistent. The spread of measurements for each data set is quite small.

But they recognised that the first experiment with 1.00 mol/dm³ of lactic acid – circled in the table – does not fit the pattern of the next four results. Their decision was to carry out the experiment again, rather than base the average on just four results.

A result that doesn't fit the pattern is called as an **anomalous result** or **outlier**.

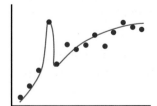 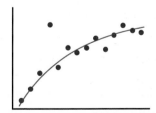

The left-hand graph shows the effect of including an anomalous result. Look at other points. It is clear that these display a trend. Exclude the anomalous result, as shown on the right-hand graph

... anomalous results

Carrying out repeats

When making measurements, in most instances it's essential that you carry out repeats. Just one set of results from your investigation may not reflect what truly happens.

More than one measurement will also reduce **random error**. Random error is the type of error introduced by the investigator. Two possible sources in this investigation are being inconsistent on each run when starting the stopclock, or determining when 50 cm³ of gas had been produced.

Displaying data in graphs

Jodie draws a graph of their results. A graph gives a clear picture of relationships and trends.

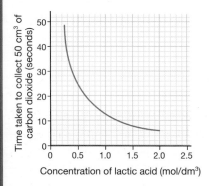

The graph shows the relationship between the time taken to collect 50 cm³ of carbon dioxide and the concentration of lactic acid

Trends in data

Jodie calculates the rate of production of carbon dioxide. She made a **quantitative hypothesis** based on her knowledge of chemistry. She says, "The reaction between lactic acid and calcium carbonate depends on successful collisions between particles. If we double the concentration of lactic acid, we're doubling the particles that can react. So the rate of reaction will double."

$$\text{Rate of reaction} = \frac{\text{amount of product formed (or reactant used up)}}{\text{time}}$$

Using the data on page 257, for 2.00 mol/dm³ lactic acid, if:

in 60 seconds, 50 cm³ of carbon dioxide is collected,

in 1 second, $\dfrac{50 \text{ cm}^3}{60}$ of carbon dioxide is collected = 0.83 cm³

So, the rate of carbon dioxide production for this concentration is 0.83 cm³/second.

Jodie calculates all the reaction rates. She then draws a graph of the rate of reaction against concentration.

Exam tip

When drawing graphs:

- the independent variable is almost always plotted on the x-axis; the dependent variable on the y-axis

- use suitable scales for the axes; try to fill the graph paper; work in 1s, 2s, 5s, 10s, 20s, etc.; that way, you can work out the value of one of the smallest divisions. Don't work in 3s, even if you waste some space on the page

- make sure that the divisions on the axes represent equal divisions in values

- label the axes so that they give an accurate description of the variables

- include units, where appropriate

- it is usual to plot means; you can use range bars to indicate the upper and lower range of your data sets

- sometimes it's helpful to plot all the data, not just the means; circle any anomalous results

- decide whether to link the points with a line of best fit or a curve of best fit.

... drawing graphs in science

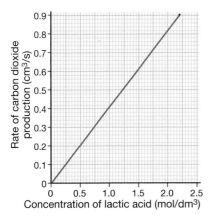

Jodie's graph of the relationship between the rate of reaction and concentration shows that as the concentration doubles, the rate of reaction doubles

During this chemical reaction, there is a change from colourless to blue

There is a **positive correlation** of the data. Her line of best fit goes through the origin of the graph (at a concentration of 0 mol/dm³ lactic acid, there is no reaction). The rate of reaction is **directly proportional** to the concentration of lactic acid.

From the data, she can find a **quantitative relationship**. She works this out by reading the reaction rates at 1.00 and 2.00 mol/dm³ lactic acid from the graph (see left).

Other methods of finding the rate of reaction

It's not always possible to measure the volume or mass of a product formed or reactants used up in a chemical reaction. Other methods of investigating chemical reactions are:

- measuring the time taken for a colour change

- measuring the time taken for the formation of precipitate, e.g. by the reaction mixture turning cloudy.

The rate of reaction and the time taken for a reaction to occur are inversely related, so rate of reaction = (1 ÷ time taken).

Factors that affect the rate of chemical reactions

Aaron is investigating the effect of temperature on the reaction.

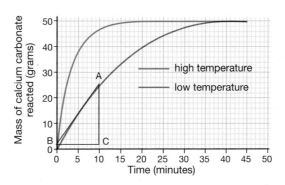

Aaron plots graphs of mass of calcium carbonate reacted over time

He finds the rate of reaction at any time by calculating the **gradient** of the graph. The steeper the gradient, the faster the reaction. You can see the reactions are fastest at the beginning.

Aaron wants to find the reaction rate at 5 minutes. For the low temperature graph, he draws a tangent (line AB) on his graph. He draws lines AC and BC where the tangent intersects with lines on the *x*- and *y*-axes.

He carries out the following calculation:

$$\text{gradient} = \frac{\text{AC}}{\text{BC}} = \frac{(26-2)\,\text{g}}{(10-0)\,\text{min}} = \frac{24\,\text{g}}{10\,\text{min}} = 2.4\,\text{g/min}^{-1}$$

... correlation in graphs

Water quality

Your learning aims:

A.1	Produce a good plan for an investigation
B.6–B.9	Draw graphs, identify anomalous results, draw lines of best fit and read off values
B.12	Describe trends and patterns in data
B.13	Analyse evidence and draw a conclusion

The water supply turns brown

Consumers contact the local water company. They say the water supply is discoloured. Is it safe to drink?
A few people, who did not notice it was discoloured, drank some. They say they now feel ill. But is this connected to the water?

Are microorganisms present in the water?

The water company thinks that the colour is probably the result of metal ions in the water. But the water must also be checked for microorganisms. It *may* have become contaminated with soil or sewage.

Oliver is a water analyst. One of his team has collected water samples from one of the houses affected. Oliver **inoculates** a Petri dish containing nutrient agar with a water sample. It is essential that, throughout the process, he uses **aseptic technique**.

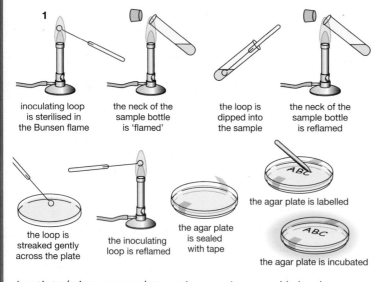

1 inoculating loop is sterilised in the Bunsen flame — the neck of the sample bottle is 'flamed' — the loop is dipped into the sample — the neck of the sample bottle is reflamed

the loop is streaked gently across the plate — the inoculating loop is reflamed — the agar plate is sealed with tape — the agar plate is labelled — the agar plate is incubated

Aseptic technique ensures that no microorganisms are added to the samples. It also makes sure that no microorganisms escape into the environment

Quick diagnostic tests for chemicals

Flame tests, or quick chemical tests, can quickly reveal the presence of metal ions in water.

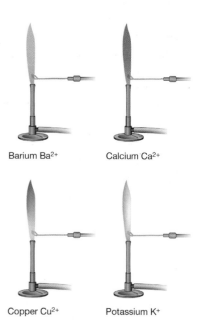

Barium Ba^{2+} Calcium Ca^{2+}

Copper Cu^{2+} Potassium K^+

Flame tests can indicate the presence of some metal ions

... aseptic technique

Potassium thiocyanate gives a blood red colour with iron(III) ions

Question

A member of the public has brought in a water sample in a jam jar. Explain why Oliver is cautious about any microorganisms found in this sample.

Exam tip

*So that equipment gives accurate readings, it has to be **calibrated** against standards of known accuracy. Chemical equipment such as pH meters must be calibrated using solutions of known pH (buffers) before use.*

Question

Suggest two reasons why Oliver chooses the range of his standard solutions to be 0.00–1.00 mg/dm³.

Exam tip

***Error** is the difference between the measured value and its true value. Error leads to uncertainty in measurements.*

Testing for iron(III) ions

Some ions do not give a flame colour. Oliver carries out a test specific for iron(III) ions. He adds some potassium thiocyanate solution to a sample.

Finding the concentration of the ions

Oliver makes up a series of samples containing known, different concentrations of iron(III) nitrate. These are called **standard solutions**. Oliver adds potassium thiocyanate solution to each solution and transfers them to a glass chamber called a cuvette. He places these, one by one, into an instrument called a colorimeter.

In this reaction, the intensity of the red colour in each sample is proportional to the concentration of iron(III) ions present. The colorimeter determines the intensity of colour by measuring how much light is absorbed by each of the samples.

Oliver plots the absorbance of each standard solution over concentration.

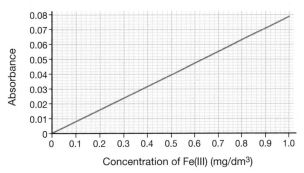

*Oliver uses the readings to plot a graph called a **calibration curve***

Oliver says, "I measure the absorbance of the water samples treated with potassium thiocyanate in exactly the same way as the standard solutions. By drawing a horizontal line on the graph to indicate the absorbance of the sample, I read off a value of the concentration of iron(III) ions from the graph." This is called **interpolation** from the graph.

Accuracy and precision

The standard solutions that Oliver makes up must be prepared accurately to reduce error.

Oliver first prepares a stock solution containing 100 mg/dm³ of iron(III) ions. He dilutes this stock solution to prepare the standard solutions. He says, "I measure the liquids using graduated pipettes and volumetric flasks. The volumetric flask is of high accuracy and precision. It measures 500 cm³ to ±0.02 cm³. This is a relative uncertainty of 0.02 ÷ 500, which is 4×10^{-4}."

Lenses

A visit to the optician

Sarah is finding it difficult to see objects a short distance away.
She visits her optician. The eye tests carried out show she is long-sighted.
She will need glasses to correct this defect in her vision.

Your learning aims:

A.1   Produce a good plan for an investigation

B.1   Tabulate data in a clear, logical way

B.4,   Perform calculations
B.5   from data, using significant figures to an appropriate level of accuracy

B.6,   Draw graphs with lines of
B.8   best fit

B.12,   Describe trends and
B.13   patterns in data, analyse evidence

Sarah is long-sighted

The optician tells Sarah, "Long-sightedness is when light rays are focused behind the retina when looking at near objects. We use lenses with positive values to correct this. The larger the number, the more powerful and thicker the lens has to be."

In her physics lesson, Sarah is investigating lenses. She is carrying out some practical work on their focal lengths. She learns that the power of a lens is (1 ÷ focal length). We say that lens power is **indirectly proportional** to focal length:

$$\text{power of a lens (in dioptres)} = \frac{1}{\text{focal length (in metres)}}$$

Measuring focal length

Sarah tests how focal length varies with lens thickness. She measures the maximum thickness of a range of convex lenses using a micrometer. She sets up a ray box and places a comb in front of it to produce light rays. She measures the focal length of the different lenses. All the lenses she investigates have the same diameter.

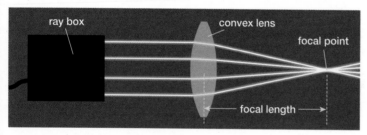

ray box   convex lens   focal point   focal length

Sarah measures the focal length of a lens

She constructs a table to record her results. She ensures that the headings of the columns are clear and define the measurements she is recording, and she includes units. She arranges the values of her independent variables so that they are in ascending order. In other words, she starts with the smallest value first.

Question

Sarah's prescription for her left eye requires a lens of power 4.25 dioptres. Calculate the focal length of the lens.

🔍 ... indirectly proportional

Thickness of lens (mm)	Focal length (mm)
2.6	250
2.9	175
3.1	150
3.3	125
3.6	100
4.1	75
4.7	60
5.2	50
6.1	40
6.8	35
7.7	30
9.0	25

Sarah's completed results table

Exam tip

Although Sarah's graph doesn't show it, when there is a directly proportional relationship, the line goes through the origin of the graph.

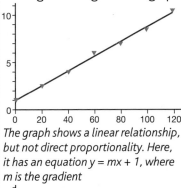

The graph shows a linear relationship, but not direct proportionality. Here, it has an equation y = mx + 1, where m is the gradient

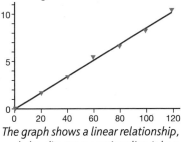

The graph shows a linear relationship, and also direct proportionality. It has an equation y = mx, where m is the gradient

Sarah plots her data on a graph. She draws a **curve of best fit** through the points.

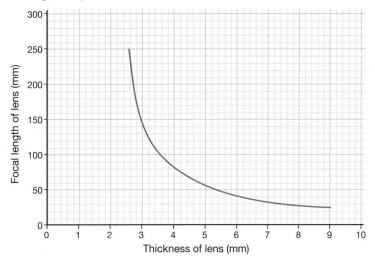

Relationship between the thickness of a lens and its focal length

The graph shows a **negative correlation** – as values of the independent variable *increase*, those of the dependent variable *decrease*.

Sarah thinks that the curvature of the lenses might be a better factor to investigate than the maximum thickness. She measures the radius of the curved surface of each lens. She uses an instrument called a spherometer. She plots a graph of focal length against radius of curvature.

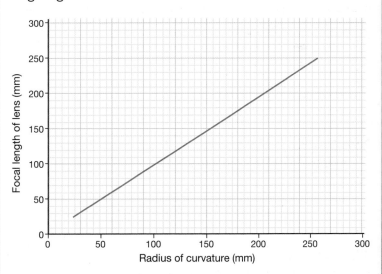

Relationship between the radius of curvature of a lens and its focal length

There is a **positive correlation** between the two variables. The graph shows a **linear relationship**. Focal length is **directly proportional** to the radius of the lens.

🔍 ... directly proportional

Analysing glass

Your learning aims:

A.1 Produce a good plan for an investigation

B.4 Perform calculations from data

B.6 Draw bar charts

C.1 Draw inferences from a conclusion

Ram raid at the bank

A van is driven at high speed into a bank, smashing the front glass window. Masked men jump out of the van and wrench the cash machine from the wall. The men drive off with the cash machine and the van is later found abandoned. A team of scene-of-crime officers collect tiny fragments of glass from the abandoned van and remove the van's headlamp, which has been broken in the ram raid.

Analysing glass

When glass is smashed, it breaks into many pieces of different sizes. Large pieces may be produced, but it is also likely that a large area is showered with tiny fragments. Glass fragments can help to confirm that suspects were present at a crime scene.

Different types of glass have different densities. Density is therefore important in matching glass fragments. Density is mass per unit volume, and is calculated using the formula:

$$\rho = \frac{m}{V}$$

where ρ = density (in kg/m³)

   m = mass (in kg)

   V = volume (in m³)

Because the glass fragments may be very small, forensic scientists can't find their density by simply measuring their mass and their volume. Instead, a fragment is put in a series of mixtures of liquids having different densities, to see which one it is suspended in.

The refractive index of glass

One of the most useful investigations carried out on glass is to find its **refractive index**. When rays of light pass from air through a piece of glass, they are bent, or refracted, by the glass.

Question

The mass of a piece of glass found at the bank is 0.416 g. Its volume is 0.16 cm³. A glass fragment found in the shirt pocket of a suspect has a mass of 0.078 g. Its volume is 0.03 cm³. Calculate the densities of the two glass fragments (in g/cm³). What can you conclude?

Exam tip

Scientists often need to rearrange equations and formulae to carry out calculations. Think of an equation as being like a set of balanced scales. Whatever you do to the left-hand side of the equation, you must also do to the right.

Using the equation $\rho = m/V$, to calculate mass m, you must multiply both sides of the equation by V.

So $m = \rho V$.

$\mathcal{P}$... rearranging equations

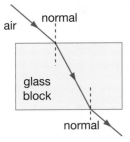

Light enters the glass block at an angle. It slows down in the glass and refracts towards the normal.

Refraction of light as it passes from air into glass

Question

For her block of glass, Shila measures the angle of incidence as 35° and the angle of refraction as 71°. Calculate the refractive index of the block.

You will need some sine tables, either from your Maths teacher or the Internet, or use a sine function on a scientific calculator or on the Internet.

We can easily measure the refractive index of a large piece of glass, such as a glass block, in the school laboratory. We measure the angle at which a light ray enters the glass, and the angle at which it leaves. The refractive index can then be calculated.

Calculating refractive index

Shila has been measuring the refractive index of a block of glass in the school lab. She calculates its refractive index using the formula:

$$\text{refractive index} = \frac{\sin i}{\sin r}$$

where i is the angle of incidence and r is the angle of refraction.

As fragments of glass from a crime scene are often very small or irregular in shape, forensic scientists find their refractive indices using specialist equipment – a 'GRIM3'. This compares the refractive index of the sample with oil at different temperatures.

What the refractive index can tell us

Different types of glass each have a slightly different refractive index. So it's possible to identify and match a sample of glass collected from a crime scene or a suspect.

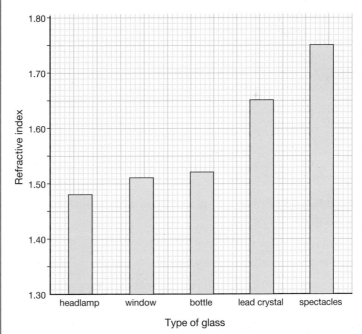

A bar chart to show the refractive indices of different types of glass

We use **bar charts** to display data where one of the variables is **categorical** rather than continuous.

The dietician

Working with people on their diet

Juliette is a dietician. She says, "I carry out theoretical – and sometimes practical – research on the science of nutrition. I work with people so that they can make informed choices about the food they eat and their lifestyle. I also put information from my research into a format that is understandable to the public with no scientific background."

The obesity epidemic

Juliette talks about her job, "Obesity rates in Britain have soared in the past few years. Nearly a quarter of adults are now classed, clinically, as being obese. Many more are overweight."

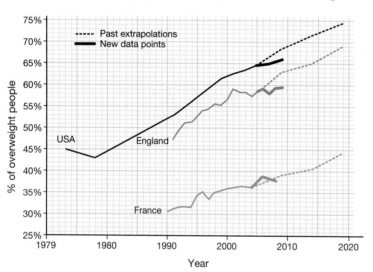

The percentage of overweight people in England is increasing, but not at the rate predicted for the mid-2000s

"I calculate a person's body mass index, or BMI, to find out if a person is a healthy weight."

$$BMI = \frac{\text{mass in kilograms}}{(\text{height in metres})^2}$$

There are many BMI calculators on the Internet. People's BMIs are compared with the following information:

- less than 18.5 = underweight
- 18.5–24.9 = healthy weight
- 25–29.9 = overweight
- 30 or greater = very overweight or obese

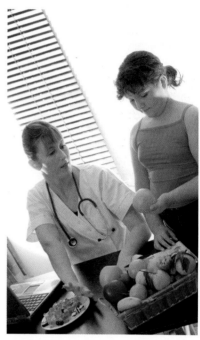

Juliette advises a 12-year-old girl about her diet

Exam tip

Scientists often look at the trend in a graph, and extend the graph beyond the data they've already collected. This is called extrapolation. It helps to predict what might happen.

Question

Calculate the BMI of a person whose mass is 99 kg and height is 1.7 m. How is this person classified?

...extrapolating data

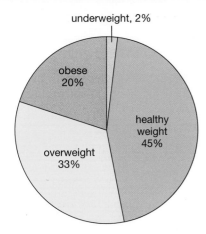

*Juliette uses a **pie chart** to show the proportions of people of different weights*

Question

Calculate the angle required to represent the 45% of people of healthy weight.

Providing information to the public

Juliette says: "I put information from my research into leaflets. These are distributed to people in health centres locally. These include the results of BMI measurements I've made on my visits or in the clinic over the past year. I think it's a good 'snapshot' of the health of the local community."

Constructing pie charts

You can generate pie charts using various spreadsheet packages, but in an exam you would have to draw them by hand. You will need a protractor. There are 360° in a circle. You must convert your data to angles. So, if the percentage of obese people is 20%:

The angle to represent the proportion of obese people $= \dfrac{20}{100} \times 360 = 72°$

Calculate the angles for all your data. Check that they add up to 360° before you draw the pie chart.

Obesity and other diseases

Juliette continues: "Many people think of being overweight as a 'cosmetic' issue. They don't realise all the health problems it is linked with."

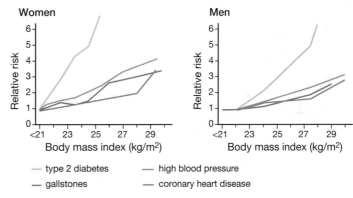

Juliette says, "I try to show people the correlation between BMI and various diseases, such as type 2 diabetes, heart disease and cancer"

Monitoring food and energy intake

Juliette asks her patients or clients to monitor their food intake over a day or a week. "I ask them to list the foods they've eaten. We work out – or maybe they've recorded – the portion sizes eaten. We then use food labels, packets or food tables to look up the energy content of the foods, in kilocalories per 100 g."

"We can calculate a person's energy intake for the day (or week) they have monitored their food. IT-literate people could use a spreadsheet to do this; others can complete a table."

Food	Energy content, kcal/100g	Size of portion eaten	Energy intake food, kcal
Bread	200	50	
Margarine	500	2	
Cheese	400	25	
Steak	200	100	
Oven chips	200	200	
Peas	70	50	
Tea (without milk or sugar)	0	200	
TOTAL ENERGY INTAKE:			

Brewing

Your learning aims:

A.1 Produce a good plan for an investigation

B.6, B.8, B.9 Draw graphs with lines of best fit and read off values

B.12, B.13 Describe trends and patterns in data, analyse evidence and draw a conclusion

C.1 Draw inferences from a conclusion

C.2 Comment on the extent to which the evidence supports the conclusion

A new beer is brewed

Stewart is a brewer. He is producing a new beer. He starts by brewing it on a small scale. When he is satisfied with its quality, he sets up a tasting panel. Members of the public volunteer. They like his new beer.

The fermentation process

Beer is produced as yeast feeds on the sugars in malted barley. As the oxygen runs out in the fermenter, the yeast switches to **anaerobic respiration**. Ethanol (alcohol) and carbon dioxide are produced instead of water and carbon dioxide.

glucose → ethanol + carbon dioxide

This process is called **fermentation**. The production of a successful alcoholic drink depends on the healthy growth of yeast. There are several ways in which to monitor the process.

Quality control

Effective quality control is required at all stages during the brewing process.

Stewart collects samples from the fermentation vessels during all stages of the brewing process. He sends these to a laboratory for analysis. The lab measures various factors important in quality control.

To check that the yeast is growing healthily, a cell count is measured over 3½ days using an automated process. A curve is fitted to the measurements made using a computer.

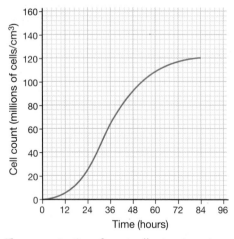

The concentration of yeast cells at various stages of the fermentation

Question

Describe the trend in yeast cell numbers over the course of the fermentation.

Suggest:

* *why the graph does not pass exactly through (0, 0)*
* *what is happening between 72 and 84 hours*
* *what the yeast cell count might be at 96 hours.*

...fermentation

Stewart also monitors the temperature during the growth of the yeast.

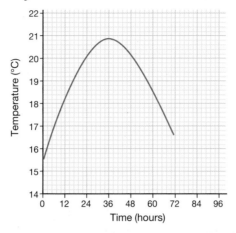

The temperature of the fermentation during the brewing process

Question

Describe how temperature changes as the fermentation proceeds.

Drawing conclusions

Stewart can draw conclusions about the growth of the yeast in his brew. The growth curve is typical of all microorganisms and shows the usual phases of growth. And so is the change in temperature during the fermentation process.

Scaling up

Stewart has made his first product successfully on a small scale, by brewing several litres of the new beer. This process must now be reproduced when he moves production to his 20 000-litre brewing vessels. The yeast must grow properly and the beer must look and taste the same. It must be of exactly the same quality.

Question

Explain this change in temperature.

Sampling during fermentation in the brewery

The process is called **scaling up**. Stewart says, "I have four main problems with scaling up. The temperature will be more difficult to control on a large scale. When fermenting beer, the only microorganism I want to grow is yeast. I must sterilise the brewing vessels and avoid contamination of the beer. This is far more difficult when using large fermenters. Lastly, aeration is more difficult. Although fermentation is an anaerobic process, oxygen is essential at the beginning of the process."

The effectiveness of antibiotics

Your learning aims:

A.1 Produce a good plan for an investigation

A.2 Provide a hypothesis based on relevant scientific ideas

B.6, Draw graphs with
B.8, lines of best fit and
B.9 read off values

B.12, Describe trends and
B.13 patterns in data, analyse evidence and draw a conclusion

C.1 Draw inferences from a conclusion

C.2 Comment on the extent to which the evidence supports the conclusion

C.3 Comment on the extent to which the hypothesis is supported by evidence

C.4 Evaluate the method, suggesting ways of extending the investigation

Antibiotic-resistant bacteria

Laura works in the microbiology department of a hospital. She is called to a particular ward by hospital consultants. Several patients with severe infections of their respiratory systems are not responding to their antibiotic treatments. The consultants suspect that there is a strain of bacteria in the ward that is resistant to antibiotics.

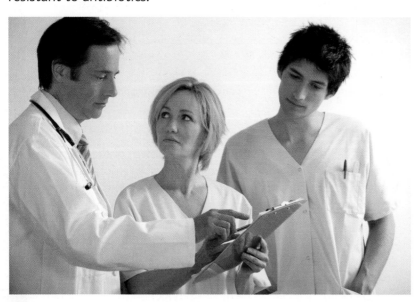

The susceptibility of the bacteria to the antibiotic

The patients are known to be infected with the pneumonia bacterium, *Streptococcus pneumoniae*. They are being treated with an antibiotic called levofloxacin. Laura knows how the antibiotic normally performs against this bacterium. It is usually very effective.

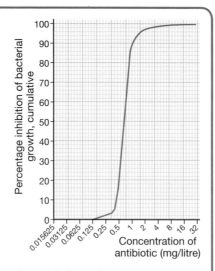

The graph shows the minimum dose of the antibiotic that has any effect against the bacterium. It also shows the concentration of antibiotic able to kill all the bacteria in a population

Question

What is the minimum concentration of levofloxacin required to produce any inhibition of growth of the bacterium?

... antibiotic resistance

Laura's hypothesis

Laura suggests that the pneumonia bacteria in the ward have become more resistant to the antibiotic. She makes a prediction: "I think that the minimum concentration of antibiotic that will inhibit the growth of the bacterium will be higher than normal. It is also likely that the concentration that will produce no growth of the bacteria, or kill the bacteria, will be higher. The graph will shift to the right."

The investigation

Laura cultures bacteria from one of the patient's lungs in nutrient broth. This gives her sufficient numbers of the bacteria to work with. She then makes up a series of dilutions of the antibiotic in separate tubes. She inoculates each tube of the antibiotic with an equal volume of the culture.

Laura incubates the tubes for 20 hours. She looks for growth.

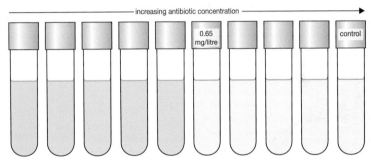

The tubes that are cloudy, or turbid, have bacteria growing in them. The tube on the far right is the control

Laura finds the minimum inhibitory concentration (MIC) of antibiotic by simply looking at the tubes. This is the first tube that is clear, and shows no bacterial growth. The tubes suggest that the MIC for the antibiotic on this strain of bacterium is 0.65 mg/litre.

Taking the investigation further

Laura would like more information about how the growth of the bacteria has been affected. She would also like to make the study more quantitative. A tube with no visible growth does not mean that all the bacteria have been killed. They could just have been inhibited from growing.

Laura is extending the investigation. She wants to find the concentration at which all the bacteria have been killed. She repeats her experiment, but this time transfers some of each dilution to a clean agar plate with no antibiotic. She is then able to determine the concentration at which all the bacteria were killed.

Question

Look closely at Laura's investigation.

Can you suggest ways in which the investigation could be improved?

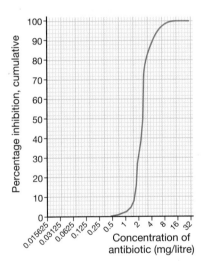

Laura draws a graph of her results

Question

Compare the shape of this graph with the previous one. Describe the effectiveness of the antibiotic against this new strain of bacterium. Is Laura's hypothesis supported by the data?

Biodiesel

Your learning aims:

A.2 Provide a hypothesis based on relevant scientific ideas

B.4 Perform calculations from data

B.6–B.8 Draw graphs, identify anomalous results, draw lines of best fit

B.12, B.13 Describe trends and patterns in data, analyse evidence and draw a conclusion

C.1 Draw inferences from a conclusion

C.2 Comment on the extent to which the evidence supports the conclusion

C.3 Comment on the extent to which the hypothesis is supported by evidence

C.4 Evaluate the method, suggesting improvements

Going green

Abishek wants to set up in business growing biofuel crops. He has identified 15 potential crops that could be processed to produce biodiesel. Biodiesels are esters of long-chain acids (fatty acids) with alcohols such as methanol or ethanol.

The energy content of biodiesel

The energy content of different biodiesel fuels depends on the fatty acids they contain. Abishek is investigating the energy content of biodiesels containing different numbers of carbon atoms. He suggests that the longer the carbon chain, the greater the energy stored in the biodiesel molecule. He carries out the investigation by burning the biodiesel fuel and using the energy released to heat water. He produces a graph of his results.

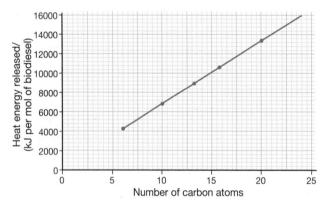

The heat energy released on burning biodiesel fuels with different numbers of carbon atoms

Burning fuels in the school laboratory

In his school lab, Jake is investigating another type of biofuel – ethanol. He is doing this is in a similar way, but using the equipment shown in the diagram. He lights the ethanol. He allows it to burn until the temperature of the water has risen by 40 °C.

Jake measures and records:

- the mass of water used

- the mass of ethanol at the beginning and end of the investigation, so he knows how much has burned

- the temperature rise of the water, i.e. 40 °C.

He calculates the heat energy absorbed by the water using the following equation (see page 157):

Question

Suggest how Abishek could extend his investigation.

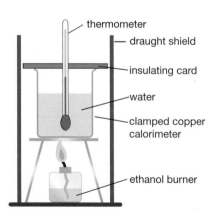

The equipment Jake uses to determine the energy in ethanol

... biodiesel

273

heat energy absorbed by water (in J)	=	mass of water (in g)	×	specific heat capacity (in $JK^{-1}g^{-1}$)	×	temperature change (in K)
	=	50.98	×	4.2	×	40
	=	8565 J				

Jake calculates that this is equivalent to 214 125 J per mole of ethanol. He looks up the value of the heat of combustion of ethanol in a data book. He calculates that his value for the heat of combustion is only about one-tenth of that in the data book.

Jake says, "The main problem with this method is that it relies on the transfer of all the chemical energy in the fuel to heat energy, which is used to warm the water. But using this equipment, the transfer is nowhere near 100%. I think the reasons for this are:

- poor transfer of heat energy from the burning fuel to the water

- the energy in the fuel is not all converted into heat energy

- incomplete combustion of the fuel.

My measurements of the temperature rise may also be inaccurate because without stirring, the heat energy is not evenly distributed through the water."

Improving the investigation

Jake says, "I could improve the investigation by modifying my method or by using different equipment. The transfer of heat to the container holding the water (in this case, a boiling tube) can be improved. I could also insulate the container."

Question

Convert this value to kilojoules.

Question

Using Jake's finding, calculate this as a percentage of the true value.

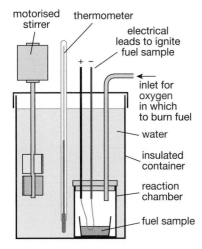

motorised stirrer   thermometer

electrical leads to ignite fuel sample

inlet for oxygen in which to burn fuel

water

insulated container

reaction chamber

fuel sample

Many investigators use a device called a bomb calorimeter, in which to burn a fuel and make their measurements, to overcome these problems

Exam-style questions

1 A bus sets off from the bus station. It takes 80 seconds to travel to the first bus stop, 500 m away. It stops for 30 seconds to pick up passengers. The bus then travels to the next bus stop, 1000 m away. This part of the journey takes 100 seconds.

   a Draw a table to display these data. [2]

   b Display the data in a distance–time graph. [5]

      i How far had the bus travelled after 2 minutes? [2]

      ii Which part of the graph is steepest? What is the speed of the bus during this part of the journey? [2]

2 Aiguo is testing how corrosive various acids are on the metals in a kettle element. The metals react with the acids and are converted into soluble metal salts.

   a He converts his results to a 'corrosive index', shown below.

Acid	Corrosive index
citric acid	1.15
ethanoic acid	4.25
lactic acid	1.00
phosphoric acid	2.90
sulfamic acid	2.95

   Display the data in the most appropriate chart or graph. [7]

   b Plan an experiment to test the effect of temperature on the reaction rate between lactic acid and a metal. [5]

3 When blood droplets hit a surface, a number of 'spines' form around the edge.

On observing many droplets, a forensic scientist suggests that the number of spines is related to the speed at which the blood hits the surface.

He carries out an investigation to test this.

   a What is the name given to a suggested explanation based on observations? [1]

   b Give **two** variables that he would control in this investigation. [2]

   c His results are shown below.

Speed of blood (m/s)	Number of spines					Average number of spines
	Experiment 1	Experiment 2	Experiment 3	Experiment 4	Experiment 5	
2.0	20	21	19	20	20	
2.3	24	21	24	22	24	
2.8	29	25	26	26	28	
3.1	31	21	32	31	30	
3.4	33	33	35	36	32	
4.0	40	40	36	36	39	
4.2	42	43	41	40	39	
4.4	43	42	42	43	44	
4.6	45	46	47	44	43	
4.9	46	47	48	45	48	

      i Identify the anomalous result. [1]

      ii How do anomalous results come about? [1]

      iii How do you treat anomalous results? [2]

   d Calculate the average number of spines for each speed. [5]

   e Give **two** reasons why your averages are whole numbers. [2]

f Draw a graph of the results. [6]

g What conclusions can you draw from the data? [1]

h Give **one** way in which the investigation could be extended. [1]

4 A roller-coaster ascends to a height of 60 m. The car and the people onboard have a total mass of 500 kg.

a Calculate the gravitational potential energy of the car at the top of the roller-coaster using the formula:

$$\text{GPE (J)} = \underset{\text{(kg)}}{\text{mass}} \times \underset{\substack{\text{field strength} \\ \text{(N/kg}^1)}}{\text{gravitational}} \times \underset{\text{(m)}}{\text{height}}$$

where gravitational field strength = 10 N/kg^1 [2]

b The roller-coaster moves down the slope. Assuming all of the gravitational potential energy is converted to kinetic energy, calculate the speed of the roller-coaster at the bottom of the slope. Use the equation:

$$\text{KE} = \frac{1}{2} \times \underset{\text{(kg)}}{\text{mass}} \times \underset{\text{(m/s)}^2}{\text{velocity}^2}$$

c Explain why in reality all the gravitational potential energy is not converted to kinetic energy. [2]

5 A scientist is testing a new biodegradable polymer. She cuts a strip of the polymer. She hangs masses from the strip and measures its length as the masses are increased.

a In this investigation, which is the:

   i dependent variable [1]

   ii independent variable? [1]

b Give **two** variables that she should control to make the investigation a fair test. [2]

c Her results are shown in the table.

Mass (g)	Length of polymer (mm)	Extension (mm)
0	50	0
100	51	1
200	52	
300	56	
400	60	
500	65	
600	68	
700	71	
800	76	
900	80	
1000	83	

Calculate the extension (the new length compared with the original length) for each mass. One has been done for you. [1]

d Plot a graph of extension against mass. [4]

e Describe the relationship between extension and mass. [3]

f The scientist's hypothesis was that 'as the mass increases, the extension of the polymer increases'. Does the graph support her hypothesis? Explain your answer. [2]

g Suggest how the investigation could be improved to add further support to the hypothesis. [3]

6 A forensic scientist analyses a sample from a crime scene. It is thought to contain drugs. He uses chromatography. Chromatography separates mixtures of substances according to the distance they move in a solvent. His results are shown below.

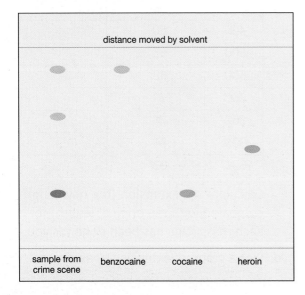

distance moved by solvent

| sample from crime scene | benzocaine | cocaine | heroin |

The forensic scientist can calculate what is called the R_f value:

$$\text{value} = \frac{\text{distance moved by spot}}{\text{distance moved by solvent}}$$

a Calculate the R_f values of benzocaine, cocaine and heroin, and the spots in the sample. [4]

b What conclusions can you draw? [2]

c Samples of cocaine on the street often contain a drug called lignocaine. In the solvent used in this analysis, lignocaine has an R_f value of 0.65. What can you conclude from the evidence? [2]

7 Jason is investigating the release of energy from foods as they burn. He sets up the equipment below:

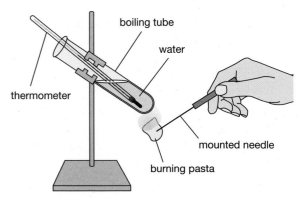

He uses 20 cm³ of water in the boiling tube. He burns three pieces of pasta and measures the temperature rise each time.

a Some of his results are shown below.

Temperature rise (°C)		
Experiment 1	Experiment 2	Experiment 3
37	35	39

  i Explain why he carried out repeats. [2]

  ii Calculate the energy contained in each piece of pasta. Use the formula:

  heat energy absorbed by water (J) = mass of water (g) × specific heat capacity (J/K/g⁻¹) × temp. change (K)

[6]

  iii Jason calculates the energy content of the pasta per 100 g. His value is one-tenth of that given on the packet. Suggest why. [4]

b The nutrient breakdown on the packet is:

Content per 100 g:

protein 7.0 g; starch 18.0 g; sugars 0.5 g; fat 0.4 g; fibre 8.0 g

  i Display the information in a table. [5]

  ii Display the information in a pie chart. [4]

Preparing for exams

Unit 1 and Unit 8 are assessed by exams. The information below will help you prepare to do your best.

Revising before your exam

The aim is to remember what you have learnt so you can answer questions when you get into the exam room. Revision works best when you make yourself notes or draw pictures to help you remember, rather than just reading and hoping it sticks. Here are some ideas to help you revise.

- Prepare a revision timetable to make sure you have time to cover all the topics you need to.
- Find a quiet and comfortable space where you won't be disturbed. It's best if there's fresh air and plenty of light to keep you alert.
- Take regular breaks and try not to revise when you are feeling tired.
- Write short summaries of each topic as you read through your class notes.
- Check anything you don't understand with your teacher or look for the explanation in this book.
- Draw mind maps covering the basic information on each topic.
- Set up revision cards showing key points to remember.
- Ask yourself questions, or try the questions in this book, as you're revising.
- When you think you've revised everything in the unit, test yourself using the practice exam style questions in this book or those that your teacher gives you.

On exam day...

A little bit of nervousness before your exam can be a good thing, but try not to let it affect your performance. When you open the exam paper keep calm.

- Don't spend so long on some questions that you don't have time to answer others.
- If don't understand a question, move on and complete the ones you're able to do first, then go back to the ones you found difficult.
- Read all questions carefully to make sure you understand exactly what you need to do.
- Make sure that you highlight key words in a question.
- Look at how many marks are allocated to each part of a question. In general, you need to write at least as many separate points in your answer as there are marks.
- Use correct scientific vocabulary.
- Make sure that your writing is neat. An examiner can't award marks for answers that he or she can't read.
- If you have time, go back and check your answers at the end of the exam.

Finally, good luck!

Research, predict and and investigate

Science affects all our lives. It affects the world around us, by trying to answer big questions such as:

- How did the world get to be the way it is?

- How can we make the world safer for its inhabitants?

- How can we look after it for future generations?

So what do scientists do? They gather **data**. Data is information. Scientists observe, collect information, and use it to find out things about the world.

Reliability

*Scientists always need to consider whether the data is **reliable**. They ask themselves: how confident are we about it? Can we trust it? These are the questions you have to ask yourself when dealing with your data.*

Events and variables

Things change, and this interests scientists. They like to explain changes, so that they can be managed and predicted. They call the things that change **variables**.

Unlinked events

Sometimes things cannot be predicted and managed. This is a **chance occurrence**. While you are brushing your teeth in the morning, a baby is born somewhere in the world – but it is unlikely that these events will be linked.

Linked events

Sometimes, though, events are linked. If they are, the link can be explained. If you exercise for a period of time, your heart will beat faster. Here, one **variable** (how active you are) changes another **variable** (your heart rate). Usually, in science, several variables are involved and linked. If they are linked, they can be explained.

Internet research

There is lots of information for professional scientists on the internet. Get information at the right level for you by typing in the following words and phrases after your search: GCSE, KS4, KS3, for kids, easy, simple.

Keyword searches are usually the best way to find what you need. Use several words and try to be specific. A search for asthma will bring up thousands of results about all aspects of asthma. A search for asthma causes or asthma treatment will bring more specific useful information. The first few pages of results will always be the most relevant.

For example...

You might notice that the sandwich you bring from home is drier at lunchtime than it is at breakfast. Why is this? You might decide to investigate whether it has lost moisture. You could then reach a conclusion about how the sandwich changes over time, and why.

Observations

Scientists spend a lot of time making observations. Observations raise questions, and these may lead to an investigation.

Investigations

What is an investigation?

If you change an object, and keep track of how it is different, you are seeing the effect of your actions. You are measuring the amount that it has changed. This is an investigation!

Scientists use a lot of different ways to measure things. If they do it correctly, the results of these measurements can tell them something about the world.

Many investigations have an important real-life purpose, like:

- Searching for new drugs to combat cancer or heart disease
- Trying to make mobile phones that work on the Underground
- Finding alternative energy sources and solutions of global warming

To carry out your investigation you need to think about what your scientific purpose is.

When getting your results, leave room for human error – nobody is perfect.

Ask yourself...

- *What are you trying to find out?*

- *What do you need to do to find this out?*

- *How are you going to do it?*

When you know the answer to these questions, you're ready to start your investigation.

Always be sure what you are trying to find out.

Start investigating

To start, you need to think about the **big question**. What are you trying to find out?

The 'big question' will lead to other questions. Finding a way to answer all these smaller questions will give you a way to answer the big question.

You can answer questions through tests. The tests you use must be **fair tests**. It's usually better to do them in a lab, where it's easier to control variables. (Though that's not always possible, so some tests have to be carried out 'in the field'.)

An investigation must be designed to give data that is reliable and precise – not vague. After your investigation you should think about and write about the reliability of the measurements you have made. You should **evaluate** this reliability in your conclusion.

Display your results

It is useful to display the data that you have found in your investigation, because you will be able to think about it more easily when making a conclusion.

Scientists arrange data in ways that help them to spot patterns and trends. How they do this depends on the type of data.

How to display data

You can display data in three ways:

1. **Tables** – these set out data clearly so that you can see it all at once.

2. **Bar charts** – these show how something you are measuring changes, whether it's over time, with rising heat, with rising pressure, and so on. The time, heat or pressure goes along one axis (the x-axis), and the **variable** – the thing that changes – goes along the other axis (the y-axis).

3. **Line graphs** – these display data from investigations where you are looking at two variables, both of which change.

Graphs are really useful. When you look at them you can see a pattern in your results quickly. You can also see results that are out of place.

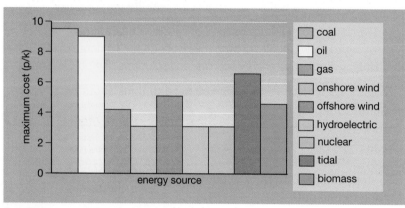

Bar chart

Looking at results

- Look for results that don't look like they belong with the rest of the results. They could be extremely high points, extremely low points, or points with completely random locations. Try to work out why this is.

- Leave room for human error. An anomaly can be there because you made a mistake in measurement. You should ignore these results, as they won't tell you anything useful.

Thinking about what you've found

- If you've been asked to find a value, remember to include the unit that it's measured in.

- If you've made a graph, try to say something about its shape and what that indicates.

- If you can see a pattern on your graph, try to explain it in a short sentence.

Tables

- Do not forget to head table columns with quantity and unit.

- Make sure that your readings are reliable and recorded to the same degree of accuracy.

Charts and graphs

- Make sure graphs are as large as possible. Balance this with finding sensible scales for both axes.

- Make sure that you have placed the correct objects and quantities along the x- and y-axes.

- Look for a pattern in the points you plot on the graph.

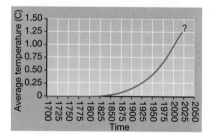

Line graph

When drawing a graph, always remember to label both axes and use the right units.

The units that your answer is in may not always be the same as the units that the question is in.

Remember the limitations of your data. An investigation conducted on members of your own school may not mean that your conclusions are true for the whole world!

Evaluate your data

Scientists use data for **evidence**. It's like police work. Fingerprints, marks at the scene of the crime and DNA samples are all data that can be gathered. They are evidence that will later be used in court to get a conviction. Likewise, you will use your data to make a **conclusion**.

The big question

You should have asked yourself the following questions by now:

- Which areas of my data are the most reliable?
- Is there a pattern in the results I have got?
- Are there any unexpected results?
- Does this mean I have found something that answers my **big question**?

Your conclusion

If the answer to the last question is 'yes', you can make a conclusion. In your conclusion you evaluate the results you have produced.

To do this, you have to ask yourself:

- What pieces of evidence did I use to form my conclusion?
- Does the rest of my evidence support my conclusion?
- Were there any anomalies, and where?
- Why are they there? Was it human error, or something else?
- Is there any way I could have improved my data?

Watch out

- You must base your conclusion entirely on the results you have.
  If you don't, it isn't a conclusion. It's just an opinion.

- There's no place for prejudice or hearsay when evaluating your results. Try not to let any outside factors influence your results, or what you think about them.

Conclusion or opinion?

Your **conclusion** must relate to the question asked: it is the answer to that question. You should explain why you have thought of this conclusion, and how sure you are that it is correct. You might not be so sure about it if your measurements are not very reliable, for example. Even if you're not sure about this, you can still have an opinion.

Remember your data

You should make your conclusion when thinking about the data you've collected and investigated. What has this told you?

You can (and should) talk about the data in your conclusion. This is how you back up your opinion. This is what makes it a **conclusion**, instead of just an **opinion**.

Health and Safety

Health and Safety is an important aspect of life today. This includes when we are working as scientists.

The number of injuries and deaths in science laboratories and workplaces where science is used is very small. But the risk is still present.

Dangers

Heat burns and scalds

Burns are caused by dry heat, like a Bunsen burner flame; scalds are caused by wet heat, such as boiling water.

The burned person will experience pain and possibly shock. Symptoms include swelling, blisters and redness.

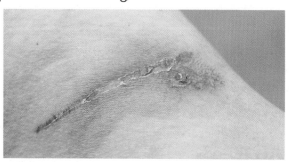

Chemical burns

Some chemicals can burn the skin if they come into contact with it. These may be liquids, such as a concentrated acid, or powders, such as lime.

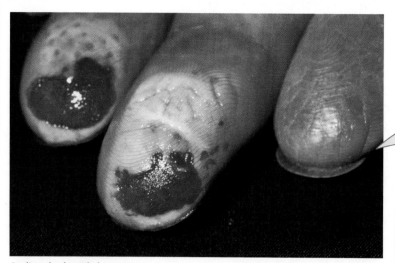

Sodium hydroxide burn

What to do

The priorities are to try to reduce the pain and the risk of infection. Cold water should be applied for several minutes and a dressing pressed to the affected area. If the burn is at all serious (the redder the skin, the more serious the burn), call 999.

Nothing should be applied to the injury other than water or a dressing.

What to do

The priorities are the remove the cause of the injury, and take steps to prevent infection. The cause of the burn should be removed, either with cool running water for at least 15 minutes in the case of a liquid, or brushing in the case of a powder. Any contaminated clothing or jewellery should be removed and the affected area wrapped loosely in a clean dressing or cloth.

Minor chemical burns usually heal themselves; however if there are symptoms of shock – or if the burn is deeper, you should seek expert attention.

What to do

The priorities are to ensure that the casualty's airway is open and to call an ambulance. If the casualty isn't responding, resuscitation may be necessary. If the chemical that has caused the injury is known, this should be communicated when making the call and to the ambulance crew as well.

What to do

Recovery cannot begin if the casualty is still in contact with the source of the current. In this case, additionally, the first aider is at risk of shock as well.

Removing the source of current may be done by switching off the supply using an insulator such as a wooden broom. If unconscious, a casualty's airway should be opened and resuscitation may be appropriate. An ambulance should be called.

Injury from breathing in fumes or swallowing chemicals

Many chemicals in scientific laboratories are potentially dangerous if swallowed. Some chemicals, such as ammonia, release fumes that are dangerous.

Symptoms vary according to what has been swallowed, but may include drowsiness, unconsciousness, nausea and vomiting, and even cardiac arrest.

Electric shock

Low voltages (typically around 12 V) present few risks in the laboratory. Mains voltage, however, can be lethal. If an electric current passes through the body, it can cause a person's breathing and heartbeat to stop.

Cuts and damage to the eyes from particles or chemicals

If foreign particles enter the eye, the priority is to remove them. It is important not to allow the casualty to rub his or her eyes as this will increase the damage or allow any other liquids to be introduced.

There are three established ways of removing particles. Let tears wash out the particle. Use an eye wash or Pull the upper lid down onto the lower lid and let the lower eyelashes sweep away the particles by blinking rapidly.

If this doesn't work, the eye should be closed and immediate expert attention sought. It is essential that the eye is not rubbed.

Glossary

ABS braking system known as Advance Braking System which helps to control a skidding car

absorb the small intestine absorbs food molecules – they pass from the small intestine through the thin walls into the blood stream

accelerate an object accelerates if it speeds up

acceleration a measurement of how quickly the speed of a moving object changes (if speed is in m/s the acceleration is in m/s2)

accuracy how close a reading is to its true value

acid rain rain water which is made more acidic by pollutant gases

adaptation a feature of an organism that helps it survive

addiction when a person becomes dependent on a medicine

addition polymer a very long molecule resulting from polymerisation, e.g. polythene

addition reaction reaction in which a carbon double bond (C=C) opens up and other atoms add on to each carbon atom

adrenal glands glands which make the hormone adrenaline and also corticosteroid hormones

adrenaline hormone which helps to prepare your body for action

aerobic respiration respiration that involves oxygen

agar plate a solid jelly that contains all the nutrients and other substances microorganisms need to grow and multiply

agile being able to move in bursts in different directions

air bags cushions which inflate with gas to protect people in a vehicle accident

air resistance the force exerted by air to any object passing through it

alkali substance which produce OH- ions in water

alkali metals very reactive metals in group 1 of the periodic table, e.g. sodium

alkanes a family of hydrocarbons found in crude oil with single covalent bonds, e.g. methane

alkenes a family of hydrocarbons with double covalent bonds, e.g. ethene

allergic reaction excessive reaction of the body to a substance (pollen, dust or certain foods)

alloy mixture of two or more metals – used to make coins

alpha particles radioactive particles which are helium nuclei – helium atoms without the electrons (they have a positive charge)

alternating current (a.c.) an electric current that is not a one-way flow

ammeter meter used in an electric circuit for measuring current

amniotic sac fluid-filled sac within the uterus – inside this the baby is protected from knocks

amplitude the maximum distance of a point on a wave from its rest position

amps units used to measure electrical current

anaemia disease where the body does not have enough red blood cells and therefore can't carry enough oxygen

anaerobic respiration respiration without using oxygen

analgesic therapeutic drug used to reduce pain

analytical chemist someone who studies the chemical composition of materials

anomalous result a result that doesn't fit with the pattern of the rest of the results

anorexia nervosa eating disorder where the person eats less and less because they see themselves as being overweight (even though they may be underweight)

antenatal screening method for seeing if an unborn baby has abnormalities

antibacterial something which acts to kill bacteria, but is toxic to ingest e.g. antibacterial soap

antibiotic therapeutic drug acting to kill bacteria which is taken into the body

antibody protein normally present in the body or produced in response to an antigen which it neutralises, thus producing an immune response

anti-fungal medicine that kills fungi that cause disease, such as athlete's foot

antigen any substance that stimulates the production of antibodies – antigens on the surface of red blood cells determine blood group

antistatic an antistatic particle cannot spark a fire in dangerous conditions

antiviral therapeutic drug acting to kill viruses

appendicitis inflammation of the appendix

arc-discharge an industrial process for producing nanotubes

arteries blood vessels that carry blood away from the heart

aseptic technique precautions taken, when working with microorganisms, to ensure a culture doesn't become contaminated, or microorganisms don't escape into the environment

asteroids small objects in space which orbit a larger mass

atherosclerosis build up of fatty deposits on artery walls that reduce blood flow and can lead to heart attacks

atom the basic 'building block' of an element which cannot be chemically broken down

atom economy a way of measuring the amount of atoms that are wasted or lost when a chemical is made

atomic number the number of protons found in the nucleus of an atom

auto-immune disease disease caused by the immune system of the body attacking the body, e.g. type 1 diabetes

average velocity how fast an object is travelling in a certain direction: velocity = displacement ÷ time

bacteria single-celled microorganisms which can either be free-living organisms or parasites (they sometimes invade the body and cause disease)

bacterial infection infection caused by bacteria invading the body

balanced diet eating foods (and drinking drinks) which will provide the body with the correct nutrients in the correct proportions

balanced equation chemical equation where the number of atoms on each side of the equation balance each other

balanced forces forces acting in opposite directions that are equal in size

bar chart a graph/chart where values on the x-axis are categoric, i.e. in groups, rather than a continuous scale

basal metabolic rate (BMR) amount of energy that someone needs just to keep their body processes ticking over

base solid alkali

bases in a DNA double helix, the two strands are held together by bases in base pairs

bauxite mineral which contains aluminium compounds

beta particles particles given off by some radioactive materials (they have a negative charge)

bioaccumulate chemicals that increase in concentration as they are passed from one organism to another along a food chain

biodegradable a biodegradable material can be broken down by microorganisms

biodiesel fuel made from rapeseed oil

biodiversity range of different living organisms in a habitat

bioethanol ethanol made from fermented corn or sugar cane

biofuels fuels made from plants – these can be burned in power stations

biological cause when a pathogen infects the body causing disease

biological indicators organisms which live in water – their presence or absence tells scientists how polluted water is

biomass waste wood and other natural materials which are burned in power stations

bladder sac inside the body which acts as a temporary store for urine

blast furnace furnace for extracting iron from iron ore

blood fluid that is pumped through the body by the heart; contains plasma, blood cells and platelets

blood groups blood falls into one of four groups: A, B, AB or O

blood pressure force with which blood presses against the walls of the blood vessels

body mass index (BMI) measure of someone's weight in relation to their height

bone marrow transplant bone marrow is taken from a healthy person and put into another person

braking distance distance travelled while a car is braking

breast screening method of checking for breast cancers at an early stage

breathing process which involves the exchange of gases between lung and air

buckyballs carbon molecules containing many carbon atoms which form large hollow spheres

buffer an aqueous solution of a mixture of a weak acid and a weak base (the pH of the buffer changes very little when a small amount of strong acid or base is added to it)

bulimia eating disorder where the sufferer alternates between eating too much and vomiting to keep to a chosen weight

calibration confirming a scale, e.g. using a known weight to draw up a scale of spring extension

cancer life-threatening condition where body cells divide uncontrollably

capillaries small blood vessels that join arteries to veins

carbon sink carbon-containing organisms, such as trees, that remove carbon dioxide from the atmosphere as they grow

carbon-neutral fuel fuel grown from plants so that carbon dioxide is taken in as the plants are growing – this balances out the carbon dioxide released as the fuel is burnt

carboxylic acid an organic acid with a carboxyl group

carboxylic acid group the molecular group COOH which is found in organic acids

carcinogen something which causes cancer, e.g. chemicals in cigarettes

cardiovascular fitness the fitness of the heart and circulatory system

cardiovascular system organ system made up of the heart and blood vessels

carrier someone who carries an abnormal gene but does not have the disease

catalyst substance added to a chemical reaction mixture to alter the speed of the reaction

categorical a type of variable where the values are not a continuous range of numbers, but are groups, e.g. blood groups; type of food, etc.

cell (biology) smallest unit of living things

cell (electrical) a device used to generate electricity

cell membrane layer around a cell which helps to control substances entering and leaving the cell

cell wall a thick wall found around plant cells that keeps their shape

central nervous system (CNS) collectively the brain and spinal cord

cervical screening method of detecting abnormal cells (cancerous cells) taken from the cervix

cervix opening of the uterus (the baby passes through the cervix and down the vagina)

CFCs gases which used to be used in refrigerators and which harm the ozone layer

characteristic the features of an organism, including its structure, the chemistry of its cells and its appearance

chemical barrier substance in the body that can kill or limit the effect of a pathogen

chemical bond very strong force attracting together atoms in a compound

chemical change any process in which one or more substances are changed into one or more different substances

chemical energy energy found in fuels and foods

chemical property property which can't be observed just by looking at a substance – a chemical property depends on how that substance reacts chemically with other substances

chemical reaction a process in which one or more substances are changed into other substances –chemical reactions involve energy changes

chemical therapy type of treatment that uses drugs to treat an illness

chemotherapy drug treatment which kills or damages cancer cells

chloride ion when a chlorine atom gains an electron it becomes a chloride ion with a negative charge – it is written as Cl-

chlorophyll pigments found in plants which are used in photosynthesis (give green plants their colour)

chloroplast a cell structure found in green plants that contains chlorophyll

cholesterol fatty substance which can block blood vessels

cholesterol level amount of cholesterol in the blood. high cholesterol levels are linked with cardiovascular disease

chromatography process used for separating mixtures using differences in their absorbency

chromosomes thread-like structures in the cell nucleus that carry genetic information

cilia tiny hair-like structures which help to keep mucus and dust out of the lungs

circulatory system a transport system in the body that carries oxygen and food molecules

classify when we classify something we put it into a certain group

coal fossil fuel formed from plant material

collision theory idea that relates collisions between particles to their reaction rate

combustion process in which fuels react with oxygen to produce heat

comets lumps of rock and ice found in space – some orbit the Sun

commensal organisms that live together and benefit each other

complementary base pairs bonding between the bases of each strand of a double-stranded DNA molecule – each base on one strand of DNA bonds with its complementary partner on the other strand: adenine always bonds with thymine; guanine always bonds with cytosine

complete combustion when hydrocarbon fuels burn in excess of oxygen to produce carbon dioxide and water only

component (cell) the parts that make up a cell

component (circuit) the parts of an electric circuit

compound two or more elements which are chemically joined together, e.g. H_2O

compressive force a force which squashes something

concave lens lens which is thinner in the middle than at the edges

concave mirror mirror that curves inwards i.e. the middle is further away than the sides

conclusions opinions reached after studying all the evidence

conduction heat transfer caused by particles in a solid vibrating and passing on thermal energy to nearby particles

conductors materials which transfer thermal energy easily; electrical conductors allow electricity to flow through them

conserve energy is conserved when it is used – it is not lost but transferred to a different form of energy

contaminants pollutants which affect land, sea or air, e.g. chemicals from factories

convection heat transfer in a liquid or gas – when particles in a warmer region gain thermal energy and move into cooler regions carrying this energy with them

convex lens lens that is thicker in the middle than at the edges

convex mirror mirror that curves outwards i.e. the middle is closer than the edges

cornea transparent outer covering to the eye

cosmic background radiation radiation coming very faintly from all directions in space

cost-effective a cost-effective drug is one that works, but at the same time is not extremely expensive

covalent bond bond between atoms where some of the electrons are shared

coverage the coverage of a screening programme means what percentage of the target population has been screened

critical angle angle at which a light ray incident on the inner surface of a transparent glass block just escapes from the glass

crude oil black material pumped from the Earth from which petrol and many other products are made

crumple zones areas of a car that absorb the energy of a crash to protect the centre part of the vehicle

crust surface layer of the Earth made of tectonic plates

current flow of electrons in an electric circuit

curve of best fit curve best suited to experimental results when plotted on a graph

cuticle outer, protective layer of a hair

cystic fibrosis genetic condition where the lungs become clogged with mucus

cytoplasm part of the cell where most chemical reactions take place

dative covalent bond type of covalent bond where both shared electrons come from the same atom

decelerates an object decelerates if it slows down

defibrillator machine which gives the heart an electric shock to start it beating regularly

deforestation removal of a large area of trees

density the density of a substance is found by dividing its mass by its volume

dependent variable variable that is being measured; it depends on the input variables

depression condition where people feel unhappy or worthless for most of the time

diabetes disease where the body cannot control its blood sugar level

diagnosis identifying the nature or cause of a medical problem

diameter distance across a circle, from one side to the other passing through the centre

diet what a person eats

digestive system the 9-metre long system that handles and digests food (starts at mouth, ends at anus)

diminished a diminished image is smaller than the object

dioxins polluting chemicals produced during the manufacture of PVC

direct current (d.c.) an electric current that flows in one direction only

directly proportional a link between two variables that shows they are directly related; if a relationship is directly proportional as one variable increases, the other also increases

displacement distance moved in a certain direction

displacement reaction chemical reaction where one element displaces or 'pushes out' another element from a compound

displayed formula when the formula of a chemical is written showing all the atoms and all the bonds

distance–time graph a plot of the distance moved against the time taken for a journey

distribution living organisms are found in certain places – they have a distribution, e.g. some plant species are only found in warmer areas of the UK

DNA molecule found in all body cells in the nucleus – it's sequence determines how our bodies are made (e.g. straight or curly hair), and gives each one of us a unique genetic code

dominant an allele that will produce the characteristic if present

double covalent bond covalent bond where each atom shares two electrons with the other atom

double helix two strands of the DNA molecule face each other in a way that looks like a ladder, these are then twisted around each other to form a double helix – like a spiral staircase

drag energy losses caused by the continual pushing of an object against the air or a liquid

dwarf planets objects orbiting the Sun which are smaller than planets but larger than asteroids

earthquake shaking and vibration at the surface of the Earth resulting from underground movement or from volcanic activity

eating disorder abnormal eating habits that may involve taking in too little or too much food

ecosystem a habitat and all the living things in it

effectors cells that respond to a stimulus by moving the body, e.g. muscle cells

efficiency a measure of how effectively an appliance transfers energy into useful effects

efficient a process in which losses are minimised

egg female sex cell

elastic potential energy energy gained and stored when an elastic object is stretched

electric current when electricity flows through a material we say that an electric current flows

electrical conductors materials which let electricity pass through them

electrical energy energy from the flow of electrons through a circuit (e.g. devices with plugs or batteries use electrical energy)

electrical insulators materials which do not let electricity through them

electrolysis when an electric current is passed through a solution which conducts electricity

electromagnet a magnet which is magnetic only when a current is switched on

electromagnetic spectrum electromagnetic waves ordered according to wavelength and frequency – ranging from radio waves to gamma rays

electromagnetic waves a group of waves that carry different amounts of energy – they range from low frequency radio waves to high frequency gamma rays

electron small particle within an atom that orbits the nucleus (has a negative charge)

electron structure a way of writing down the arrangement of electrons in an atom

electrostatic attraction attraction between opposite charges, e.g. between Na+ and Cl-

element substance made up of only one type of atom

endocrine glands organs that make hormones

endocrine system the body system that is made up of endocrine glands (these secrete hormones)

endoscope device using optical fibres which allows doctors to look inside the human body

endothermic reaction chemical reaction which takes in heat energy

energy the ability to 'do work' – the human body needs energy to function

energy profile diagram diagram showing energy taken in or given out during a chemical reaction

energy transfers when energy moves from one object to another or from one region to another

energy transformations when energy changes from one type to another

environmental variation the differences between individuals caused by their environment (not by their genes), e.g. bad diet making you obese

enzyme biological catalyst that increases the speed of a chemical reaction

epidemic when a disease spreads throughout a community

epithelium cells which line a surface, e.g. epithelial cells lining the lungs

esters chemical substances that give us fruit flavours

ethanol another name for pure alcohol

eutrophication when waterways become too rich with nutrients (from fertilisers) which allows algae to grow wildly and use up all the oxygen

evidence data resulting from scientific trials

evolution the gradual change in organisms over millions of years caused by natural selection

exercise physical activity (running is a form of exercise); exercise can be of mild intensity, moderate intensity or high intensity

exothermic reaction chemical reaction in which heat energy is given out

extinction the process or event that causes a species to die out

fatty acids the building blocks of fats (together with glycerol)

fermentation a type of respiration in microorganisms that produces a useful product, e.g. the conversion of carbohydrates to ethanol (alcohol) by yeast

fertiliser chemical put on soil to increase soil fertility and allow better growth of crop plants

fever when the temperature of the body rises above a 'normal' temperature of about 37°C

fitness ability to do what your body requires you to do – includes speed and flexibility

flame test test where a chemical burns in a Bunsen flame with a characteristic colour – tests for metal ions

flammable a substance that burns easily

flavouring a substance that gives flavour to food

flexible a person who has a wide range of movement around their joints

fluid any substance which flows, e.g. water and air

focal point the point where light rays refracted through a convex lens meet up

foetus unborn baby in the uterus

food additives substances, such as flavourings, added to food

food chain flow chart to show how a living thing gets its food

food web flow chart to show how a number of living things get their food (more complicated than a food chain)

forensic scientist scientist who helps the police investigate crimes by gathering and analysing scientific evidence

fossil fuels fuels such as coal, oil and gas

fractional distillation column found in a refinery, this sorts the hydrocarbons in crude oil according to size of molecules

fractions the different substances collected during fractional distillation of crude oil

fragments very small pieces, e.g. fragments of glass

frequency the number of waves passing a set point per second

friction energy losses caused by two or more objects rubbing against each other

fullerenes cage-like carbon molecules containing many carbon atoms, e.g. buckyballs

functional group the atom or group of atoms in a molecule of an organic compound that is responsible for its characteristic chemical reactions

fungal infection infection caused when the body is invaded by a pathogenic fungus

fungi living organisms which can break down complex organic substances (some are pathogens and harm the body)

fungicide chemical used to kill fungi

galaxy a group made of billions of stars

gamma rays ionising electromagnetic waves that are radioactive and dangerous to human health – but useful in killing cancer cells

gene section of DNA that codes for a particular characteristic

gene mutation a change in the DNA in a cell resulting in a gene functioning differently from normal

gene therapy medical procedure where a virus is used to 'carry' a gene into the nucleus of a cell (this is a new treatment for genetic diseases)

generator a device for generating electricity

genetic adaptation the way in which biological species adapt genetically to changing environmental conditions

genetic code all of the base sequences of the genes that give instructions for an organism

genetic disorders inherited diseases passed on from parents to children

genetic variation the differences between individuals (because we all have slight variations in our genes)

genome all the genes in an organism

genotype the genes that an organism has for a characteristic

genus a group consisting of more than one species (used in classification of living things)

geologist scientist who studies rocks and the formation of the Earth

geothermal energy energy obtained by tapping underground reservoirs of heat (energy form 'hot rocks')

giant ionic structure sodium chloride forms a lattice, also called a giant ionic structure

glands organs within the body which produce hormones

glucagon hormone produced by the pancreas which converts glycogen stored in the liver to glucose

glucose a simple sugar (when combined with oxygen, glucose releases energy)

glycerol together with fatty acids, these make up fats

glycogen substance that stores glucose molecules linked in a long chain

Gore-Tex™ synthetic fibre which keeps you dry inside and out

gradient a slope, such as in a graph. Scientists calculate gradients of graphs to give them a quantitative relationship between the variables on the y- and x-axes

graphite a black solid formed from carbon atoms joined to make flat sheets

gravitational potential energy the energy an object gains due to its height

gravity the attractive force between objects (dependent on their mass)

greenhouse gas any of the gases whose absorption of solar radiation is responsible for the greenhouse effect, e.g. dioxide, methane

group within the periodic table the vertical columns are called groups

haemoglobin chemical found in red blood cells which carries oxygen

half-life the average time taken for half of the unstable nuclei in a sample to decay

halogens reactive non-metal elements in group 7 of the periodic table , e.g. chlorine

hardness describes water with lots of sodium or magnesium compounds dissolved in it

hazard something that is likely to cause harm, e.g. a radioactive substance

heart disease blockage of blood vessels that bring blood to the heart

heart rate the number of heartbeats every minute

herbicide chemical used to kill weeds

hertz (Hz) unit for measuring wave frequency

heterozygous a person who has two different alleles for an inherited characteristic, e.g. someone with blond hair may also carry an allele for red hair

high intensity exercise that is much harder than normal for an individual and causes their heart rate and breathing to increase so much it is difficult for them to talk

homeostasis the way the body keeps a constant internal environment

homozygous an individual who has two alleles that are the same for an inherited feature, e.g., a blue-eyed person will have two blue alleles for eye colour.

hormones chemicals that act on target organs in the body (hormones are made by the body in special glands)

host the organism on which a parasite lives (a parasite takes food from its host)

hydrocarbons compounds made of molecules containing only carbon and hydrogen atoms

hydroelectricity electricity generated by harnessing the power of moving water

hydrogen fuel cell a device which produces electricity from hydrogen

hydroxide ion consisting of oxygen and hydrogen atoms (written as OH-)

hypothalamus small gland in brain, detects temperature of blood

hypothesis a possible explanation for some observations

identification key pathway used to help in identification of an organism

image an image is formed by light rays from an object that travel through a lens or are reflected by a mirror

immune system a body system which acts as a defence against pathogens, such as viruses and bacteria

immunise to protect against infectious disease by causing production of antibodies in response to a vaccine

immunity you have immunity if your immune system recognises a pathogen and fights it

impulse electrical signal that passes along a neurone

incomplete combustion when fuel burns in a reduced concentration of oxygen so that carbon monoxide and water are produced

independent variable input variable that affects an outcome

indicator (chemical) chemical which changes colour according to pH (indicators show how acidic or alkaline a substance is)

indicator (electrical) in electric equipment an indicator shows whether a device is switched on

indicator (biological) organisms or chemicals whose presence or absence can indicate pollution

indirectly proportional a link between two variables that shows they are related, where as one variable increases, the other decreases

inert an inert substance is one that is not chemically reactive

infection when the body has been invaded by pathogens (disease-causing organisms)

infectious if someone is infectious they can pass on a disease caused by pathogens to another person

inflammation swelling due to an immune response causing redness and swelling

ingest to take something into the body (we can ingest medicine)

inhale breathe in

inoculate to transfer microorganisms, for instance, to an agar plate, or to vaccinate against an infectious disease

insecticide chemicals used to kill insects

insulator a material that transfers heat or electrical energy only very slowly

insulin hormone made by the pancreas which controls the level of glucose in the blood

intermolecular force force between molecules

interpolation making an estimate within the range of results

invertebrate animal without a backbone

involuntary response an automatic response to a stimulus that you do not think about

ionic bond a chemical bond between ions with opposite charges

ionic compound in an ionic compound positive and negative charged particles are held together by ionic bonds, e.g. sodium chloride

ionising radiation electromagnetic radiation given out as an unstable radioactive element decays; it has enough energy to ionise the material it is absorbed by

ions charged particles (can be positive or negative)

iris surrounds the pupil in the eye and controls the amount of light entering

iron core partly molten inner part of the Earth made up of molten and solid iron and other metals

irreversible reaction a reaction that cannot go backwards

isotopes atoms with the same number of protons but different numbers of neutrons

joule unit of work done and energy

keyhole surgery surgery carried out using an endoscope, which means that the doctor need only make small cuts on the body

kinetic energy the energy that moving objects have

kingdoms classification of all living things into one of 5 groups – each group is called a kingdom

lactic acid a substance produced in anaerobic respiration

laser therapy treatment using lasers, e.g. some eye surgery involves lasers

lattice ordered structure formed by ions in an ionic compound, e.g. NaCl forms a lattice

lava magma which has erupted onto the surface of the Earth

law of conservation of energy in all energy transfers, no energy is lost or created – energy is conserved

law of reflection the angle of reflection is the same as the angle of incidence

lenses pieces of glass or plastic shaped to bend and control the way light travels through them

leukaemia cancer of the white blood cells – it means that you are likely to catch many infections

life cycle the stages that some things go through as they age, e.g. a fly goes through egg, larva, pupa and adult stages

lifestyle the way that someone chooses to live their life – this can be assessed in a lifestyle evaluation

light-emitting diode (LED) a very small light in electric circuits that uses very little energy

light-dependent resistor (LDR) device in an electric circuit whose resistance falls as the light falling on it increases

light energy anything that glows (such as a light bulb) gives out light energy

lime water calcium hydroxide dissolved in water – this clear liquid turns milky in the presence of carbon dioxide

limescale hard white substance found inside 'furred up' kettles (mostly calcium carbonate)

linear relationship when the relationship between two variables is proportional. It is shown by a straight line on a graph

litmus indicator that goes red with acids and blue with alkalis

long-sighted where you cannot see close objects clearly and the image forms behind the retina

long-term goals targets which take some time to achieve

LPG fuel mixture of fuels such as propane and butane (short for liquefied petroleum gas)

lung cancer when cells in the alveoli divide in an uncontrollable way and destroy lung tissue

lymphocytes white blood cells that surround pathogens and make antibodies to destroy them

magma molten rock found below the Earth's surface

magnetism the attraction that some materials, known as magnets, have for iron

magnified an image is made larger than its object

mammogram X-ray of breast to detect cancer

mantle semi-liquid layer of the Earth beneath the crust

mass number total number of neutrons and protons within the nucleus of an atom

melanic form a form of moth which has dark colouration

melanoma dangerous type of skin cancer

mental illness things going wrong with the mind

meteors bright flashes in the sky caused by rocks burning in the Earth's atmosphere

microorganism very small organism (living thing) which can only be viewed through a microscope – also known as a microbe

microwaves non-ionising waves used in satellite and mobile phone networks – also in microwave ovens

mild intensity exercise exercise that does not cause a significant increase in heart rate

mitochondria structures in a cell where respiration takes place

mixtures one or more elements or compounds which have been mixed together – they can be separated out fairly easily

mobility ability to move

moderate exercise exercise that causes an individual to have a raised heart rate and break a sweat, but they are not so breathless they cannot talk

molecular formula the formula of a chemical using symbols, e.g. methane has a molecular formula of CH_4

molecule two or more atoms which have been chemically combined

monoculture when a single crop is grown in a huge field

monomer small molecule that may become chemically bonded to other monomers to form a polymer

moon large natural satellite which orbits a planet

motor neurone nerve cell carrying information from the central nervous system to muscles

mucus sticky material consisting of a mixture of substances produced by special 'goblet' cells in the lings

mutated a mutated cell is one where the genes have been altered

mutation where the DNA within cells has been altered (this happens in cancer)

nanochemistry the study of materials in the nanoscale range (1-10 nanometres)

nanometre units used to measure very small things (one billionth of a metre)

nanomotor very small motor to drive a nanoscale vehicle

nanoparticles very small particles on the nanoscale

nanoscale scale which deals in nanometres

nanosilver nanoparticle containing silver

nanotube carbon molecule in the form of a cylinder

nanowire microscopic wires that can conduct electricity in tiny circuits on microchips

narrow spectrum antibiotics antibiotics effective against only a few types of bacteria

National Grid network that carries electricity from power stations across the country (it uses cables, transformers and pylons)

natural fibres fibres from animal or plant sources

natural flavouring flavour that comes from natural materials

natural gas mixture of gases formed from animals and plants which lived millions of years ago (it is a fossil fuel)

natural selection process by which 'good' characteristics that can be passed on in genes become more common in a population over many generations ('good' characteristics mean that the organism has an advantage which makes it more likely to survive)

nebulae clouds of dust and gases from which stars form

negative correlation a link between two factors that shows they are related, (but one does not necessarily cause the other); a negative correlation shows that as one variable increases, the other decreases

neonatal screening health checks carried out on newborn babies

nervous system system for conducting messages (via nerves) around the body

neurone a nerve cell

neurotransmitter chemical that passes between nerve cells

neutral a neutral substance has a pH of 7

neutralisation reaction between H+ ions and OH- ions (acid and base react to makes a salt and water)

neutron small particle which does not have a charge – found in the nucleus of an atom

newton unit of force (abbreviated to N)

non-biodegradable living organisms cannot break down non-biodegradable objects – many plastics are non-biodegradable and so last for very, very long times in the environment

non-infectious a disease that is not caused by pathogens and cannot be passed to another person (unless it is inherited)

non-rechargeable a non-rechargeable battery runs from a chemical reaction within the battery and cannot be topped up using mains electricity

non-renewable something which is used up at a faster rate than it can be replaced e.g. fossil fuels

non-specific a general immune response designed to prevent infection, for example a cut scabbing over

normal a line at right angles to a boundary

nuclear energy energy that is stored inside atoms

nuclear fission energy released when nuclei of atoms are split

nuclear fuels radioactive fuels, such as uranium and plutonium, which are used in nuclear power stations

nuclear fusion energy released when two small atoms combine to make a larger atom

nuclear power energy which comes from slowly releasing the energy stored inside an atom (by nuclear fission)

nucleons protons and neutrons (both found in the nucleus)

nucleus (atom) central part of an atom that contains protons and neutrons

nucleus (cell) part of the cell that controls the cell

nutrients substances in food that we need to eat to stay healthy, e.g. protein

nutrition the way the body takes in and uses food

obesity a medical condition where the amount of body fat is so great that it harms health

object something which we view and from which light rays reflect

oestrogen female hormone secreted by the ovary and involved in the menstrual cycle

OH group an oxygen atom bonded to a hydrogen atom – found in all alcohols

ohm unit used to measure resistance to the flow of electricity

ohmmeter a device used to measure electrical resistance across a component in an electrical circuit

oil fossil fuel formed from animals and plants that lived millions of years ago

oil refinery an industrial plant that heats crude oil to separate it into its chemical components, which are then made into useful substances

optic nerve nerve leading from the retina to the brain

optical fibre thin and flexible tubes of transparent material for transmitting light from one end to another

ore rock which contains a metal, e.g. iron ore

organ a collection of tissues that work together e.g. the heart

organ transplant where an organ from one person is transplanted into another person, e.g. liver transplant

organic acid a naturally found acid, e.g. vinegar

organic compound chemicals containing carbon, e.g. toxins found in animals and plants

organic solvent a liquid containing carbon that dissolves a solid, e.g. alcohol

outlier a result that doesn't fit with the pattern of the rest of the results

ovaries organs (in females) which make eggs

overnutrition when a person eats too much

oxidation reaction reaction that increases the amount of oxygen in a compound

oxide a molecule containing oxygen

oxidising agent chemical that adds oxygen atoms

ozone gas found high in the atmosphere which absorbs UV rays from the Sun

pancreas organ which makes the hormones insulin and glucagon

parallel circuit electric circuit formed by more than one loop so that the electrons can go through different paths

parasite organism which lives on (or inside) the body of another organism

pathogen harmful organism which invades the body and causes disease

pedigree chart a chart that shows the genetic line of descent from generation to generation

percentage yield comparing the actual amount of useful product made to the amount calculated

period horizontal row in the periodic table

periodic table a table of all the chemical elements based on their atomic number

peripheral nervous system (PNS) the nerves leading from the brain and spinal cord to all parts of the body

pesticide chemical used to kill living organisms which are pests, e.g. rats or insects

petrochemical industry industry concerned with crude oil and the materials produced from it

pH meter a device which measures the pH of a solution accurately

pH scale scale running from 0 to 14 which shows how acidic or alkaline a substance is

phagocytes white blood cells that surround pathogens and digest them using enzymes

phenotype the characteristic that an organism has

phloem tissue made up of long tubes that transport glucose made in the leaves to all other parts of a plant

photochromic photochromic materials react to the stimulus of light

photosynthesis process carried out by green plants where sunlight, carbon dioxide and water are used to produce glucose and oxygen

physical barrier something that stops pathogens entering the body, e.g. the skin

physical cause when an illness is caused by an injury

physical change change from one state (solid, liquid or gas) to another

physical illness things that can go wrong with the body – either infectious disease or non-infectious

physical property property that can be measured without changing the chemical composition of a substance, e.g. hardness

physical therapy treatment that does something physically to the body

physiological to do with the way the body works

physiological effects something which influences the way the body works, e.g. exercise has a physiological effect when it strengthens heart muscle

physiological investigation taking measurements about a person's level of fitness, e.g. pulse rate

physiological measurements measurements about a person's level of fitness, e.g. pulse rate

physiotherapy exercises and massage to treat muscle problems

pie chart a circular chart divided into sectors. Each sector is proportional to the amount it represents

piezoelectric a piezoelectric material produces a voltage when under stress

pigment material which gives something its colour

pituitary gland gland at the base of the neck which makes many different hormones

placenta organ that develops in the female during pregnancy through which the foetus obtains oxygen and food

planet large ball of gas or rock travelling around a star (planets orbit our Sun)

plastic compounds produced by polymerisation, capable of being moulded into various shapes or drawn into filaments and used as textile fibres

plasticisers small molecules which fit between polymer chains and allow them to slide over each other

pollutant gases gases released into the air which damage the environment (gases in car exhausts)

pollution contaminating or destroying the environment as a result of human activities

poly(ethene) also called polythene, this useful plastic is made from ethenes

polymer large molecule made up of chains of monomers

polymerisation chemical process that combines monomers to form a polymer: this is how polythene is formed

positive charge when an atom loses an electron it become an ion with a positive charge, e.g. Na+

positive correlation a link between two factors that shows they are related, (but one does not necessarily cause the other); a positive correlation shows that as one variable increases, the other also increases

potential energy another word for stored energy

power source source of electricity (a battery or mains electricity)

precipitate solid formed in a solution during a chemical reaction

precision how close a series of repeated results are to each other

predator animal which preys on (and eats) another animal

prescription a doctor's written orders for the preparation and administration of a drug

prey animals which are eaten by a predator

prism a block of glass or transparent plastic used to explore the properties of light

product substance produced in a chemical reaction

progesterone hormone produced by the ovaries which prepares the uterus for pregnancy

protein molecule made up of amino acids – we need proteins in our diet (found in food of animal origin and also in plants)

proton small positive particle found in the nucleus of an atom

psychological effect something which affects the way the mind works, e.g. regular exercise can help to fight off depression

pulse rate the movement of blood in your arteries (taking your pulse rate shows how fast your heart is beating)

Punnet square a type of genetic diagram that sets out the results of genetic crosses

pupil dark hole in the middle of the eye that allows light to enter

PVC a polymer (short for polyvinylchloride)

PVCu unplasticised polyvinylchloride

quantitative hypothesis a hypothesis that predicts an amount. for example, if I double the concentration, the rate of reaction doubles

quantitative relationship a relationship (between variables) that is described using numbers

radiation thermal energy transfer which occurs when something hotter than its surroundings radiates heat from its surface

radio waves non-ionising waves used to broadcast radio and TV programmes

radioactive decay the disintegration of a radioactive substance

radiotherapy using ionizing radiation to kill cancer cells in the body

random error errors in measurement. these can be reduced by repeating experiments

range the upper and lower limits of what you will measure

rate of reaction the speed at which a chemical reaction takes place

ray diagram diagrams showing how light rays travel

reactants chemicals mixed together to start a chemical reaction

reaction force when an object feels a force it pushes back with an equal reaction force in the opposite direction

reaction time the time it takes for a driver to step on the brake after seeing an obstacle

real image image formed on the other side of the lens to the object

receptors nerve cells which detect a stimulus, such as a hot surface

recessive two recessive alleles needed to produce the characteristic; the characteristic does not appear when a gene contains two different alleles

rechargeable a battery is rechargeable if it can be recharged using mains electricity

recovery time how long it takes for the pulse and breathing rate to return to normal after exercising

red blood cells blood cells which are adapted to carry oxygen

red shift when lines in a spectrum are redder than expected – if an object has a red shift in its light it is moving away from us

reflecting telescope telescope that reflects and focuses light using a concave mirror

reflex arc pathway taken by nerve impulse from a receptor, through the nervous system, to an effector (does not go through brain)

reflex response a muscular action that we take without thinking

reforestation planting of large areas of trees in places where forests were previously removed

refracting telescope telescope that uses two convex lenses to collect and focus light

refraction when a light ray travelling through air enters a glass block and changes direction

refractive index an indication of the amount by which a piece of glass will bend a ray of light

rehabilition the restoration of someone to a useful place in society

relative atomic mass the mass of an atom in comparison to the mass of hydrogen, which is taken as 1

relay neurone neurone that transfers a nerve impulse from a sensory neurone to a motor neurone

renewable energy that can be replenished at the same rate that it's used up e.g. biofuels

repeatability consistent results are obtained when a person uses the same procedure a number of times

replacement planting maintaining forest size by planting a new tree for every one removed

replacement therapy a physical therapy that involves replacing parts of the body that are not working well

replicating when organisms or cells make copies of themselves

representative sample sample from a scene of crime which can be used for different kinds of tests

resistance measurement of how hard it is for an electric current to flow through a material

resistant when bacteria are resistant to an antibiotic they are not killed by it (the antibiotic fails to work)

respiration process occurring in living things where oxygen is used to release the energy in foods

respiratory system body system involved in respiration (in humans these are the lungs and trachea)

resting pulse rate the normal pulse rate when not exercising

resultant force the combined effect of forces acting on an object

retina covering of light-sensitive cells at the back of the eyeball

reversible a reversible change (or reaction) is one that can also work in the opposite direction

R_f value stands for retention factor – this value is equal to the distance moved by a colour divided by the distance moved by the solvent) – used in chromatography

rhesus blood group system blood can be grouped into rhesus-positive and rhesus-negative groups

risk the likelihood of a hazard causing harm

risk assessment deciding on the level of risk in a particular course of action

salivary glands secrete a clear liquid to moisten the mouth

Sankey diagram a diagram showing the transfer of energy to different forms

scaling up where a small, trial version of a process is transferred to a larger (often commercial) scale

screening test medical test where large numbers of people are tested for a disease before the symptoms have appeared (also called screening programmes)

sedative substance that lowers a person's level of awareness

seismograph instrument for measuring and recording the vibrations of earthquakes

semiconductor substance that does not conduct electricity at low temperatures but does so at higher temperatures

sensor device that detects a change in the environment

sensory neurone nerve cell carrying information from receptors to the central nervous system

sequence arrangement in which things follow a pattern

series circuit circuit formed by a single loop of electrical conductors

shells electrons are arranged in shells (or orbits) around the nucleus of an atom

short-sighted where you cannot see distant objects clearly and the image forms in front of the retina

short-term goals targets which can be achieved fairly quickly

sickle-cell anaemia disease caused by sickle-shaped red blood cells which cannot carry enough oxygen around the body

side-effects unwanted effects produced by medicines

significant figures the number of digits in a number; in data, depends on the precision of measurements

single covalent bond bond between atoms where each atom shares one electron with the other

smart materials materials which change with a stimulus

sodium ion a sodium atom that has lost an electron from its outer shell and so has a positive electrical charge

sodium ion when the sodium atom loses an electron it becomes an ion with a positive charge, $Na+$

soil erosion where soil is worn away (for example by wind or heavy rain)

solar cells devices which convert the Sun's energy into electricity

solar energy energy from the Sun

solar panels panels which use the Sun's energy to heat water

solute substance which dissolves in a liquid to form a solution

solution when a solute dissolves in a solvent a solution forms

solvent liquid in which solutes dissolve to form a solution

sonar uses sound reflections to detect things underwater

sound energy anything making a noise gives out sound energy

sound waves vibrations which can travel through solids, liquids and gases – we detect them with our ears

species basic category of biological classification, composed of individuals that resemble one another, can breed among themselves, but cannot breed with members of another species

specific a targeted immune response against a pathogen, for example if a person has been immunised against a particular disease

spectrum pattern of light given off when a substance burns (analysed by a spectroscope)

speed how fast an object travels: speed = distance ÷ time

sperm the male sex cell

standard solution a solution with a known concentration of solute

star bright object in the sky which is lit by energy from nuclear reactions

state symbols symbols used in equations to show whether something is solid, liquid, gas or in solution in water

stem cells unspecialised body cells (found in bone marrow) that can develop into other, specialised cells that the body needs, e.g. blood cells

step-down transformer a step-down transformer changes alternating current to a lower voltage

step-up transformer a step-up transformer changes alternating current to a higher voltage

stimulant a drug that speeds up the working of the brain

stimulus something that stimulates receptor nerve cells, e.g. a hot surface

stomach acid acid produced by the stomach (helps in digestion)

stomata tiny holes in the surface of a leaf, through which gases can move

stopping distance thinking distance + braking distance

stroke sudden change in blood flow to the brain – can be fatal

structural formula formula showing the arrangement of atoms in a molecule

subscript small number in a chemical formula, e.g. in H_2O the small numeral 2 is the subscript

sub-station where transformers change the voltage in electrical cables

successful collisions when particles with enough kinetic energy react with each other

surgery operating on the body to explore, remove or repair structures

symptom a visible sign in a patient or a change in the way their body feels

synapse gap between two neurones

target organ the part of the body affected by a hormone

tectonic plate a large section of the Earth's crust which can move across the surface of the earth

tensile force a force which stretches something

terminal velocity the top speed reached when drag matches the driving force

testes organs (in males) where sperm are made

testosterone a hormone that controls the development of male characteristics

tetrahedral structure very strong three-dimensional structure (carbon atoms can be linked like this)

thermal conductors materials which allow heat to pass through them easily, e.g. metals

thermal energy another name for heat energy

thermal insulators materials which do not conduct thermal energy easily, e.g. wood

thermistor sensor in an electric circuit that detects temperature

thermochromic a thermochromic material is one that changes with heat

thermoregulation how the body keeps a constant internal temperature

thyroid gland gland at the base of the neck which makes the hormone thyroxin

thyroxin hormone made in the thyroid gland which controls metabolic rate

tissue group of cells that work together and carry out a similar task, e.g. lung tissue

total internal reflection complete reflection of a light ray within glass when the ray hits the glass/air boundary at an angle greater than the critical angle

toxic a toxic substance is one which is poisonous

toxin poisonous substance (pathogens make toxins which make us feel ill)

transformer device by which alternating current of one voltage is changed to another voltage

transfusion when blood from one person is put into another person (the two people must have compatible blood groups)

transfusion when blood from one person is put into another person (the two people must have compatible blood groups)

transmitter device which transmits waves, e.g. a mobile phone mast

transparent a transparent substance can be easily seen through, e.g. clear glass

transpiration the movement of water in plants as it is taken up through the roots and released from the leaves as water vapour

transplant when an organ is taken from one person and surgically placed into another person, e.g. liver transplant

triple covalent bond bond between atoms where each atom shares three electrons with the other

tsunami huge waves caused by earthquakes – can be very destructive

tumour abnormal mass of tissue that is often cancerous

turbine device for transferring kinetic energy (wind, water) to a generator

ultrasound high-pitched sounds which are too high for detection by human ears

ultraviolet radiation electromagnetic waves given out by the Sun which damage human skin

undernutrition when a person does not consume enough calories or nutrients

universal indicator indicator which shows the pH of a substance by changing colour (useful for the entire range of the pH scale)

Universe the whole of space

urinary system body system that produces, collects and gets rid of urine

urine liquid waste from kidneys which is excreted from the body

vaccination giving of a vaccine to provide immunity to a disease

vaccine killed micro-organisms, or living but weakened micro-organisms, that are given to produce immunity to a particular disease

vacuole a sac in a cell filled with a watery solution; plant cells tend to have large vacuoles

vagina also called the birth canal, this leads from the uterus (when a baby is born it passes down the vagina)

vascular screening health checks to find out the risk of heart disease

vasoconstriction in cold conditions the diameter of small blood vessels near the surface of the body decreases – this reduces the flow of blood

vasodilation in hot conditions the diameter of small blood vessels near the surface of the body increases – this increases the flow of blood

veins blood vessels that carry blood back to the heart

velocity how fast an object is travelling in a certain direction: velocity = displacement ÷ time

velocity–time graph a plot of the velocity of a moving object at all times during its journey

vertebrate animal with a backbone

virtual image image formed on the same side of the lens as the object; a virtual image formed by reflection can be seen but cannot be projected onto a screen

viruses very small infectious organisms that reproduce within the cells of living organisms and often cause disease

viscosity a measure of how easily a liquid flows

visible light waves in the electromagnetic spectrum that we can detect with our eyes

volatile a volatile substance evaporates easily

volcano a landform (often a mountain) where molten rock erupts onto the surface of the planet

volt unit used to measure voltage

voltage a measure of the energy carried by an electric current (also called the potential difference)

voltmeter a device used to measure the voltage across a component in an electrical circuit

voluntary response a response to a stimulus that you think about and can control

wave speed how quickly a wave carries energy from one place to another

wavelength distance between two wave peaks

white blood cells blood cells which defend against disease

wide spectrum antibiotics antibiotics good at fighting a wide range of bacteria

wind energy energy contained in moving air which spins a turbine to generate electricity

work done the product of the force and distance moved in the direction of the force

X-rays ionising electromagnetic waves used in X-ray photography (where X-rays are used to generate pictures of bones)

xylem tissue made up of long tubes that transport water and minerals from the roots to all parts of a plant

yeast single-celled fungus used in making beer and bread

yield useful product made from a chemical reaction

Index